Praise for *The Culture Cycle*

"Reading Jim Heskett's book is not some vague exercise in academic idealism. It is a well-written, practical, compelling manual of how to build an enterprise that will endure for 100 years or more. You cannot afford to ignore it."

—**John C. Bogle,** Founder, The Vanguard Group; and author, *Enough: True Measures of Money, Business, and Life*

"Jim Heskett has delivered yet another breakthrough in our understanding of how corporate cultures shape performance. If leaders take Heskett's sound advice to heart, corporate performance will improve and trust in business can be restored."

—**Bill George**, Professor of Management Practice, Harvard Business School; former Chair and CEO, Medtronic; and author, *Authentic Leadership*

"For those who might regard culture as an abstract, soft, perhaps 'hippie like' concept, Jim Heskett brings home its manifest value to both the organization and the sensibilities of its people."

—**Herb Kelleher,** Executive Chairman and CEO Emeritus, Southwest Airlines Co.

"*The Culture Cycle* inspires leaders to start with people and shape their organizations' cultures to drive engagement, inclusion, trust, innovation, and results. Jim Heskett has developed a new and valuable way to think about culture. This is a must read."

—**Jane Ramsey,** Executive Vice President, Human Resources, Limited Brands, Inc.

"Forget the squishy fluff; this book is hardcore, rooted in the numbers that drive margin. It shows the calculations…reveals the numbers for the 'report card' that predicts the future success of your company, division, or department…numbers every leader should know… and few do.

—**Scott Cook,** Co-Founder and Chairman of the Executive Committee, Intuit

"Jim Heskett's is the essential handbook for today's organizations that care about their people and are determined that theirs is an organization of the future."

—**Frances Hesselbein,** President and CEO, Leader to Leader Institute (formerly the Peter F. Drucker Foundation for Nonprofit Management)

"In his extraordinary book, Jim Heskett has nailed it. He explains the essential value and nature of organizational culture. In the vast world of management 'how to' books, this one needs to move to the top of any leader's list."

—**William J. Bratton,** Chairman, Kroll; and former Police Commissioner of Boston, New York, and Los Angeles

"Jim Heskett blends learnings from his stellar academic career with new research in this wise, beautifully written book about the most important determinant of organizational success—culture."

—**Leonard Berry,** Distinguished Professor, Marketing, Texas A&M University; and coauthor, *Management Lessons from Mayo Clinic*

"Not only a call for action, this book provides a thoughtful perspective on how best to challenge the performance hurdles managers face in today's competitive marketplace. In a very compelling way, it makes the case for culture being a primary driver for success."

—**Arkadi Kuhlmann,** CEO, ING Direct; and coauthor, *The Orange Code*

"*The Culture Cycle* defines and highlights the attributes of culture through numerous examples. It identifies a series of metrics that are meaningful proxies for seeing the impact of culture in an organization (the 'Four Rs'). It is an excellent read for leaders of organizations small or large, non-profit or for-profit."

— **John P. Morgridge,** Chairman Emeritus, Cisco Systems

"In Heskett's new book on understanding and enhancing the culture imperatives, he takes the reader step by step through complicated waters. This new piece of research and subsequent book will inspire even the most cynical managers to step up and concentrate even more to create cultures that support growth and development."

— **Thomas DeLong,** Philip J. Stomberg Professor of Management Practice, Harvard Business School; and author, *Flying Without a Net*

"Jim Heskett has put his finger on the pulse of what organizations can do to reverse a downward spin through his latest book. There is no 'spin cycle' in *The Culture Cycle*…just wisdom that can transform our organizations."

— **Ginger Hardage,** Senior Vice President Culture and Communications, Southwest Airlines Co.

"The body of literature that purports to assist us in understanding and managing organization culture suffers from a lack of systematic data supporting either the frameworks or the corresponding action agenda. Jim Heskett has managed to 'crack the code' on both fronts. This is an important book that deserves the careful attention of today's manager."

— **Leonard A. Schlesinger,** President, Babson College; and coauthor, *Action Trumps Everything*

"Jim Heskett has laid out a direction for successful organizations of the future…those that build an organizational culture founded on excellence, value their employees as assets, and see the world as their future market place."

— **William E. Strickland, Jr.,** CEO, Manchester Bidwell Corporation; and author, *Make the Impossible Possible*

"The critical role of cultural durability has been evident in sharp relief during the cathartic period since late 2008 when many leaders have put their organizations through wrenching reforms to address declining demand and rapid globalization. Those companies that have enhanced their position have done so through the embodiment of Heskett's 'culture cycle.'"

— **Gary W. Loveman,** Chairman of the Board, President and CEO, Caesars Entertainment

"Jim Heskett's new book shows how culture affects the bottom line and is the most important task a leader faces."

— **Tom Watson,** Cofounder, Omnicom Group; Vice Chairman Emeritus, Omnicom; and Dean, Omnicom University

"Jim Heskett provides us an in-depth understanding of how cultures can be developed and strengthened with a poignant reminder that they also need to be nurtured and renewed if they are going to grow and continue to flourish. As you read this book, you will be learning from a master teacher with a wealth of experience."

— **C. William Pollard,** former Chairman and CEO, The ServiceMaster Company; and author, *The Soul of the Firm*

The Culture Cycle
How to Shape the Unseen Force
That Transforms Performance

James Heskett

Vice President, Publisher: Tim Moore
Associate Publisher and Director of Marketing: Amy Neidlinger
Executive Editor: Jeanne Glasser
Editorial Assistant: Pamela Boland
Development Editor: Russ Hall
Senior Marketing Manager: Julie Phifer
Assistant Marketing Manager: Megan Graue
Cover Designer: Chuti Prasertsith
Managing Editor: Kristy Hart
Project Editor: Anne Goebel
Copy Editor: Gayle Johnson
Proofreader: Editorial Advantage
Indexer: Erika Millen
Compositor: Nonie Ratcliff
Manufacturing Buyer: Dan Uhrig

© 2012 by James Heskett
Publishing as FT Press
Upper Saddle River, New Jersey 07458

FT Press offers excellent discounts on this book when ordered in quantity for bulk purchases or special sales. For more information, please contact U.S. Corporate and Government Sales, 1-800-382-3419, corpsales@pearsontechgroup.com. For sales outside the U.S., please contact International Sales at international@pearson.com.

Company and product names mentioned herein are the trademarks or registered trademarks of their respective owners.

Printed in the United States of America

First Printing August 2011
ISBN-10: 0-13-277978-1
ISBN-13: 978-0-13-277978-4

Pearson Education LTD.
Pearson Education Australia PTY, Limited.
Pearson Education Singapore, Pte. Ltd.
Pearson Education Asia, Ltd.
Pearson Education Canada, Ltd.
Pearson Educación de Mexico, S.A. de C.V.
Pearson Education—Japan
Pearson Education Malaysia, Pte. Ltd.

Library of Congress Cataloging-in-Publication Data:

Heskett, James L.
  The culture cycle : how to shape the unseen force that transforms performance / James L. Heskett.
      p. cm.
  ISBN 978-0-13-277978-4 (hbk. : alk. paper)
  1. Corporate culture. 2. Organizational behavior. 3. Organizational effectiveness. 4. Organizational change. I. Title.
  HD58.7.H475 2012
  658.3--dc23
                              2011020182

For my beloved editor, Marilyn,
our children, Sarah, Charles, and Ben,
and grandchildren, Olivia and Sam

FINANCIAL TIMES

In an increasingly competitive world, it is quality
of thinking that gives an edge—an idea that opens new
doors, a technique that solves a problem, or an insight
that simply helps make sense of it all.

We work with leading authors in the various arenas
of business and finance to bring cutting-edge thinking
and best-learning practices to a global market.

It is our goal to create world-class print publications
and electronic products that give readers
knowledge and understanding that can then be
applied, whether studying or at work.

To find out more about our business
products, you can visit us at www.ftpress.com.

Contents

Acknowledgments

A book like this one is the product of a number of experiences and the friends and colleagues who shared them with me.

Material that I originally collected in case form supplied many ideas. It brought me into contact with case protagonists such as Luciano Benetton, Cofounder of the company that bears his name; Bill Bratton, formerly Commissioner of the Boston, New York City, and Los Angeles Police Departments; Scott Cook, Cofounder and Chairman of the Executive Committee of Intuit; Frances Hesselbein, when she was CEO of Girl Scouts of the USA (and since); James Kinnear, formerly CEO of Texaco; Arkadi Kuhlmann, CEO of ING Direct; Gary Loveman, Chairman, President, and CEO of Caesars Entertainment Corp.; John Morgridge, formerly Chairman and CEO of Cisco Systems; Bill Pollard, formerly Chairman and CEO of The Service-Master Company; Bill Strickland, CEO of the Manchester Bidwell Corporation; Lorenzo Zambrano, Chairman and CEO of CEMEX; and the people I came to know over the years and whose acquaintance I value at Southwest Airlines. Among them are Herb Kelleher, Executive Chairman and CEO Emeritus; Colleen Barrett, President Emeritus; CEO Gary Kelly; Executive Vice President and COO Mike Van de Ven; Senior Vice President Culture and Communications Ginger Hardage; Senior Vice President and Chief Marketing Officer Dave Ridley; and Vice President Network Planning John Jamotta.

Others who are not the subject of cases I've authored or coauthored, but who were instrumental in contributing ideas to the book, whether or not they are aware of it, include Pete Blackshaw, Cofounder of PlanetFeedback.com; John Bogle, founder of The Vanguard Group; James Goodnight, Cofounder and CEO of SAS; Bill Hybels, Founder of the Willow Creek Community Church; Eleanor Josaitis, CEO of Focus: HOPE; the late Will Rodgers of what was then the Management Analysis Center, with whom I conducted the early consulting work at GM that is described in the book; and Les Wexner, Founder, Chairman, and CEO of Limited Brands.

Still other executives who must remain anonymous supplied data on which analyses in Chapters 7 and 13 are based.

Those who read portions of the manuscript and contributed a number of ideas were Tom Watson, Bruce Nelson, Brian Emsell, and Brian Curran of The Omnicom Group; Jane Ramsey, Ezra Singer, Joe Simonet, and Jason Tostevin of Limited Brands; Dan Maher; and Dan O'Brien.

Coauthors of previous books and cases who have had a strong influence on my thinking are Earl Sasser, with whom I have written five books and to whom I owe a real debt of gratitude; Len Schlesinger, now President of Babson College and a coauthor on two books, always a source of stimulating ideas; and Joe Wheeler, Chris Hart, Roger Hallowell, and, of course, John Kotter, whose work on the impact of culture on performance and subsequently the management of change has helped countless practitioners and academics see issues associated with these topics more clearly.

The persons on these lists have been great teachers. I feel fortunate to still be learning from many of them.

While I'll take responsibility for any inaccuracies in the material, I was aided by an outstanding research associate, fact-digger, and fact-checker, Chris Allen. Jacqueline Archer and Janice Simmons provided important help with graphics. Throughout the project, Paula Alexander and Luz Velazquez supplied all-around assistance. All are associated with the Harvard Business School, where I have had the privilege of teaching and researching under six deans. All have provided the leadership that has enabled an inspiring group of colleagues to, as the school's mission states, "educate leaders who contribute to the well-being of society," a fitting statement for a book like this.

Near the end of the substantive work on the manuscript, I sent portions of it to three publishers. One didn't bother to reply. Of the two that gave it serious consideration, Jeanne Glasser, Executive Editor at FT Press, was most enthusiastic about it. If it hadn't been for Bob Wallace, a longtime friend and editor, and his acquaintance at FT Press, Timothy Moore, the proposal might not have even reached Jeanne's desk.

Finally, I owe the greatest debt to the person who has been at my side through at least a dozen of these book-length writing projects, my partner, Marilyn.

Jim Heskett
Cambridge, Massachusetts
June 2011

About the Author

James Heskett is Baker Foundation Professor Emeritus at the Harvard Business School. He joined the faculty in 1965 after completing his MBA and Ph.D. degrees at Stanford University and teaching at The Ohio State University. He has served as president of Logistics Systems, Inc. and on the boards of more than a dozen corporations and not-for-profit organizations. In addition, he has consulted for the management of companies in the U.S., Europe, Asia, and Latin America. He is currently a director of Limited Brands, Inc. While at Harvard Business School, he taught courses in marketing, business logistics, service management, general management, and entrepreneurial management. At one time he served as Senior Associate Dean responsible for all academic programs. He has written articles for the *Harvard Business Review*, *Sloan Management Review*, and other publications. He also cowrote *Service Breakthroughs*, *The Service Profit Chain*, *The Ownership Quotient*, and *Corporate Culture and Performance*, among other books.

Introduction

An organization's culture matters a lot. That's what John Kotter and I concluded from a three-year study of the relationship between corporate culture and performance in the early 1990s. CEOs generally agree, although I'm left wondering whether some of them really believe it or whether it's something they've been conditioned to say when reminded to do so. It's confirmed by even the best (5-star) investment analysts on Wall Street, a group that we might assume would look only to financial measures in recommending investments. They told us that culture helps corporate performance in higher performing firms and hurts it in lower-performing firms.[1]

But if culture is a force, it is an unseen force, most of the time taken for granted. Its importance sometimes rears its head when two organizations with strong and very different cultures, such as Chase Manhattan bank and J. P. Morgan, are merged. We become interested in culture when a foreign culture appears to produce especially productive behaviors, as in Japan in the 1980s. We speculate on how much of the positive difference between a company's market value and its book value is due to intangible assets such as high employee engagement,[2] productivity, and innovation. These assets are called organizational capital and are as hard to measure as they are hard to replicate.[3] We wonder about the role that the culture at companies such as Lehman Brothers, Enron, and Worldcom played in fostering behaviors that led to their downfall several years ago. And as we saw at GM, we hook our star to "a culture that can really win" as part of a herculean effort to emerge from bankruptcy.[4]

In many organizations, culture is the most potent and hard-to-replicate source of competitive advantage—far more important, for example, than technological innovation. By the time the superior performance it produces comes to the attention of competitors and the public, an organization's culture is well established and doing its job.

This book sets forth a conceptual framework—the culture cycle—that identifies relationships essential in shaping effective cultures. It demonstrates ways of calculating the economic importance of culture by means of the Four Rs: referrals, retention, returns to labor, and relationships. It describes a test of both the culture cycle and Four Rs in a real-world setting. It looks at ways in which cultures evolve and can be shaped that have a sustained positive impact on economic performance. And it examines the role of culture in the development of an organization's strategy.

Both stories and numbers serve us in this effort. Stories, of course, don't prove anything. But they provide memorable examples that make the numbers come alive. And they are an important way in which leaders communicate and reinforce an organization's culture. As neuroscientists tell us, "Given the effect stories have on us, they are one of the most useful tools one can have in a mental world, replacing the carrot and stick of the physical world. We can use them both to understand and to shape how others think and behave."[5]

The numbers themselves can be impressive too. *In studies that I will describe, as much as half of the difference in operating profit between organizations can be attributed to effective cultures.* In addition, an organization's culture provides especially significant competitive advantages in bad times, such as those we've seen in recent years. All of this is possible with little or no capital investment, yielding an infinite ROI. All it requires is the time of leaders. But this is time spent doing things that good leaders should be doing anyway. In short, it involves an investment that keeps on giving back for years and years.

The work here is a natural extension of a series of investigations into relationships that my colleagues and I characterized in 1994 as a "service profit chain" of relationships beginning with what we called "internal quality," essentially the quality of work life.[6] This, we posited, could be traced directly to employee satisfaction, loyalty, and productivity. Productivity in turn drives value for customers, which leads directly to customer satisfaction and loyalty. Customer loyalty in turn is a major determinant of profitability and growth. Numerous subsequent studies have confirmed relationships between the links in the chain through both correlation and cause-and-effect analyses.[7] Fewer have devoted much attention to the quality of work life, the first link in the service profit chain. One of the objectives of this book is to shed light on this link in the chain.

The thinking in this book really began in 1993, shortly after John P. Kotter and I completed our study of corporate culture and performance.[8] Two trips about three weeks apart took me to meet with senior executives of two organizations with strong and successful cultures, Walmart and Southwest Airlines. Much has been written about these companies. But before you conclude that this is a rehash of material you've read many times, please read on. What follows provides a lens through which many other organizations will be observed later.

Two Visits, One Story

The visits fanned an interest that didn't wane during years in which I was engaged in research and writing on other topics. In the interim, to say these companies did well is an understatement. Both would point to the effectiveness of their cultures as an important reason for that success. Because of that success, both have generated high expectations and have been held to high standards. Both have attracted a great deal of attention, both favorable and unfavorable.

A management meeting at Walmart Stores is an eye-opening experience. At 7:30 a.m. on a Saturday, nearly a thousand people gather in an auditorium at the company's Bentonville, Arkansas headquarters. The audience comprises invited store managers, employees and their guests who happen to be in the area, celebrities, CEOs of supplier companies, the class from the Walton Institute (company management training program), and other guests. Proceedings are led from the stage by a senior executive (not necessarily the CEO since founder Sam Walton's passing) selected for his dynamic personality. They include discussions of new policies, demonstrations of new products, "best-practice" examples from store managers with outstanding results, recognition of various achievements, and repeated

W-A-L-M-A-R-T cheers (with a rear-end motion to represent the "squiggly" between the L and the M, something that no longer exists in the name), capped off by the question, "Who's number one?" Answer: "The customer." The meeting is choreographed, but anyone in the audience is free to summon a microphone and contribute. Ideas get exchanged. Performance is recognized. Guests are made to feel like part of a family, albeit one of the largest in the world. Consider the following episode at a meeting I attended some years ago.

The COO at the time, Don Soderquist, introduced a regional vice president who had brought with him a "star" store manager from California. The store manager, who was sitting in the audience, was introduced and welcomed to Bentonville. After the store manager was lauded for his performance (an event captured on video by the in-company television broadcasting operation for later use on the company's satellite-linked video network to all stores), the following exchange ensued:

> Soderquist: *"If I remember right, you've been making an effort to increase your soft-goods sales as a proportion of total sales. How're you doing, Bill?"*
>
> Bill: *"With a lot of work, we've gotten them up to about 20%."*
>
> A voice from the back of the room: *"Your dad would never have settled for 20%, Bill."* (Laughter from the audience.)
>
> Bill: *"I know. In fact, Dad's been at the store trying to help me get those sales up."* (An employee sitting next to me whispers that Bill's dad is a retired Walmart store manager.)
>
> Soderquist: *"We know you're going to get the job done too, Bill. And do one more thing for us, will you? Say hello to your mom and dad when you get back."*

The significance of this exchange hit me when I remembered that Bill managed only one out of more than 1,800 Division One stores operated by the company at that time.

This management meeting was preceded by a merchandising meeting held on the previous day. Here, celebration is not one of the objectives. Operating executives have an opportunity to ask how merchandising managers could have possibly thought that the glow-in-the-dark cactus lamps bought for the stores could ever sell.

Merchandising managers, in turn, can question the way in which stores display and promote goods they've bought. Together, they plan the next big promotions. The atmosphere, however, is similar to that of a courtroom. Prosecutors and defense attorneys vigorously argue their respective cases. Then they go off together afterward, arms around each other, to continue talking shop.

What's the purpose of all this? One artifact in the meeting room makes it clear. It's a large electrified tote board on a wall of the auditorium that clicks every two seconds. It doesn't track the national debt, but instead displays the billions of dollars that Walmart has saved its customers since its founding in 1962. The mission is as clear as the values and behaviors with which it is achieved.

Talk to Walmart managers at the meeting or employees in the stores, and you get a consistent impression that they like their jobs and the people they work with. This is in spite of the fact that Walmart's starting wages are near-minimum and its salaries are modest in comparison with other multibillion-dollar companies. Store employees note that senior managers visit stores and work alongside them frequently. They are not names without faces. They are proud, for example, of the fact that during Hurricane Katrina it was Walmart that opened its stores in New Orleans; gave away products that local residents could use during the disaster; brought in additional supplies to be given away before the local, state, and national governments had figured out how to respond; and took extraordinary measures to ensure that its employees in the area were safe and solvent.

This impression is at odds with that of many outside the organization who see another picture. As one critic put it, "In 2005, Lee Scott, Walmart's CEO...committed the company to the goals of being 100% supplied by renewable energy, creating zero waste, and selling products that sustain resources and the environment. Meanwhile, Walmart paid its employees almost 15% less than other large retailers, and because of the lower pay, its employees made greater use of public health and welfare programs."[9] Those holding these views cite lawsuits charging Walmart with unfair labor practices, rather than the remarkably small number of these lawsuits, or the absence of stories about Walmart laying off employees during the recent Great Recession. Combining these two perspectives conjures the image of a cheapskate neighbor who would nevertheless enter your burning house to save you.

Much has been made of an ingenious strategy that has thrust Walmart into global prominence as the world's largest private employer. This strategy comprises everyday low prices, small-town and suburban store locations, and state-of-the-art logistics, among other things. Attention is also given to the company's ability to execute through end-of-the-week planning meetings, followed by the dispatch of senior executives into the field for four days in Walmart's fleet of aircraft, as well as the effective use of the Internet combined with a proprietary television network. The company's leading-edge information systems, well-planned logistics network, and unmatched bargaining power have enabled it to get merchandise to the right places in a timely manner at low everyday prices.

But perhaps the most overlooked and undervalued of Walmart's assets is its culture (neighborly, people-friendly, trustworthy, frugal, understated—qualities typical of a small town) propagated globally. (As someone who grew up near a town similar to Bentonville, I felt right at home having lunch at a country club just like the one where I caddied as a boy.) Yes, Walmart's continuing success is the result of a well-orchestrated strategy executed brilliantly. But a large part of its continued growth and success is due to a culture that fits the strategy and methods of execution like an old shoe.

Several days after my Walmart visit, I found myself in the modest headquarters of Southwest Airlines in Dallas, Texas. Buried in the reams of material written about the company (including several Harvard Business School case studies going back to 1975) are the reasons that the company's founders and senior executives most often cite for the industry-leading success of Southwest. They don't talk as much about strategy—point-to-point (versus hub-and-spoke) operations, on-time arrivals, frequent departures—as they do about the importance of the company's culture. It's summed up in a statement of The Southwest Way, focused around a "Warrior Spirit," a "Servant's Heart," and a "Fun-LUVing Attitude."[10] It's about values such as teamwork, individual initiative, having fun on the job, and giving back to each other and the community. The culture is supported by behaviors that include frequent celebrations and recognition, communication of achievements, and impromptu and innovative spur-of-the moment actions needed to get the job done.

In a recent conversation, I asked Southwest cofounder Herb Kelleher how he and his fellow founders had thought about mission, values, and strategy at the beginning (in 1969). His response was as follows:

> At the beginning, we said "stop wasting time on five- or ten-year plans. We want to start an airline. Culture comes first; what we're about is protecting and growing people. The questions we asked were "What do we want to be? What do we want to do for the world?"...We wanted to be the airline for the common man.[11]

This helps explain why Southwest is a way of life for Employees who put the company and their fellow Associates before themselves.[12] It helps explain how the company has been able to survive adversity and report nearly 40 consecutive years of profits in an industry that in its entire history has made very little profit. And it helps explain why Southwest, after 9/11, departed from industry practice and laid off no one; or why Employees, at a time when fuel prices were spiking, symbolically bought fuel for the company; or why Southwest now, as competitors emulate elements of its strategy, can fall back on its culture as its secret weapon in maintaining low costs while providing differentiated personal service to its highly loyal Customers.

My visits suggested several similarities in these two organizations. First, it was clear that the mission comes first in both. If Walmart is about saving money for shoppers, Southwest is about saving money for travelers.

Managers in both of these companies view themselves as acting as "agents for the customer," as David Glass, former CEO of Walmart, used to put it.[13] *This is a simple but profound thought. How did we ever forget it?* At Walmart, this is played out in such things as the negotiating stance taken with vendors (which the vendors characterize as tough but fair), as well as the way in which the stores are merchandised and managed.

Dave Ridley, who was the senior executive for pricing at Southwest Airlines at the time I talked with him, put it in a similarly memorable way. He said that the objective of his group is to come into a new market with the lowest sustainable price possible—not the lowest introductory price, the lowest sustainable price.[14]

Managers in both organizations constantly use the word "value." Contrary to what some might suppose, this includes what their targeted customers also regard as high quality.

Both companies provide prime examples of efforts to foster organizations that think and behave in the best tradition of "families." They spend a great deal of time together, enjoy each other, are visible to one another, communicate constantly, try to find ways to "let their hair down" together, fight and make up, and celebrate their triumphs and foibles.

This requires that managers spend a great deal of time in the field, at times sharing the work of the front line. To do this, both organizations incur higher-than-normal executive time and expenses for travel and communication. At Southwest, the head of the route-planning department, for example, tries to get his group into the field every six weeks for a full day of work on a counter or in a baggage-handling crew to understand the problems caused by certain kinds of scheduling moves. This is expected behavior, not an exception. Even in the age of the Internet, there is relatively low reliance on e-mail in preference to face-to-face, voice, and video communication. The culture also requires total dedication and "immersion" on the part of managers and perhaps accounts for the search for ways to involve employees' families in the affairs of the companies. This is perhaps not all that remarkable until you realize that the family at Southwest Airlines is more than 40,000 strong; at Walmart, it exceeds 2.3 million, 1.4 million of them in the U.S. alone. It may help explain why senior managers have no time to serve on the boards of other companies.

Both companies select for attitude and train for skills. Furthermore, employee attitude is taken into account in the execution of strategy. At Walmart, potentially attractive markets are relegated to lower priority if there is any question about the company's ability to staff new stores with people who have the right attitude. At Southwest, the route planners point out that one criterion stands out among others used in selecting new destinations. It is whether the new city or route will enable the company to maintain its "patina of spirituality," expressed in terms of quality of work life.[15] This is not phony talk. It goes far beyond cheers and songs. It means that people are recognized for what they do as individuals. They are taken into account when important decisions are made.

Celebration is given high priority in both organizations. Although this may often engage employees in what some would regard as "hokey" behavior, it is memorable to participants and communicates the importance of people. Celebration, to the extent that it contributes to the quality of work life, may help explain why both of these companies achieve extraordinary productivity when compared with their peers.

Both of these organizations are frugal. This fact is reflected in everything from the appearance of corporate headquarters to compensation. Although this frugality has garnered Walmart occasional unfavorable publicity for its low wages for frontline employees, it is important to point out that compensation for senior executives is similarly low by the standards of the industries in which these two firms operate.

Behaviors that support these values are important. At Walmart, they tell a lot of stories and compare a lot of information; at Southwest Airlines, they hug before they start the stories. LUV appears everywhere at Southwest, including the company's New York Stock Exchange stock symbol. Respect for others is the equivalent value at Walmart. This value is characterized by the "ten-foot greeting" accorded visitors to Walmart offices, like myself, who stray not far from employees. It is a close cousin to the welcome provided by greeters at the entrances to the company's stores. (A series of these greetings in Walmart's parking lot in Bentonville almost made me miss my plane out of Arkansas one day.) Southwest exudes a "cowboy" feeling and makes an effort to maintain an "underdog" mentality, characterized by the frequent use of the term "Warrior Spirit." Both organizations have a clear code for how one works with others. And it is consistent with, and directly related to, the values and beliefs.

At Walmart and Southwest Airlines, employees are developed and promoted from within. Rarely is a senior executive hired from outside.

The strategies of both of these organizations have both market and operational focus. Most "merely good" competitors would settle for one of these critical sources of focus. To be outstanding, I'm convinced you have to have both. The strategies, however, were not clear at the outset. They were shaped by the founders' values. Among other things, the refusal of Helen Walton to move to a larger city influenced her husband's decision to open Walmart stores in relatively small markets, avoiding larger cities for years in the company's development.[16] At Southwest, a pricing experiment to fill seats on late-night flights several months after the company began operations led to the airline's eventual low-price, high-capacity utilization strategy.[17] In both companies, the relationship between strategy and culture is complex. Attributing success primarily to either culture or strategy in these organizations (or any others) would be foolhardy. For example, both organizations are built on a set of values and a human resources business model that contributes to low cost. This includes high levels of productivity resulting from relatively high worker loyalty, low turnover, and hence low recruiting and training costs. It translates into closer relationships between employees and frequent customers, thereby contributing to sales and marketing "efficiency." Wages may or may not be lower than those of competitors (at Southwest, they're not), but combined with high productivity, they produce very low costs per unit of output.

The strategies differ on one dimension—the presence of organized labor. At Walmart, management's human resources strategy has been driven in part by a desire to operate without unions. Southwest, on the other hand, is the most highly unionized airline in the U.S. However, it has been able to maintain labor agreements that allow employees to serve as needed in a wide range of jobs.

Unlike many organizations, both companies benefit from distinctive cultures that were attractive to the "right" people almost from the moment of their founding. Their successful strategies began to show results later, before the companies ran out of money. *The point is that in these organizations, strategy (and how it is executed) and culture are intertwined and support one another.*

Both of these companies have global "brands" that are among the strongest in their respective industries. This is particularly remarkable for Southwest, because it operates only marginally beyond U.S. borders. Conversations with employees at all levels create the impression that both Walmart and Southwest Airlines, in spite of unremarkable pay practices, are good places to work. Both work hard at building distinctive cultures that contribute to their efforts to hire suprior talent. One indication of their cultures' strength and health is the number of candidates for every entry-level job opening. At Southwest Airlines, it exceeds 50. In the last pre-recession year, 2007, the company had 232,000 applicants for roughly 4,000 job openings. At Walmart the ratio is lower. But consider this: The company has to fill more than 200,000 jobs *per year*.

One other parallel is of particular curiosity to me. It is summed up in a passage in a letter I received from Herb Kelleher in response to the question of why Southwest Airlines does not employ MBA graduates of so-called "leading" business schools. (At one time, the letter might just as well have come from Walmart, although the company now has a handful of graduates from such schools in its executive ranks.) Herb wrote the following:

> I guess that we pretty generally feel that we often fare better building from the bottom up rather than from the top down. Are there exceptions? Yes, there surely are and their contributions have been both profound and substantive. Nonetheless, the overarching truth is that all of the elements that make Southwest Airlines "different," both operationally and atmospherically, were conceived and executed by people that did not have business school degrees, and in many cases, had so-called "inferior" college degrees, if any at all.[18]

I'll return to this matter in the final chapter.

Are the parallels between these two organizations coincidence, or do they reflect patterns that beg to be understood? If it is the latter, what can other organizations—especially those with internally inconsistent strategies and values that are poorly understood by employees—learn from their experiences, as well as those of other relatively successful and unsuccessful organizations? And, perhaps most importantly, what difference does it make? Of what importance is it to employees of these organizations and to their financial performance? Finding answers to these questions required the exploration of others.

Questions to Be Addressed

This book addresses the following questions:

- How does culture contribute to and detract from an organization's success?

- How, if at all, does an organization's culture affect its attractiveness as a place to work; employee loyalty, engagement, "ownership," turnover rates, and productivity; rate of new business development; client loyalty; and record of referring new business?

- To what extent can we estimate the importance of a culture's influence on performance in relation to other traits such as leadership, business strategy, the quality of execution, organization, and policies and practices?

- How is the value of a culture measured? What is it worth in terms of better performance and profitability?

- How does culture matter in fostering innovation in times of adversity and when we create organizations, perhaps multinational, with different subcultures?

- Of what special significance is culture in mission-driven organizations, both for-profit and not-for-profit?

- Going forward, how will the rate of change in the environment—influenced by such things as new communication technologies, global competition (and cooperation), and the influx of new generations of people with different interests and values into the workforce—affect the role of culture in organizations?

- What leadership behaviors and management practices are most essential in fostering, preserving, and, in some cases, reviving successful cultures?

To explore these questions, I first examined a variety of secondary sources as well as my own library of field observations. Many of them were documented in forty years worth of cases prepared with the cooperation of the managements of both for-profit and not-for-profit organizations. This provided the basis for two conceptual frameworks for measuring the quantitative and qualitative importance of an effective culture: the Four Rs and the culture cycle. They are described and applied in Chapters 5 through 7.

I was then fortunate to find an organization whose management was willing to provide an unusual level of cooperation in the data collection and analysis needed to test the Four R conceptual framework. That work is described in some detail in Chapter 7 and Appendixes B and C.

In total, the research for the book uses a variety of quantitative and other data, including interviews with leaders of a number of organizations collected over two decades. This research helped me assemble an argument for the importance of an effective culture, and ways to measure it using elements of the culture cycle, in an organization's success.

How This Book Is Organized

The book is divided into four parts. The first deals with what culture is and isn't, ways in which it is associated with performance, and how it relates to other important determinants of success over an organization's life cycle. It might as well be titled "thinking clearly about culture." The implication is that people often don't.

The second part presents results of an effort to determine just how and to what degree culture matters in fostering effective performance. In it, I set forth a Four R economic "model" that describes the information that is necessary to measure culture's impact on the bottom line. That is combined with a description of noneconomic variables (the most important indicators of culture at work) derived from case studies of many organizations and organized into a culture cycle. The Four R and culture cycle concepts are then utilized in a field study for which findings and conclusions are reported.

In the third part, the attention shifts to the impact of culture on innovation; the ability of an organization to survive during times of adversity; its capability to operate globally, possibly with several subcultures; and its ability to adapt to changing technological, social, and legal challenges.

The role of leadership in shaping, sustaining, and changing culture is the subject of the final part.

Chapters 1 through 4 cover theories behind the development of cultures. If you're interested in measuring the impact of culture on your own organization, you will benefit from a close look at Chapters 5 through 7 as well as the appendixes. Practicing managers may also be interested in Chapters 8 through 12, which explore the impact of culture from various vantage points. Senior managers may be most interested in Chapters 13 and 14. Summaries of each chapter should help you understand content you don't otherwise read in detail.

Throughout the book, you'll see cultures through the eyes of leaders in both for-profit and not-for-profit (including government) organizations. Some have failed, providing good object lessons. But others have shaped, fostered, and generally relied on cultures to achieve not only strategic goals but, more importantly, places to work that attract and inspire human beings to develop themselves.

1

A Crisis in Organization Culture?

A Conference Board survey found recently that only 45% of U.S. workers were satisfied with their jobs.[1] It was the lowest level in the 23-year history of the survey. If it's true of the American workforce as a whole, that leaves more than 85 million Americans who are not satisfied with their jobs—in short, a lot of dissatisfaction.

How could this be happening in an economy that has seen a dramatic increase in information-centered jobs that are supposedly more interesting, intellectually challenging, and higher paying than jobs they are replacing? Are these jobs outnumbered by others where the work is unvaried and uninteresting; where managers are disliked or, worse yet, distrusted; where other employees seem like they aren't carrying their share of the work; where there is little opportunity for personal development or advancement; where there is little control over how work is to be performed; and where there is no identification with an inspiring or even important mission? Is this a case of unmet expectations? If so, is it because of inflated expectations or poor experiences or both?

The phenomenon is not limited to the U.S. A 2005 study of 86,000 full-time employees in 16 countries found that only 14% of respondents answered questions suggesting that they were "highly engaged" with their work, as opposed to 25% who were identified as "disengaged."[2] The importance of this fact is reflected by the finding that those who were "highly engaged" indicated that they were more than twice as likely to stay in their jobs as those who were "disengaged." Furthermore, the report concluded that "companies with higher levels of employee engagement tend to outperform those with lower employee engagement."[3]

It's easy to conclude that these survey results quantify the fallout from a loss of trust in organizations and institutions in general. But these responses were given during a peak time for unemployment; the respondents had jobs when many other people didn't. Shouldn't they have more trust in the "system" than others? Shouldn't gratitude for their relative good fortune have had some effect on their responses? Or did uncertainty about the future color their feelings about their jobs? Or did Peter Senge put his finger on the cause when he wrote, "I believe that the prevailing system of management is, at its core, dedicated to mediocrity. It forces people to work harder and harder to compensate for failing to tap the spirit and collective intelligence that characterize working together at their best."[4]

According to Larry Senn and Jim Hart, who base their observations on continuing measurements in organizations with which they consult, "stress levels and burnout have been rising..." This may be caused in part by longer hours and greater demands on employees. But Senn and Hart note that "high stress levels are almost always accompanied by low scores in 'appreciation' of managers for those working for them and 'high performance expected but not recognized.'"[5] If they are right, dissatisfaction with work has more to do with management behaviors than it does with economic trends, technological and other types of change, and the demands and stress they create. As we'll see, these behaviors result largely from organization cultures gone awry.

Numbers and trends like this suggest trouble in the world of work. They also suggest a sizeable opportunity that awaits organizations that can take advantage of a source of competitive advantage being handed to them on a silver platter. It's the advantage that can be afforded by a culture that differentiates one competitor from another, that attracts the best talent, and that provides such a stimulating work environment that it encourages talented employees to stay and become partners in the effort to recruit more talent of the same caliber.

Culture really matters. As Lou Gerstner wrote, reflecting on his experiences in taking over the job of CEO at a failing IBM and achieving one of the most remarkable turnarounds in recent business history:

Until I came to IBM, I probably would have told you that culture was just one among several important elements in any organization's makeup and success—along with vision, strategy, marketing, financials, and the like ... I came to see, in my time at IBM, that culture isn't just one aspect of the game—it *is* the game.[6]

Culture has served some organizations so well that I am continually amazed that more don't get it. The "it" that they don't get is the subject of this book. It's why and how culture matters.

What Culture Is and Isn't

An organization's culture is complex. But it's not hard to describe. It's often explained as being "the way we do things around here"—what goes and what doesn't.[7] These behaviors reflect assumptions about people and how they think and act, as well as values and beliefs shared by members of an organization, whether or not they have been articulated. They are reinforced by artifacts—icons, stories, heroes and heroines, rites and rituals—that remind people what an organization stands for, such as IBM's famous "THINK" signs or Walmart's ubiquitous "ten-foot greeting." Stories about organizational heroes or "goats" provide added reinforcement. Finally, "the way we do things around here" is backed up by efforts to measure behaviors and take some kind of corrective action when the behaviors are unacceptable to other members of the organization. These assumptions, values, beliefs, behaviors, artifacts, measurements, and actions determine how things get done in an organization.

Stealth Weapon or Humanizing Effort?

Culture can be thought of as an element of organizational strategy. As such, it is a stealth weapon. Its returns on investment—resulting from such things as employee loyalty and organizational continuity, service to those outside the organization, increased productivity, and a selfless mentality toward others in the organization—can be impressive. Or they can be very disappointing. One study of *Fortune* 1,000 companies estimated that 20% of people's time in an organization is wasted on issues related to the corporate culture.[8] Another led its authors to estimate that in a strong culture, "a company can gain as much as one or two hours of productive work per employee per day."[9]

This view of culture as an element of organizational strategy suggests (incorrectly, I think) that it is something to be used primarily to manipulate people. Another interpretation is that culture is the humanizing element in what would otherwise be a drab and frustrating organizational existence. It can help establish expectations, foster trust, facilitate communications, and reduce uncertainty in relationships between human beings. In so doing, it can contribute to more productive outcomes. It's this interpretation that may help explain why organizations like this are often regarded as outstanding, engaging places to work.

Why is it that organizations with such cultures seem willing to share "secrets" of their success with the outside world, even competitors? For example, why has the Disney organization made a business of educating others, even competitors, in how it spreads its "pixie dust" that leads to profits in nearly everything it does? Or why is Southwest Airlines so open about its team-based methods for achieving rapid turnaround of its aircraft, thereby reducing to industry lows the costs of owning and operating aircraft? Why does Zappos.com, a large Internet shoe retailer, host ten or more groups of visitors daily to its Las Vegas headquarters, many of whom are looking for secrets to its success? I believe it's because organizations with strong, adaptive, and open cultures that foster employee loyalty and productivity are not concerned that competitors may find it possible to borrow policies, methods, and processes. They are convinced that the real key to making those policies, methods, processes, and, yes, strategies work is something much more difficult to emulate—culture. As Alfred Lin, chairman and COO of Zappos.com, puts it, "Our web sites, policies—all can be copied, but not our special culture."[10]

It's one thing for US Airways' management to conclude that the key to competing with Southwest is rapid turnaround of aircraft; it's another thing to try to achieve it, especially in the absence of a highly

productive culture based on strong employee psychological investment and "ownership" in the success of "their" airline. You can guess
the result when US Airways' management decided some years ago
to match Southwest's industry-leading aircraft turnaround time by
increasing the number of employees assigned to turning each flight
more rapidly: even longer turnaround times.

It is tempting to rhapsodize about culture and the benefits derived
from the "intrinsic" (nonmonetary) rewards experienced by employees who care about the success of their organization as well as their
own well-being. But it is easy to overlook the presence of a fine line
between pride and arrogance, especially toward customers, that can
accompany intrinsic motivation. With it comes the potential for a disruptive culture exerting a negative impact on an organization's costs,
customer relationships, and economic performance.

The question is not whether an organization has a culture. All do.
Many have more than one. Cultures form with or without leadership,
structure, or clear intent. The question is, what kind of culture naturally emerges from or is shaped by leadership?

The Development of Interest in Organization Culture

Interest in organization culture has waxed and waned in the past
80 years since a set of concepts originating in social anthropology
(studies of primitive peoples as well as species such as chimpanzees)
were applied to commercial organizations.[11] Industrial psychologists
Elton Mayo, Fritz Roethlisberger, and William Dickson carried out
research at the Hawthorne Works of Western Electric. It showed that
workers respond positively with increased output to almost any kind
of recognition or concern for their working conditions. More generally, "increased output and improved attitude...could best be associated with changes in the method of supervision" (as opposed to the
level of pay, which had been assumed up to that time).[12] This fueled
questions about assumptions underlying Frederick Winslow Taylor's
philosophy of increasing productivity by designing and paying for

work by breaking it into repetitive, boring tasks. This practice had dominated the organization of work since early in the twentieth century. As Taylor put it in a lecture he gave in 1906, "In our scheme, we do not ask for the initiative of our men. We do not want any initiative. All we want of them is to obey the orders we give them, do what we say, and do it quick."[13] So much for Taylor's grammar or state of management theory during the Industrial Revolution.

Early theoretical writings by George Homans examined the impact of norms and values on individuals working in small groups, concluding that "in some measure every group teaches its members to have the sentiments it then proceeds to satisfy."[14] Philip Selznick, without using the term culture, wrote about infusing an organization with value to create an institution to "fulfill personal or group needs."[15] Later, the work of Terry Deal, Allan Kennedy, and Edgar Schein defined the nature of organization culture.[16] Joanne Martin helped us understand how to measure it.[17] Some of this work led to an understanding of how the Japanese and a handful of U.S. firms were such successful competitors during the 1970s and 1980s.[18] It also provided the basis for efforts to explore the impact of culture on an organization's performance.[19]

The first truly blockbuster hit among business books was *In Search of Excellence*, authored by Tom Peters and Robert Waterman in 1982. It rekindled interest in the subject by providing anecdotal evidence that culture, a term rarely used in business literature before 1980, was an important factor in the success of a sample of 43 firms they observed.[20] Of equal importance was their reaffirmation of the importance of alignment of the elements of what Richard Pascale and Tony Athos had earlier termed the "Seven S Framework."[21] It comprises the "hardware" of strategy and structure as well as the "software" of style (the way we do things), systems, staff, skills, and shared values (culture). Their thesis was that extraordinary performance could be achieved through planning and execution that produces an alignment, or internally consistent reinforcement, among the S's. Significantly, when displaying the Seven S Framework in their book, Peters and Waterman arrayed the other six S's around the seventh, shared values, the unifying focus in an excellent organization.[22] A later, more systematic study of 18 American and Japanese firms with long records of success, by James Collins and Jerry Porras, attributed much of excellent performance to the organizations' cultures.[23]

Meanwhile, leaders of large corporations, such as Lou Gerstner at IBM and Jack Welch at GE, gave credence to the importance of culture in their organizations.[24] Interest was further heightened by the corporate scandals early in this century, in part resulting from stark differences between espoused values and leadership behavior. Whatever else happened at Enron and Worldcom, it stimulated efforts to explore ways in which their cultures contributed to an atmosphere of fraud and deceit. In this atmosphere, "leaders and managers were not to be questioned or second-guessed" in spite of clear and public statements of admirable values to the contrary.[25] Similar allegations have been made more recently about the leadership of the now-defunct Lehmann Brothers in helping trigger the Great Recession of 2008.[26] They arose yet again from alleged differences between public declarations by BP's leaders regarding safety and protecting the environment and actual cost-cutting decisions leading to such personal and environmental disasters as refinery explosions and the Gulf of Mexico fire and oil leak.[27]

Anecdotal evidence from seven case studies led Charles A. O'Reilly III and Jeffrey Pfeffer to conclude in 2000 that an organization's culture helps it leverage the abilities of what they termed ordinary people to achieve extraordinary results.[28]

Some of these ideas are reflected in the recent writing of Nobel prize-winning economist George Ackerlof and Rachel Kranton. They wrote about the causes of seemingly irrational economic decisions by large numbers of individuals that call into question one of the basic economic assumptions of formal economics—rational behavior on the part of individuals and organizations. They coined the term *identity economics* to explain why people get tattoos and elect to work for less money than they could make elsewhere. They concluded that these people are motivated by the value they derive from sharing the same norms and identity as others in a group or organization. In a sense, they "fit in" and use the group's shared norms to advance its goals. It's a belated recognition by "behavioral economists" of the value of an effective culture. They go so far as to assert that identity economics "transforms our understanding of what makes economies work or fail."[29]

Future waves of interest in the importance of culture and organizational performance are inevitable. Culture can foster organization stability and facilitate changes in strategy. Both will be increasingly important in an environment evolving ever more rapidly due to changes in technology and the outlook and work patterns of those capable of using it. In addition, interest will grow in the rise and fall of enterprise in countries around the world, particularly India and China, with organization cultures distinctly different from those developed in the Western world.[30] We'll come back to these matters later.

The Nature of an Organization's Culture

Charles Jacobs has described an organization's culture as "the collective story the group tells itself" that "drives the thinking that drives behavior."[31] A more formal set of lenses through which culture can be viewed by managers is made up of shared assumptions, values, beliefs, behaviors, and artifacts. For those who believe that cultures can be shaped and managed, two other related elements, measurement and action, also are critical.

Shared Assumptions

Shared assumptions provide the basis from which other elements of culture are derived. Edgar Schein goes so far as to define culture as "a pattern of shared basic assumptions that was learned by a group as it solved its problems of external adaptation and internal integration, that has worked well enough to be considered valid and, therefore, to be taught to new members as the correct way to perceive, think, and feel in relation to those problems."[32]

Douglas McGregor, who contributed Theory X and Y philosophies (to be discussed shortly) to the management lexicon, was one of the first to highlight the importance of shared assumptions. He commented that "it is not possible to reach a managerial decision or take a management action uninfluenced by assumptions, whether adequate or not."[33]

Often the assumptions are those of an organization's founder, the "rightness" of which is confirmed through success. Assumptions that relate to customers, competitors, suppliers, communities, and the legal and regulatory environments influence an organization's strategy and how it executes that strategy.

In order to change a culture at its roots, these assumptions have to be understood and altered. This takes time. In part for this reason, few practitioners can accomplish this task during their tenure on the job. This explains why nearly all change deals with other elements of culture.

Assumptions are influenced by personal experience. O'Reilly and Pfeffer provide an interesting example of this in their study of Cypress Semiconductor and its founder and CEO, T. J. Rodgers.[34] Rodgers' first job was at a company called American Microprocessors, Inc., which later failed. He remembered it as "the ultimate hypocrisy of warm-and-fuzzy cultures that don't deliver... Winning is what matters. And if winning means being tough, demanding, impatient, then that's what you have to be."[35] Vowing not to let that happen to his company, Rodgers created an organization based on five values:[36]

- Cypress is about winning.
- Cypress people are "only the best."
- We do what's right for Cypress.
- We make our numbers.
- We invent and make state-of-the-art products.

In short, little is "warm and fuzzy" about them.

Assumptions that relate to people, their motivations, how they work, and how they relate to one another have a profound influence on an organization's culture. Table 1-1 shows two contrasting sets of shared assumptions, the policies and practices with which they are associated, and the results they produce. They result in two very different cultures, both of which can be successful if they are internally consistent and aligned with strategy and execution. Over the years they have become associated with what has come to be known as Theory X and Theory Y management.[37] I've purposely stated the assumptions to provide maximum contrast. They represent two extremes on a spectrum of possibilities.

Table 1-1 The Impact of Shared Basic Assumptions on Culture, People, and Management: Two Alternative Sets of Shared Basic Assumptions About People, Motives, Work, and Organizational Performance*

Assumption Set X	Assumption Set Y
The average human being	The average human being
• inherently dislikes work.	• regards work as being as natural as play or rest.
• avoids work if he can.	• exercises self-direction and self-control when committed to goals.
• prefers to be directed.	
• wants to avoid responsibility.	• is rewarded in part by needs for satisfaction of ego and self-actualization.
• has relatively little ambition.	
• wants security above all.	
• therefore must be coerced, controlled, directed, and threatened with punishment to get him to put forth adequate effort.	• learns, under proper conditions, to accept and even seek responsibility.
	• has potential that is only partially realized.
	The capacity to exercise imagination, ingenuity, and creativity in problem solving is widely distributed in the population.
Resulting Policies and Practices	
Break work into tasks that	Break work into tasks that
• require few skills and little training.	• require skills and cross-training.
• can be performed by individuals.	• can be performed by teams.
Limit training to the minimum necessary.	Provide good training and encourage personal development.
Pay low compensation.	Pay market or higher compensation.
Provide close supervision.	Allow use of judgment on the job, with limited supervision.
Expect high turnover of people and staff, and organize for it.	Expect employee loyalty.
Minimize promotions from within.	Promote from within.

Results Produced

High employee turnover (confirming the correctness of assumptions and expectations)	Low employee turnover (confirming the correctness of assumptions and expectations)
High recruiting and supervisory costs	Low recruiting and supervisory costs
Low wages and per-person training costs	High wages and per-person training costs
Low job satisfaction	High job satisfaction
Highest potential for success is in a low-cost competitive strategy	Highest potential for success is in a differentiated competitive strategy

* Assumption sets X and Y are adapted from Douglas McGregor, *The Human Side of Enterprise*, 25th Edition (New York: McGraw-Hill Book Company, 1985), pp. 33–47.

Theory X

Proponents of Theory X management trace their roots at least back to the work of Frederick Winslow Taylor and so-called scientific management. Scientific management advocated breaking a job into its tasks and training a person to do one of them. By structuring repetition into a job and coupling it with incentives for production, the goal was to increase productivity. And it helped American industry achieve significant productivity gains in the early twentieth century. Although Henry Ford did not acknowledge any influence from Taylor, who in turn regarded Ford's autos as "roughly made cars," Ford's engineers were probably influenced by Taylor's writings when they designed the first Ford assembly line, which revolutionized the production of automobiles.[38] Because of its emphasis on one best way of doing things, "Taylorism" became associated with command-and-control management.

In its most extreme form, Theory X assumes, I believe, that frontline people work only because they have to. If not provided with extrinsic incentives (money) and supervised, they will not work well. They have limited skills and aptitudes and are hard to train beyond a certain point. But they are more affordable than versatile, skilled people. Worst of all, workers are not loyal; they will leave for a small increase in pay.

As shown in Table 1-1, this results in policies and practices reflecting these assumptions. First, break work into repetitive tasks that require few skills and little training, as Taylor advocated. Pay wages tied to output, a practice called piecework. Limit training to the minimum necessary. Provide close supervision. Expect high turnover, and prepare for it by not promoting from within. Results confirm the assumptions, leading to a continuation of the policies and practices.

Before we conclude that this set of shared assumptions is passé, consider that frontline employees of many firms providing services such as security, catering, and even basic health care experience Theory X management today. And it works—at least for a time.

The theory is alive and well. After I coauthored an article suggesting that a strategy of more careful selection and training; hiring fewer, better-paid people for broader job responsibilities; and encouraging their loyalty, among other things, could produce higher employee loyalty leading to service differentiation, greater customer satisfaction, and higher long-term profit, I received a communication from the founder and owner of a successful business. It informed me that my view of the world was naïve. As he put it:

> Our experience is that people basically do not want to put in a day's work for a day's pay. So we have to watch them closely. We design jobs that don't require much training and are easier to supervise. People no longer are loyal either. I have plenty of evidence that my view is right. The minute our people get a better offer, they leave."[39]

Several very successful organizations have adapted Theory X concepts. For example, UPS, the large, global package-delivery organization, was founded in 1907, just as the popularity of Taylorism was on the rise, and it is essentially managed today much as it was then. But instead of assuming that people don't want to work, its management seeks drivers and package sorters who are willing to do whatever it takes to make sure that packages are delivered punctually by adhering to an extensive and strict set of recommended methods accompanied by reasonably close supervision. In addition, UPS has flourished from the application of carefully engineered "time and motion" processes that were introduced with the hiring in 1923 of a Frederick Taylor disciple by UPS founder Jim Casey.[40] Ensuing industrial engineering introduced methods that apply to nearly every component of the company's delivery "cars" and even prescribe the gait that a successful UPS driver uses to deliver packages most efficiently.

In return for their loyalty and productivity, UPS employees, unlike their less fortunate predecessors in the Taylor movement, have a good chance to be promoted into supervisory ranks. Generous opportunities for ownership of company stock have made many UPS employees over the years quite wealthy.

The CEO of auto glass installer Safelite, which has employed piecework-based compensation systems similar to those advocated by Taylor, has commented that it wasn't piecework that made Safelite profitable. As he put it, "It requires a fundamental change in the business culture ... based on trust."[41]

Trust is at the core of the success of Lincoln Electric, a leading manufacturer of welding equipment that has prospered for many years. Founded during the era of Taylorism, Lincoln Electric has applied the concepts of time-and-motion study and compensation based on piecework, the anathema of much of organized labor because of the pressure it puts on workers. In this case, it has been applied to good advantage for both the organization and its members because it has been combined with a guaranteed employment policy that fosters trust and mitigates some of the stresses of Theory X.[42]

Theory Y

The lineage of this theory passes through the studies conducted over an eight-year period beginning in 1924 at the Chicago Hawthorne Works of Western Electric, mentioned earlier. The researchers concluded that effective working relations between operators and supervisors had a greater impact on production "efficiency" than incentives or changes in working conditions. Even more profound was the conclusion that "An industrial organization may be regarded as performing two major functions, that of producing a product and that of creating and distributing satisfactions among the individual members of the organization."[43]

Abraham Maslow pointed out later that people have nonmonetary needs for "self-realization" long after basic needs for such things as food and shelter are met.[44] Work fulfills several needs for them. In addition to recognition, they seek personal training and advancement, broader responsibilities, and a sense of community. They will be loyal to organizations that can provide those things in addition to reasonable compensation.[45]

It was left to Douglas McGregor to put a memorable stamp on these issues by naming and elaborating on Theories X and Y at a convocation at the Massachusetts Institute of Technology in April 1957. As Warren Bennis put it, the book emanating from the speech "changed an entire concept of organizational man and replaced it with a new paradigm that stressed human potential, emphasized human growth, and elevated the human role in industrial society."[46]

Policies and practices reflected in this philosophy often involve organizing work into tasks that have varying degrees of complexity and tasks that may be performed by teams. Strong emphasis is placed on recruiting and training frontline people who will fit with the culture for some time and require only limited supervision. Training and personal development also are emphasized. Employees are paid at or above market levels with the expectation that their higher productivity will offset high wages.

Results from these policies and practices include the following:

- Low employee turnover
- Low recruiting and supervisory costs
- High per-person training costs
- High productivity
- Compensation that is no higher than that of the competition, adjusting for productivity
- High job satisfaction
- A potentially successful strategy of differentiating products or services from those provided by competitors
- In some cases, relatively low costs

Note that shared assumptions underlying both Theories X and Y produce results that confirm the assumptions; they constitute self-fulfilling prophecies. And if they are consistent with other elements of an organization's strategy and execution, both can produce positive results—such as high productivity and low costs—for the organization, if not the individual. The question they pose, however, is: In which of these organizations would you like to work? In which would you like to be a manager? Your answer provides a clue to the durability of each approach in developing an effective culture.

Shared Values and Beliefs

Values and beliefs in young organizations often reflect those of the founder. In such cases they are influenced by personal experience. A classic example is Thomas Watson's beliefs at IBM, as articulated by his son:

- Respect for the dignity and rights of each person in the firm
- Giving the best customer service of any company in the world
- Pursuing all tasks with the objective of accomplishing them in a superior way[47]

Values and beliefs may be revisited occasionally to reflect the views of subsequent leaders, efforts to revive flagging performance, or a merger with another organization. For example, when John A. Allison IV became CEO of BB&T, the 11th largest bank in the U.S., in 1989, he began placing strong emphasis on the values—reason, independent thinking, and decisions based on facts—articulated in Ayn Rand's book, *Atlas Shrugged*, to which he strongly subscribes. New managers began receiving copies of the book. The company's values as well as its philosophy are set forth in some detail in a 30-page pamphlet distributed to all employees.[48] The values themselves reflect a set that Allison found more appealing when he took over.

An organization without a statement of mission or values has come to be seen as deficient. But the way in which many of those statements are formulated renders them practically useless. "Excellence," for example, is often listed as either a pursuit (as in a mission statement) or a value. But what does it mean to believe in the importance of excellence? Even when care is taken to vet the values throughout an organization, they often wind up as a set of words or notions that are so vague that they provide little guidance about how things are done. The authors of one study of several securities firms and investment banks concluded that "mission statements provide a familiar example of how executives allow talk to substitute for action... The executives assumed that saying something made it so."[49]

Behaviors

Statements of shared values and beliefs, if supplemented by suggested behaviors that are associated with each value, can provide clarity to "how" things are done. At Cisco Systems, for example, frugality—along with dedication to customer success, innovation and learning, partnerships, and teamwork—has been a value of the organization at least since the early days of this relatively young corporation. Recently, this has been modified to "doing more with less." But the definition doesn't end there. It translates into the following:

> As a core component of our culture, frugality is one of the values that has made our company great. It doesn't mean being cheap; it means getting the best value for what we do. I look to all Cisco employees to work with outsource partners on projects that fall beyond our realm of expertise, and to do so effectively. This allows Cisco to continue spending money on the two most important things—our customers and employees.[50]

It is also reflected in day-to-day policies, such as reimbursement only up to coach fare for air travel, regardless of the length of the flight. Whether or not this saves Cisco any money, it is a constant reminder of how the company does business.

Values and beliefs can be taught and memorized as part of a welcoming orientation to the organization. Accepted behaviors have to be learned over time, often through an on-the-job trial-and-error process. They influence and reflect how an organization functions. Edgar Schein cites an interesting example from his experiences some years ago at Digital Equipment Corporation (later acquired by Compaq) and Hewlett-Packard (which later acquired Compaq). At the time, both organizations placed strong emphasis on teamwork. But similarities ended when it came to practicing teamwork. According to Schein:

> At DEC, to be a team player meant to be open and truthful and trustworthy.... If you did not agree, you did not promise to do something that you did not intend to do (even if it meant delaying a decision). At HP, on the other hand, the assumption grew up that groups should reach consensus...that arguing too much or sticking to your own point of view too much was equivalent to not being a team player. Consequently,

decisions were reached much more quickly (than at DEC), but they did not stick. People agreed in public to uphold the norms but then in private failed to follow through, forcing the decision process to start all over again.[51]

Anyone transferring between these two organizations might have experienced some pain learning what teamwork meant in each.

Values, beliefs, and behaviors set forth at the corporate level, if shared and practiced consistently, can provide reassurance that things will be done in a certain way for a particular reason, one on which colleagues can rely during times of stress. As we will see, that does not preclude the development of subcultures peculiar to particular subsidiaries or departments (say, engineering versus sales). This will work as long as such subcultures don't produce dysfunctional conflict or depart from corporate values, beliefs, and behaviors.

Artifacts

Artifacts are important in providing constant reminders to members of the organization what is really important in how they do what they do. At MTV, the media empire aimed primarily at the 18-to-24-year-old crowd, television sets pervade the offices and hallways. They may be turned down but not off. And, of course, they're tuned to the MTV channel, where advertising spots designed for MTV by its young associates, a powerful nonmonetary "perk," often appeared early in the development of the business.[52]

An absence of artifacts where they are expected can be just as important. At Willow Creek Church, a megachurch located in a Chicago suburb, there are no religious icons in the sanctuary during so-called Sunday "seeker" services designed primarily for guests of church members who have not yet committed themselves to the church's beliefs.[53] The rostrum from which the minister speaks is transparent, eliminating a barrier and conveying a sense of trust between the pastor and those in attendance.

Artifacts that really count include stories, heroes, rites, and rituals. Organizations rich in stories and heroes invariably have strong cultures. Walmart employees still tell the story of how Sam Walton lost a bet to his management colleagues that Walmart could not achieve an ambitious sales target and, as a result, danced in a hula skirt on Wall Street.[54] Former ServiceMaster CEO Ken Hansen's lecture to new management candidates on "desk skills," which only incidentally dealt with the topic but really concerned conduct expected of a ServiceMaster manager, became legendary long after Hansen had departed the company. John Rollwagen succeeded legendary founder Seymour Cray as president of Cray Research in 1980, when Cray left to head a spin-off company. When Rollwagen was asked, "What will Cray Research do now that Seymour Cray is no longer around?" he replied, "I'm not going to tell anyone that he's gone. It will give me more freedom to invoke Seymour's philosophy of management."[55]

Companies with strong cultures have important rites and rituals. Bill George, former CEO of medical equipment maker Medtronic, is a no-nonsense leader (and teacher) who nevertheless has written emotionally about the company's Mission and Medallion ceremony. As he describes it:

> Shortly after I joined Medtronic, Earl Bakken (then-CEO) asked me to come to one of these (Mission and Medallion) ceremonies...(along with) thirty other new employees.... Earl started by describing the founding of the company and the invention of the pacemaker. Next he took considerable care to go over every word of the mission.... Finally, he invited each of us to come up individually to receive our medallion.... I still recall Earl's words as he handed me my medallion: "Bill, this medallion is only given to Medtronic employees, not even our customers. Put it on your desk and look at it while you're working. If you get frustrated with your work, remember that you are here to help restore people to full life and health, not just to make money for yourself or the company."[56]

At Rackspace Hosting, a company that manages web sites for customers, a rather bizarre form of ritual is used to recognize employees, called Rackspace Fanatics, who have done unusual things to serve customers. They are honored by having their photo taken in a straitjacket with the words "Customer Fanatic" on the front.

Artifacts are a means of communicating in memorable ways the kinds of things that are important to a culture. Given their nature, they can be changed occasionally to reflect ways in which an organization's culture relates to a changing environment. They provide powerful ways of communicating the essence of a culture.

Measurement and Action

Behaviors count only if they are monitored and if the measures trigger corrective action when behaviors are out of alignment with values.

The study of several securities firms and investment banks cited earlier concluded that executives in several organizations who had spent a great deal of time carefully constructing mission statements stressing such values as teamwork, integrity, and respect for the individual were basically wasting their time. For example, even though respect for the individual was a frequently cited value, there was little respect for individuals at lower levels in several of these organizations. Instead, there was more of a "churn and burn" mentality regarding young talent. When confronted with the evidence, the leadership expressed surprise.[57]

The most valid measurements of behavior are perceptions of people reporting to those whose performance is being measured. This is a case where perceptions trump facts, because people form their impressions and take actions about the workplace based on their perceptions. Of course, measurement in the absence of action may make a bad situation worse by raising expectations that aren't fulfilled.

Measurements and actions help ensure that saying something does make it so when it comes to an organization's culture. A classic example of this occurred at GE in 1992, whose shared values at that time included reality, candor, speed, empowerment, globalization, and acting in a boundaryless fashion. (This means the willingness and ability to share ideas and talent while working across organization lines to help and get help from sister departments and other companies.) For the first time, a process was put in place in which those who couldn't manage by the values and didn't respond to counseling were asked to leave even if they were meeting their financial goals. It's easy to say but tough to do, especially in a timely manner. But the policy, requiring both measurement and action, was cited by Jack Welch, CEO at the time, for its importance. In his words, "we could not afford the...person who delivers on all the commitments, makes the numbers, but doesn't share the values—the manager who typically forces performance out of people, rather than inspires it."[58]

I quoted Marvin Bower earlier in commenting on culture as "the way we do things around here." He could just as well have said "how we do things," suggesting the importance of "know how" as the essence of culture. Figure 1-1 shows one way of thinking about an organization's culture and its components. Each component—assumptions, values, beliefs, behaviors, artifacts, measurements, and actions—has its own properties. For example, shared assumptions, values, and beliefs are harder to influence, change, and "manage" than behaviors.[59] Much of their strength lies in the fact that they are relatively timeless in how they are stated. They constitute the bedrock on which changing strategies are based. This view maintains that unless you understand the assumptions underlying values and beliefs, it is difficult to understand what makes a culture work or, if it isn't working, how to change it. The roots of these assumptions run deep. They may have religious, psychological, or sociological origins. They are particularly relevant when one organization's culture is merged with another's, when organizations with different national origins (and assumptions) are attempting to cooperate or deal with one another, or when one element of culture becomes misaligned with others.

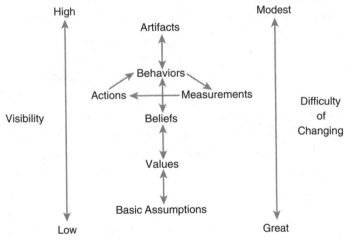

Figure 1-1 Elements of culture

The most visible aspects of culture—artifacts and behaviors—are also most easily changed in the shortest amount of time. Such efforts are often confused with basic culture change, but they can in themselves impact performance positively. We'll return to this topic when we address issues of leading culture change in Chapter 13.

Culture and the Workplace

Some people associate with an organization in order to change the world. Others do so primarily for the money. Whatever the motive, policies and behaviors associated with an organization's culture are among the primary determinants of a good workplace according to surveys of thousands of employees in many types of organizations. Here's what they tell us:[60]

I like my job for the following reasons:

- My boss is fair. She hires, recognizes, helps, and replaces the right people.
- I have ample opportunities for personal development.
- My work is recognized.
- My coworkers are winners. (Everyone likes to work with winners; winners don't like to work with losers.)
- I have the latitude (within limits) to deliver results to coworkers, customers, and others.
- My compensation is reasonable.

This is the approximate order in which reasons often are stated. Note that the first five reasons relate to behaviors resulting from values associated with an organization's culture. The sixth is associated with the success of a strategy and the execution of a business model (of which culture is a part) that enables management to return ample compensation to everyone in the organization. The first five reasons are called "intrinsic" motivators, as opposed to the "extrinsic" motivation of money.[61]

We're concerned about the workplace because we spend so much of our waking hours there. Good workplaces foster more productive work.[62] They encourage loyalty, leading to continuity and relationships among employees and between employees and customers. Studies have shown that these relationships reduce the costs of "friction" and thus are valuable.[63] Perhaps in part for these reasons, organizations offering the best places to work produce better returns on shareholder equity than their more ordinary counterparts.[64] (I say "in part" because to some degree, workplace quality may be associated with the economic results of a successful competitive strategy.)[65] One of the most comprehensive annual calculations of these reported that the annual returns to shareholders of the publicly held firms that were among the "100 best places to work" were more than 5 percentage points higher than those in the Standard & Poor's 500 and the Russell 3000 (smaller firms) from 1998 to 2008.[66]

Good places to work are found in all kinds of industries, as shown in Table 1-2. Over the past four years, retailers have been mentioned most frequently in *Fortune* magazine's annual rankings of the top ten places to work. But they are followed by organizations developing software, providing health care, and engaging in OEM manufacturing. The two companies making the list all four years were Wegmans Supermarkets and Genentech. Just try to find an industry pattern here. Nor are such workplaces associated with certain kinds of work. Rather, they occur in organizations where individual behaviors (often related to core values) are regarded as very positive and attractive, where an effort is made to measure those behaviors, and where timely action is taken to resolve situations where individuals don't practice the behaviors. The fact that good places to work are also associated with economic success suggests several other things:

- Good places to work do not have to be prohibitively costly to maintain. In fact, just the opposite may be closer to the truth.
- They rely to some extent on the degree to which the culture reflects the organization's strategy; the rate of change required to remain competitive; and the ability to adapt to the external demands of the changing social, legal, and economic environment.
- To some degree, good places to work depend on strategic success, creating a self-reinforcing benefit for both.

Table 1-2 Principal Businesses of Organizations Included on Fortune's List of Top Ten Best Places to Work, 2006 to 2009*

Principal Business	Number of Listings**
Retailing	9
Software development	5
Health care	5
OEM manufacturing	5
Consumer manufacturing	4
Biotechnology	4
Retail financial services	3
Investment banking	2
Management consulting	2
Energy	1
Total	**40**

 * Source: *Fortune* magazine for each of the four years
 ** Forty entries comprise the Top Ten list for four years.

It should be no surprise that effective cultures foster good places to work. In large part, an employee's perception of the quality of a workplace depends on the fit between what he has encountered on the job and what he expected. Effective cultures provide clear choices for prospective employees. This enables them to self-select into the organization. Thus, what is a great place to work for one person may be a terrible fit for another. It doesn't depend so much on the nature of a specific set of values as it does on the clarity of an organization's values, beliefs, and behaviors; how these are made clear to prospective employees to help them select themselves into the organization; the extent to which they reflect preferences of those employees; and the degree to which the organization can deliver on the promises they contain.

Culture and the Long-Term Erosion of Job Satisfaction

There are many possible explanations for the long-term decline in job satisfaction throughout the world. Not all concern culture. But they are rooted somehow in the shared assumptions with which managers approach their tasks. One such assumption is that today's world requires greater organizational "agility," too often used as a code word for the ability to upsize and downsize as needed. This assumption may satisfy investors' short-term needs but can wreak hardship on a workforce. It can lead to a shift in priorities away from behaviors and practices associated with organizational long-term stability, such as ensuring a good fit between the prospective employee and the job.

Agility as a strategy may be outweighed by other factors affecting job satisfaction. The same Conference Board study citing the decline in job satisfaction concluded that "increasing dissatisfaction is not just a 'survivor syndrome' artifact of having coworkers and neighbors laid off in the recession" and "this increasing worker unhappiness is not cyclical."[67] Furthermore, findings suggest a common reaction among all age or income groups. The primary reason given for a loss of job satisfaction is simply a loss of "interest in work," a factor outranking even concerns about job security at a time when you might have thought this would be paramount in everyone's mind. In addition, declining employee engagement was found to be associated with dissatisfaction about job design, organizational health, managerial quality, and extrinsic rewards.

We're led to conclude that a crisis of organization culture must be accounting for a substantial portion of the decline in job satisfaction. This underlines the importance of examining just how culture affects performance and what can be done about it.

Summary

Workers around the world are experiencing less job satisfaction. In the U.S., it has declined over a number of years, reaching the lowest point in the 23-year history of The Conference Board survey.

Although declining job security is one factor in the survey result, it is exceeded by the decline in interest in the work, leading to a loss in employee engagement as well as worker perceptions of such things as organizational health and managerial quality. It suggests the presence of a possible culture crisis in the workplace.

Every organization has a culture, whether or not it is clearly defined or communicated. Cultures ultimately reflect what works for the organization, as indicated by success. As a result, what we tend to observe are the survivors, organizations whose cultures have contributed to their success at least at certain critical points in their history.

An organization's culture comprises underlying assumptions, values, beliefs, behaviors, and artifacts.

At its heart are underlying assumptions about human nature and attitudes toward work. Two contrasting assumptions, for example, are associated with the so-called "X" and "Y" theories of management. Theory X is based on the assumptions that the average human being has an inherent dislike of work, requires a great deal of regimentation, and responds to monetary incentives. Theory Y, on the other hand, starts from the assumptions that human beings regard work as being as natural as play or rest, will exercise self-direction, and respond to nonmonetary as well as monetary incentives. Either of these theories may support good performance, depending on whether they are aligned with an organization's strategy and its methods of executing the actions that the strategy requires.

Values and beliefs shared by an organization's members follow from such assumptions. Values and beliefs are reflected in accepted behaviors of organization members. A culture is expressed to the world beyond the organization and to its members by behaviors and what have been called "artifacts" (dress, building design, signs).

The least visible elements of culture—shared basic assumptions and values—are the most difficult to change. But they are essential to the long-run health of an organization's culture and the foundations on which fundamental changes in culture are based.

Related elements of measurement and action provide a means by which cultures are achieved and maintained. Key to the maintenance of effective cultures are the measurement of behaviors as well as actions intended to ensure that behaviors reflect an organization's values. This includes the dismissal of those unable to manage by the values.

Trying to establish shared assumptions, values, and beliefs without defining associated behaviors or implementing measures and corrective actions can lead to confusion and disillusionment among an organization's members.

Achieving and maintaining a high-performance culture is one of the most important responsibilities of leadership. Examples of effective cultures, if the results of surveys to identify "best places to work" are any indication, are found in all kinds of businesses and endeavors.

Failure to communicate the nature of an organization's culture to prospective members or to ensure that elements of a culture are in alignment can result in unmet expectations—a gap between what is expected and what is experienced. It may account for some of the decline in job satisfaction in the U.S. and other countries.

Of course, there is more to an organization's success than its culture. An effective culture exists only in the context of, and in alignment with, strategies and how they are executed. That's our next concern.

2

Culture as "Know How"

Some very successful leaders believe that culture is the foundation on which the success of their organizations is based. Arkadi Kuhlmann, CEO of ING Direct, an online-banking organization, is a strong believer in this theory. In his words: "With the right culture, the problems of commitment, alignment, and motivation go away and hierarchy becomes irrelevant.... [Managers] tend to set strategy and plans first and then try to put the right people in place. Great companies do it the other way around."[1] Tony Hsieh, CEO of Zappos.com, an Internet shoe retailer, puts it this way: "...our belief is that if you get the culture right, most of the other stuff—like great customer service, or building a great long-term brand, or passionate employees and customers—will happen naturally on its own."[2]

A culture does not exist in a vacuum. If it is not aligned with an organization's strategy and execution, the inconsistent signals sent to its members will seriously handicap it in achieving its goals.

Culture is critical to the development and execution of a strategy. Just how critical is suggested by the experiences of the leadership of upstart bank ING Direct.

ING Direct: Shaping a Culture

Not all financial institutions regard "making money" as their primary purpose. ING Direct, a multinational purveyor of simple financial products such as high-interest-paying savings accounts, competitively priced mortgages, and certificates of deposit through direct channels such as the Internet and telephone, is one that doesn't. That's one reason why it makes so much money.

ING Direct's mission in the U.S. is "Leading Americans back to savings."[3] It's a mission about which current and prospective employees can get excited. ING Direct's founding management sought to pursue the mission by redefining financial services through "relentless simplification," starting with its simple advertising plea to "save your money." It pioneered offering savers high rates (as much as eight times the average for savings accounts at full-service banks), no fees, and no minimums (on deposit balances). In fact, the ING Direct story provides a good example of how "know why" (purpose), "know what, when, where" (strategy), and "know who" (execution) can come together with "know how" (culture) to produce extraordinary value.

Since ING Direct's founding in the U.S. in 2000, others have emulated its strategy. But, in the meantime, Arkadi Kuhlmann, its CEO, has concentrated on building an organization with an especially strong external brand and internal culture. The shared assumptions, values, beliefs, and behaviors of its culture are expressed in something ING Direct calls The Orange Code, which consists of 12 statements:

1. We are new here.
2. Our mission is to help people take care of the wealth they make.
3. We will be fair.
4. We will constantly learn.
5. We will change and adapt and dwell only in the present and in the future.
6. We will listen; we will invent; we will simplify.
7. We will never stop asking why or why not.
8. We will create wealth for ourselves too, but we will do this by creating value.
9. We will tell the truth.
10. We will be here for everyone.
11. We aren't conquerors; we are pioneers. We are not here to destroy; we are here to create.
12. We will never be finished.

To foster adherence to the purpose, values, and behaviors, the company seeks out potential employees who are "orange"—that is, people who are convinced (or willing to be convinced) that

- Conventional banks are "evil" because of the low interest they pay on savings.
- Credit card companies are "evil" because they encourage spending while charging high interest rates on unpaid credit balances.

It's ironic, but by no means a surprise, that a financial institution that pays so little attention to the purpose of making money makes so much. ING Direct has been the fastest-growing bank in the U.S. over the last ten years. Some of this is explained by its practice of paying high interest rates to savers. Strong word-of-mouth marketing results not only from its policies but also from its reputation for outstanding service (from "orange" employees). This has produced low marketing costs (one-fourth that of its competitors to acquire a customer) and a volume of new business that has raised productivity at ING Direct to six times the industry average. The low costs that these strategies have delivered have enabled the company to return substantial profits to its Dutch parent while maintaining its focus on customers and employees. ING Direct's success is a product of the alignment of its purpose, "know why," with its strategy, constituting "know what, when, where." The strategy is in turn supported by ways of executing "know who" that includes organizational form, policies, and practices as well as the Orange Code with its shared values and behaviors.

Culture, execution, and strategy together explain much of an organization's performance. Figure 2-1 shows one way of thinking about the relationship. Shared assumptions regarding such things as the "right" customers, competitors, and suppliers; communities to be served; the legal and regulatory environment; and people, work, motivation, and the social environment influence elements of culture, strategy, and execution. That explains why these basic elements of management typically have more overlap than theory leads us to believe.

Although extraordinary technologies or products may afford short-term success, the degree of alignment between elements of culture, strategy, and execution is a major factor in determining an organization's long-term performance, as shown in Figure 2-2.

Figure 2-1 Culture's role in organizational performance

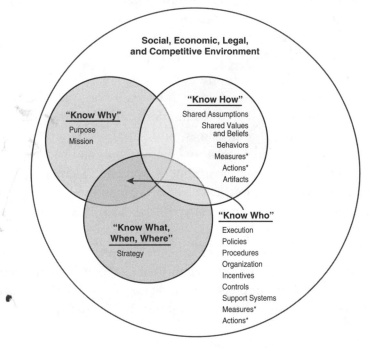

Figure 2-2 Culture as "know how"

* Areas of significant overlap between culture and execution

Culture and Purpose ("Know Why")

Culture is a reflection of the organization's purpose— its "know why." A culture in tune with an organization's purpose can be a powerful force. C. William Pollard, former CEO of ServiceMaster, has commented that "People want to work for a cause, not just for a living. When there is alignment between the cause of the firm and the cause of its people, move over—because there *will* be extraordinary performance."[4]

Certain objectives may foster and perhaps require a stronger sense of purpose than others. For example, does an organization whose prime purpose is to make money (both for itself and for clients, as in many financial institutions) require the same sense of mission as one devoted to "leading Americans back to savings"?

Nikos Mourkogiannis cites four possible types of purpose that provide "sources of energy" for an organization:

- Discovery, the challenge of adventure and innovation characterized by dot-com entrepreneurs willing to work 24/7 in search of the new or unknown
- Excellence, in which high standards are not compromised for short-term performance, as with Berkshire Hathaway and Warren Buffett
- Altruism, in which the primary purpose is to serve customers, employees, and others first and assume that profit will follow, as at Nordstrom
- Heroism, typically involving grand plans to change entire industries or even the way we live, as with Bill Gates and Microsoft[5]

These purposes provide reasons for people to affiliate with the organization.

Making money may be the result of any of these purposes but does not itself provide "the ultimate moral basis for an action" that is at their core. Mourkogiannis argues that putting mere goals, such as making money, before purpose gets us an Enron or Worldcom. The pity, as he sees it, is that true purpose could have enabled these organizations to make even greater "real" profits than those they reported. For example, Google has as its purpose "to organize and make accessible all the world's information," a heroic purpose if there ever was one. This doesn't prevent Google from being one of the most profitable of all companies. More important, it's one that is attracting a generation of outstanding talent combining idealism with economic goals. Of course, the attractiveness of this mix of idealism and economics will be tested as Google approaches maturity and offers less opportunity for its employees to build wealth through stock ownership.

Culture and Strategy ("Know What, When, Where")

Interactions between an organization's culture and its strategy are continuous. Each influences the other in ways that are easy to imagine but impossible to measure. In concentrating here on culture, I run the risk of blowing its importance out of proportion to strategy and other elements of the context in assessing its impact on performance. Can a great culture survive a poor strategy? At the extreme of poor performance over a long period of time, probably not. But, as you will see later, it can help an organization bridge a period of poor performance while it seeks more successful strategies. Can an organization with a great strategy or product survive a dysfunctional culture? Perhaps for a time. But dysfunctional cultures drive away talent. To the extent that talent is critical to the long-term success of a strategy, eventually that combination must fail.

Culture and Execution ("Know Who")

Culture and strategy are linked by policies, processes, organization, incentives, controls, support systems, measurement, and action—elements of what often is referred to as "execution"—as shown in Figures 2-1 and 2-2. Misalignment of these elements of execution can undermine desired behaviors and even values, with serious effects on long-term results. For example, an organization that rewards individuals solely for financial results may find it difficult to encourage adherence to values and accepted behaviors of any kind.

Similarly, personnel policies that foster lifetime specialization and discourage people from moving across departmental, functional, or even subsidiary company boundaries will contribute little to either personal development or the kind of customer focus characteristic of many successful cultures.

Organizations with effective cultures share one thing in common. They devote extreme care to whom they hire. They place at least as much emphasis on attitudes of potential hires and their likely fit with others in the organization—characterized by beliefs and likely behaviors—as on skills. They involve employees in the hiring process.[6] And then they make an effort to choose initial assignments that will immediately immerse the new recruit in the organization's culture.

Larry Bossidy and Ram Charan emphasize the importance of aligning people with jobs in the process of execution this way: "...the same leaders who exclaim that 'people are our most important asset' usually do not think very hard about choosing the right people for the right job."[7] This suggests that much of execution involves "know who." Assigning responsibilities is so critical to employees' overall job satisfaction and success that some of the best places to work try to allow employees to seek and shape their own jobs. For example, this happens at W. L. Gore and Google, as we will see later.[8]

Research cited in Chapter 1 tells us that every personnel move is observed and judged by a "jury" of interested observers—peers, subordinates, and others. Was the right person hired, recognized, or fired? Are assignments fair and appropriate?

As a highly successful restaurant manager told a Gallup organization interviewer, documented by Marcus Buckingham and Curt Coffman: "A manager has got to remember that he is on stage every day... pick the right people...once you've picked them, trust them...don't overpromote people...never pass the buck...make very few promises to your people, and keep them all...(when necessary, fire a hiring mistake) fast, the faster the better."[9]

Controls play an important role in executing a strategy. They help define the limits of responsibility. Whether they do so in a way that allows for judgment and exhibits a certain degree of trust determines, for many employees, the quality of a workplace. For example, when Southwest Airlines says to its employees, "Do whatever you feel comfortable doing for a customer," it is giving them significant latitude in how they execute their jobs. When the Ritz-Carlton hotel chain allows its lowest-paid employees to commit the organization to spending up to $2,000 on the spot to correct a problem with a guest, it places a significant amount of trust in their judgment.

How Successful Managers View the Importance of Culture

During the course of the research leading to this book, I have had the opportunity to talk with a number of managers about the degree to which culture contributes to their organizations' performance. After several such conversations, I (at first reluctantly, because I feared that respondents would find the questions too hard to answer) began asking each of them three questions intended to put numbers on the conversations:

1. If your organization's performance (operating income) equals 100%, roughly what percentage is accounted for by the quality of the organization's strategy (clients we target; products, services, and results we offer; the way we organize and compensate people) versus the quality of the organization's execution of its strategy (the quality of our people, work, processes, decisions)?

2. If your organization's strategy equals 100%, roughly what proportion of its effectiveness is dependent on and accounted for by the organization's culture (widely shared values, beliefs, behaviors, rites and rituals; i.e., "the way we do things around here")?

3. If the execution of your organization's strategy equals 100%, roughly what proportion of its effectiveness is dependent on and accounted for by the organization's culture?

The results were both remarkable and remarkably consistent. First, the managers didn't hesitate to provide estimates in response to the questions. Several found the questions of enough interest that they circulated them to others. In one case, at ING Direct, Arkadi Kuhlmann used the questions as the subject of a management meeting; nearly 40 of his most senior managers provided estimates before discussing the results.

Second, I found that those attributing higher importance to the organization's execution than to its strategy generally assigned a greater importance to the impact of culture on performance. Most remarkable, the vast majority of respondents assigned a combined percentage[10] of 70% or more to the impact of culture on performance.

Curious about these results, I posted the same set of questions along with a value-neutral explanation on a monthly blog that I write on the Harvard Business School's Working Knowledge web site. Responses from a diverse, nonscientific sample produced roughly the same results. About 60% of those responding to the questions cited culture as having the highest impact on performance, about three times the number citing either strategy or execution.[11]

Culture in the Context of Purpose, Strategy, and Execution

ING Direct is typical of many of the firms we'll study later. These organizations make outsized profits without using profit as a purpose or even a starting point in planning efforts. They practice what John Kay has termed "obliquity"—achieving a goal, such as profits, by concentrating on the things that produce profits.[12] They achieve extraordinary results by concentrating on values-based strategies. And they care little about dividing lines between purpose, strategy, and culture—thereby rendering the message of Figure 2-1 somewhat curious to them—as long as there is internal consistency in how elements of purpose, strategy, execution, and culture come together. Consider this description of what goes on at the widely acclaimed Mayo Clinic by its CEO, Dr. Glenn S. Forbes:

> What makes Mayo Clinic distinct is that we have said, "The needs of the patient come first," from the beginning. Over generations, we have driven the needs of the patient into our thinking about how policies were developed. We've driven it into our thinking about how we structure ourselves and our governance and how we allocate resources. We've driven it

into our thinking when we recruit people and form staffs. We've driven it so broadly and deeply into our management and operations that it becomes part of a culture. Thus, when we bring an issue forward, it's not a thin layer of, oh yes, that was the marketing mantra that somebody thought of last week. No, this is driven much more deeply into the fabric of the organization. That's what makes us different.[13]

Is "the needs of the patient come first" a strategy or a value that is an integral part of the Mayo Clinic's culture? Is it part of the mission and purpose as well? It is hard to sort this out. But this isn't necessary when it implies a purpose, strategy, and culture that are in alignment. Leonard Berry and Kent Seltman, in their study of the organization, concluded that "Mayo Clinic teaches that excellent organizations can have one or more strategies that are so central to their belief system (such as "the patient comes first"), so integral to who they are, that they rise to the level of a core value."[14]

The Container Store (TCS), a Dallas-based organization that has been named one of the 100 Best Companies to Work For in the U.S. every year since 2000, provides a locus for summing up much of what we have discussed. At first glance, TCS appears to offer an unlikely example to illustrate these points. After all, what is the potential for an inspirational mission, deeply held shared assumptions, and inspiring values in a store that sells storage items and tools to help organize things? But read its story, told in the following sidebar.

Know Why, What, When, Where, Who, and How at The Container Store

There was little time to formulate mission statements or values in the early days of The Container Store (TCS). In the beginning, it was hard to generate excitement about a new retail concept centered around selling storage devices and other products intended to help people organize their possessions. But Garrett Boone, Kip Tindell, and John Mullen realized that in a relatively affluent society that had accumulated a lot of "stuff," a mission of "helping people simplify their lives" would resonate with a large group of potential customers. It gave them the focus for a product line that represented the core of a retailing strategy. More important for TCS, it was a mission to which employees could devote themselves with enthusiasm. It took some time to prove it. But when the company opened a store in Houston in 1988, it faced the crisis of sales three times greater than expected. To meet demand, it hired people who were unsuitable for the company. As a result, the founders decided to sit down and articulate what they were missing ten years after the company's founding. They had a mission and strategy; what else did they need? They needed something that could be communicated simply to increasing numbers of employees.

They drew on the "philosophy epistle file" that current chairman and CEO Kip Tindell calls "almost corny." He began it as a student at a Jesuit high school in Dallas, creating what became known as the Foundation Principles™. These principles, seven in all, can be viewed in terms of their emphasis on strategy, execution, and culture.

Strategy:

- "Man in the desert" selling is characterized by bringing together in one place—for example, in the desert, such things as water, palm trees, pith helmets, and cell phones—things that people have needed for some time to simplify their lives.

- "Fill the other guy's basket" refers to vendors whose products TCS sells, but this principle has meaning for employees as well.[*]

- "One great person equals three good people." According to Tindell, "one great person could easily be as productive as three good people. So we try to pay 50% to 100% above industry average."[**] By implication, TCS tries to avoid hiring merely good people.

---

[*] The phrase is attributed to Andrew Carnegie, who wrote "Fill the other guy's basket to the brim. Making money then becomes an easy proposition," cited recently in Adam Bryant, "Three Good Hires? He'll Pay More for One Who's Great," *New York Times*, March 14, 2010, p. BU1.

[**] *Ibid.*, p. BU2. The quote is from Kip Tindell.

Culture:

- Communication is leadership. "We believe in relentlessly communicating everything to every single employee...except for individual salaries."***

- Intuition does not come to an unprepared mind. Therefore, extensive training is needed.

- An air of excitement. Fun and surprises are an important element of work at TCS, as illustrated by a "National We Love Our Employees Day," a surprise party announced on the day of the celebration in the *New York Times* and on billboards.

Execution:

- Service, selection, pricing.

Other practices related to the Foundation Principles™ include an intense effort to select the right people and up to 30 times as much training as other retailers offer.

*** *Ibid.*

Note how well the elements of strategy, culture, and execution complement one another at The Container Store, guiding everyday efforts to meet the mission of "helping people simplify their lives" through internally aligned elements of strategy, culture, and execution. The results include frequent employee references to such things as strong talent, diversity, organizational empathy, "family first," the company as "home," and love. This helps account for a turnover rate that is one-tenth that of comparable retailers, closer relationships with more highly satisfied customers, and above-average profits.

By setting such high standards for organization culture and its alignment with strategy and execution, the leadership team at TCS also escalates the cost of a failure to adhere to the standard. We'll have more to say about that later.

Summary

If an organization's mission is its "know why," its strategy is its "know what, when, where," and how it executes its strategy its "know who," its culture is its "know how."

Successful managers asked to assess the relative importance of strategy, execution, and culture in the success of their organizations attributed a great deal of their success, as much as 70%, to the effectiveness of their cultures. Those attributing higher importance to their organizations' execution than to strategy also generally assigned greater importance to the impact of culture on performance.

An organization's culture can provide a competitive edge in such things as acquiring and holding talent, building long-term relationships with customers, and achieving high productivity. But to the extent that culture encourages inward-looking attitudes and an unwillingness or inability to respond to a changing environment, it can become a liability for an organization and its leadership. That's our next concern.

3

Culture: A Multi-edged Sword

Clarence Darrow, paraphrasing Charles Darwin, once said, "It is not the strongest of the species that survive, nor the most intelligent, but the one most responsive to change."[1] The same is true for organization cultures.

Strong cultures contribute to superior performance—until they don't. Pride in the organization is constructive until it turns into arrogance toward customers and others outside the organization. Carefully hiring people who "fit in" and subscribe to a common set of values is great until it suppresses the diversity of backgrounds and ideas necessary for an organization's capability to adapt to changes in the environment. You might wonder why anyone would allow this to happen.

Strong cultures relate to performance in the manner shown in Figure 3-1. An organization whose members are dedicated to a clearly understood set of values and behaviors that appear to be working are not likely to change. They develop pride in their organization and its capabilities. A David-versus-Goliath mentality forms in the small but growing organization, with everyone associating with David. In order to improve, they are open to the outside world and what they can learn from it. They are encouraged to engage in a lot of external benchmarking and internal best-practice work. They make strategic hires from the outside and spend time listening to what these new people say. Innovation and a mentality of "working for the customer" are emphasized. As a result, planning starts from commonly shared assumptions about such things as innovation, service, and products. If proposed strategies or tactics don't reflect shared values, they are put aside. Performance is tracked by nonfinancial as well as financial measures. This all works, confirming the "rightness" of an organization's strategy and culture. In some cases, it produces real wealth among those associating early on with the organization. They begin to have more and more at stake in its success.

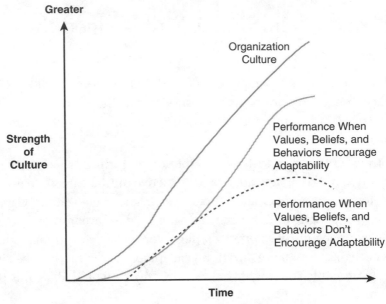

Figure 3-1 Strength of culture and organizational performance

Leadership becomes more and more confident of the organization's success, even as new leaders ascend to the top ranks. Success is attributed to great product and service ideas, superior talent, and a first-rate strategy. The beliefs to which early hires subscribed are taken for granted. They are assumed to be in place, even though there are no sanctions when individual behaviors don't reflect them. Newcomers get the idea that beliefs and behaviors don't count, that the things that count are more closely related to the "bottom line." Planning starts with financial goals and works back toward strategies and the "soft stuff" of people and culture, rather than vice versa. We're now Goliath. "What we can learn from others" turns to "what others can learn from us." As a result, barriers to the outside competitive world are established, making benchmarking and other continuous-improvement efforts more difficult. A sincere belief in the superiority of our talent leads to jobs being filled almost exclusively from within. Time formerly spent listening to others (including customers) is now spent on improving what we believe we're really good at doing. A "not invented here" mentality arises. For a while, the strong culture is perceived to be helping deliver success. Why change it? Furthermore, why not erect barriers for those who would change it?

This may help explain why fewer than one in five of the Fortune 500 largest U.S. firms in 1970 are still found there, including only 40 of the largest 100. It reinforces the finding of one comprehensive study of more than six million U.S. firms that a fraction of 1% survive 40 years.[2]

At Texaco, a proud, successful oil company for nearly all of its history, those applying for expense money to attend industry conferences were told, "Here's the money, but don't bring any of those ideas back here."[3] As late as the 1970s, unlike Texaco's suppliers and competitors, "only three company executives belonged to Houston's famed Petroleum Club." As one senior executive commented some years later, "There was no need to belong. Texaco people kept their own counsel. There was a Texaco way and a wrong way of doing things."[4] This culture contributed to a decline extending over many months and years. It culminated in a botched hostile takeover attempt of Pennzoil that produced a judgment against the company that would have frozen its operating assets. One of Jim Kinnear's first actions after assuming the role of CEO in 1987 was to declare bankruptcy for the company in order to preserve those operating assets. Other important initiatives would follow shortly. Efforts to change Texaco's culture of isolation had already begun among managers of local company operations who realized that something had to be done to cope with difficult labor relations. Among other things, they implemented quality initiatives, even relying on the benchmarking of policies and practices against those of other organizations, with or without the encouragement of top management. The new mantra of middle managers, one that Kinnear encouraged, was that "if corporate senior management didn't request information on something, there was no reason to get them involved."[5] In addition, Kinnear used the crisis of bankruptcy to shake up senior management, introduce a statement of vision and values, improve communications with the field, and introduce new performance-based compensation methods, budgeting processes, and planning systems.

Similarly, at Coors Brewing Company, a singular devotion to product quality combined with a disdain for ideas from the outside caused a serious "moment of truth" for Peter Coors, president at that time.[6] Coors Brewing, based in Golden, Colorado, had developed a mystical reputation for the quality of its beer. Beer lovers in the Eastern U.S. believed that the reason Coors was not distributed there was that temperature control during the distribution process could not meet the company's exacting standards. The company did nothing to dispel the belief. As a result, people traveling through the region would purchase six-packs of Coors to take back east with them for special occasions.

The leadership of Coors concentrated its efforts on producing the highest-quality beer possible. Travel to compare beer-making methods with other producers was discouraged. After all, it was unnecessary. People were beating down the doors to get all the beer that Coors could make. But in the mid-1980s, this penchant for quality with, among other things, a disregard for other customer-oriented values caused wrenching difficulties when the company produced a can that customers found hard to open. Institutional customers such as airlines complained first, citing their customers' problems with the cans. Then Coors' distributors began complaining. But the message coming out of Golden was, "We make the best beer; people will find a way to get to it."

Management finally responded when a group of vociferous distributors threatened to refuse deliveries. Among other things, Peter Coors saw to it that quality was redefined to include other elements of the beer-drinking experience, including the packaging. He organized a course in continuous quality improvement, including benchmarking and the importing of best practices from outside the company, for the senior executives. And he decided to teach it himself.

Savvy managers understand that strong cultures operating "on the edge" between pride and arrogance offer opportunity for outstanding performance. Organizations do not "flip" from positive to negative cultures overnight. But they require leaders who carefully nurture and police behaviors, both their own and those of others, to ensure that arrogance and associated attitudes and behaviors don't take root. They also require the "right" values, as we will see.

Nature and Results of the 1992 Study

The goal of a 1992 study[7] that John Kotter and I conducted (there were others) was to shed light on the relationship between corporate culture and performance. We thought we could meet our goal by establishing an index of the strength of an organization's culture and comparing it with the company's economic performance (average yearly increase in net income, average yearly return on investment, and average yearly increase in stock price) over a period of ten years leading up to the study. The thinking was that ten years was a sufficiently long time to counter short-term perturbations in performance while not so long as to be irrelevant. In addition to compiling the economic data, we prepared a "strength-of-culture" index for each company based on responses from the top six officers in 207 of the largest U.S. companies in 20 industries. Six hundred of them provided ratings of the strength of each of their *competitors'* cultures (not their own) based on the following criteria:[8]

- To what extent have managers in competing firms commonly spoken of a (company name) "style" or way of doing things?
- To what extent has the firm both made its values known through a creed or credo and made a serious attempt to encourage managers to follow them?
- To what extent has the firm been managed according to long-standing policies and practices other than those of just the incumbent CEO?

The resulting correlation of these two sets of data, which we had hypothesized would be high, *yielded basically no relationship*. We found organizations with strong cultures that had both strong and weak performance. There were also organizations with weak cultures and strong performance. Eighteen months into our study, we had little to show for our efforts.

Overcoming our discouragement, rather than quitting we decided to continue with what turned out to be three additional explorations:

- Noting firms with strong cultures and both good and poor performance in many of the same industries, we studied in some depth (in many cases including field visits) 22 companies comprising matched pairs (in two cases, "pairs" consisted of three companies) with contrasting performances in ten very different industries.

- We also took an in-depth look at 20 firms with both weak cultures and poor economic performance to determine how they had reached this state.
- Finally, we focused on ten firms that appeared to have experienced culture changes and improved economic performance.

In total, all of this was done over a period of about two and a half years of research "highs" and "lows." It provided the basis for several conclusions or, depending on your point of view, hypotheses for further investigation:

- Strong cultures affect performance.
- The strength of an organization's culture, however, is not correlated with good performance.
- Cultures that support adaptability foster long-term success.
- A culture's fit with the competitive, social, and legal environments is important.
- "Outsider-insiders" often lead culture change.

Strong Cultures Affect Performance

This assertion is confirmed by even the best (Five Star) investment analysts on Wall Street, a group that apparently does not look only to financial measures in recommending investments. We asked 75 of them to tell us whether they thought culture had helped performance in the 12 high-performing firms and had hurt performance in the ten low-performing firms in our matched pairs of companies in ten different industries. They told us that culture had caused these effects on the performance of our sample of companies. *Only one analyst out of the 75 said that "culture has had little or no impact on performance."*

Strength of Culture Is Not Correlated with Good Performance

For years, it was assumed that very good long-term organization performance was very difficult, if not impossible, to achieve without a strong culture. Some have gone further to imply that strong cultures are correlated with good performance. The authors of one often-quoted book pointed out that "The early leaders of American business such as Thomas Watson of IBM, Harley Procter of Procter & Gamble, and General Johnson of Johnson & Johnson believed that strong culture brought success ... In fact, a strong culture has almost always been the driving force behind continuing success in American business."[9]

But our measures of economic performance in 207 U.S. firms over a ten-year period and the strength of their cultures at the end of that period of 1977 to 1988 convinced us that a strong culture is no guarantee of good economic performance. The performance of firms judged by competitors to have the strongest cultures in 1988 (led by Walmart, J.P. Morgan, Procter & Gamble, Northwestern Mutual, Dow Chemical, Shell Oil, DuPont, IBM, Delta, and Boeing) varied widely during the preceding ten years, as it has since then.

Adaptability Keys Long-Term Success

Confounded by the findings of our first study, we examined in depth the cultures of ten matched pairs of firms, all of which were found to have strong cultures. Each pair comprised firms of approximately the same size from the same industry, one with solid performance and one with relatively weak performance over the previous ten years. All were organizations with time-honored names and reputations.

Our examination included visits to many of the firms and a compilation of information about values and accepted behaviors in each.

The objective was to establish patterns of differences between the successful and the unsuccessful. The differences, conveyed by fact and story alike, were quite clear. Organizations with the best performance in each case were those with values and leadership that encouraged behaviors such as innovation, continuous quality improvement, benchmarking against the world's best, and efforts to import good ideas from anywhere outside the organization as well as to generate them from within. We deemed these values and behaviors typical of an adaptive culture, one that supports an organization's ability to adapt to changes in the competitive, social, and regulatory environments.

Values alone were not enough. Of greater importance to success was the presence of leadership constantly reminding the organization of the values and the expected behaviors they implied. Values without leadership appeared not to produce the desired behaviors and results.

The Question of Fit

It stands to reason that if culture is to have a positive impact on an organization's performance, it should set forth values and encourage behaviors to which people at all levels of the organization subscribe. The culture should support behaviors that attract the "right" people to the organization—people who can carry out the organization's strategy. It should reflect the beliefs of a leadership team that occasionally revisits and reconfirms the organization's culture. And, of course, it should support the organization's strategy and methods of executing that strategy.

Fit Between Culture and People

Strong cultures take on many forms. Deal and Kennedy, for example, characterize them as "tribes," describing four:

- The "tough-guy, macho culture," populated by individualists who take big risks and seek quick feedback.
- The "work hard/play hard culture," in which risk-taking is downplayed in preference to small daily wins involving hard work and fun, as is the case in many retailing or sales-oriented organizations.

- The "bet-your-company culture," in which large commitments are made with great uncertainty and long-term payoffs, characteristic of big pharma, defense, and other project-oriented businesses.
- The "process" culture, characterized by an emphasis on how things are done—and, in extreme cases, politics and bureaucracy. Deal and Kennedy cite banks, insurance companies, utilities, and regulated industries as having great potential for this kind of culture.[10]

Managers may find it difficult to move from one type of strong culture to another. One study, based on a relatively small sample of executive recruiters and management consultants, concluded that they generally avoid recruiting management talent from certain large organizations. One reason was the strong cultures in these organizations, combined with their poor track record in developing senior executive talent.[11] The list of companies cited contains some very successful companies, as we will see later. The point is that managers have demonstrated difficulty in moving from organizations with such strong cultures, regardless of their success. Strong cultures mold people. The fit between people and culture does matter.

An extended study of "star" investment analysts (as rated by *Institutional Investor* magazine each year) found that it was difficult for those moving from one organization to another to maintain their "star" status. This was especially true if they moved from organizations encouraging the development of "firm-specific human capital" (strong cultures fostering a dedication to the firm and its ways, such as at Goldman Sachs) to those that encouraged "general human capital" (with an emphasis on individual performance and limited reliance on the firm's resources, such as at Morgan Stanley).[12]

Fit Between Culture, Strategy, and Competitive Environment

Earlier, I mentioned that in a survey of the highest-rated investment analysts, they told us that culture is an important influence on performance. They told us something else when we asked, "How well has the culture at (company name) fit the market, competitive, technological, and other environments in which the firm has found itself?" For each of the firms among the matched pairs of competitors in ten different industries, they told us that the best performers had a much better "fit" between culture and the respective environments in which these firms competed. The contrast was striking. In every one of the ten pairs, fit was judged to be greater in the better-performing firm. The best performers in all pairs, taken as a group, were rated 6.1 on a 7-point scale (with 7 being perfect) on culture/environment fit. The poorer performers were given a rating of 3.7. To test these judgments, we conducted our own extensive research of documents and field interviews to arrive at our own conclusions. Our research resulted in conclusions similar to those of the analysts.[13]

To summarize, research and experience suggest that fit between a culture, a strategy, and the environment in which an organization functions is a powerful concept. They suggest the following:

- Culture and strategy develop together, ensuring some degree of fit from the moment of their founding for successful organizations.
- Strategies are easier to change than cultures.
- Culture can constrain or facilitate strategic change.
- A good fit between a culture and strategy does not ensure success if both represent a poor fit with the competitive environment.
- Lack of fit results from one of the following:
  - Poor definition of either a culture or strategy
  - "Drift" in the leadership of either the culture (actions that contradict shared values, for example) or strategy (initiatives that contradict successful strategic directions of the past, for example)
- "Slack" resulting from such things as the outstanding success of a product or a very large market opportunity provides an umbrella over both effective and ineffective competitors. It can obscure a lack of fit between culture and strategy for some time. Such conditions may delay, but not prevent, declines in performance.

Typical of explorations of the nature of the "fit" between an organization's competitive environment and its culture are those of Rob Goffee and Gareth Jones. They have categorized cultures on dimensions of "sociability" (people-oriented, highly social, but political) and "solidarity" (task-oriented, meritocratic, but potentially ruthless).[14] Using a 2×2 matrix, they came up with four types of cultures: "fragmented" (low on both dimensions), "networked" (high on sociability), "mercenary" (high on solidarity), and "communal" (high on both dimensions). Using this scheme, you might conclude that communal cultures represent the ideal, combining the benefits of both high sociability and high solidarity that are typical of successful new ventures. And in fact they can provide formidable competitive advantage, as evidenced by a number of examples described in this book. Goffee and Jones, however, observe that communal cultures, comprising a balance of solidarity and sociability, are hard to sustain. They require unusually sensitive and adept leadership all too rarely found on a consistent basis. Too often, communal cultures are allowed to morph into "networked" cultures typical of bureaucracies with growing tolerance for poor performance. To combat the disadvantages of such cultures, leaders sometimes resort to a kind of "shock treatment." It emphasizes performance to the point that the culture swings to a strongly mercenary character with an attendant loss of talent.

The idea of "fit" implies that no one type of culture is superior to another. It depends instead on the degree to which a culture's members subscribe to the basic assumptions on which it is founded, as well as its values and behaviors. It also depends on the degree to which the resulting culture is appropriate for the competitive situation in which the organization finds itself.

To complicate matters further, a culture, the people comprising it, a strategy, and the competitive environment are in a constant state of flux. Even the strongest culture can succeed only so long when it falls out of alignment with an organization's competitive environment and strategy. This underlines the importance of a culture that supports adaptability, a subject to which we will return repeatedly.

The Role of Leadership

It should be apparent that the most important functions of a leader are ensuring the creation and maintenance of a strong and adaptive organization culture as well as a clear strategy. But a rapidly changing world requiring constant review and adjustment adds significant complexity to the task. Too often leaders must sense the inevitable "drift" in organizational behaviors producing the misalignment that occurs between an organization's culture, its competitive environment, and the strategic responses that change requires. Leadership demands a clear sense of the relative difficulties and risks involved in changing either a strategy or a culture to bring them into alignment with each other.

Too often, in the views of some, organizations in need of new leadership turn to "outsiders," those who have been successful in other organizations, to lead efforts to change either a strategy or culture.[15] This is a natural reaction in societies that revere the "CEO superstar," attributing successes to a leader while overlooking the importance of the "surrounding system" in producing success.[16] Such mistakes in judgment are discovered only when the superstar is introduced to a new competitive environment.

Many of the successful efforts to change cultures that John Kotter and I observed in our 1992 study were led by people who are regarded as "insider-outsiders."[17] These are people who proved themselves as leaders inside the organization but were often regarded as having led peripheral businesses or departments. For example, before assuming the job of CEO of GE, Jack Welch made his mark in General Electric's plastics business, not regarded as core to the corporation's success. Herb Kelleher, even though he was a cofounder, served for a number of years as Southwest Airlines' legal counsel before assuming the job of CEO in 1982 and becoming the "poster boy" for the organization's now-famous culture and strategy.

I'll return to issues of leadership in greater depth in Chapter 13.

Summary

A strong culture can contribute to an organization's success or its failure. More important is whether an organization's values and the behaviors they encourage contribute to its adaptability, agility, and ability to cope with change.

A great product, service, or other significant competitive advantage can carry the performance of an organization that has a weak or counterproductive culture for only so long.

There is no one ideal culture. Rather, its contribution to an organization's long-term success is determined by the extent to which it does the following:

- Sets forth values and encourages behaviors to which people at all levels in the organization can subscribe
- Attracts people who can carry out the strategy chosen for it
- Reflects the beliefs of a leadership team that occasionally revisits and reconfirms the organization's culture
- Promotes behaviors that meet the demands of the organization's competitive environment

A good fit between a culture and strategy does not ensure success if both represent a poor fit with the competitive environment.

Lack of fit results from the following:

- Poor definition of either a culture or strategy
- "Drift" in the culture (actions that contradict shared values, for example) or strategy (initiatives that contradict successful strategic directions of the past, for example)
- Beliefs and behaviors on the part of leadership that don't reflect the assumptions and values held by others in the organization

The primary roles of a leader are

- Building and maintaining a strong culture that supports adaptive behavior
- Sensing when the capabilities fostered by an organization's culture are falling out of alignment with its competitive environment and strategic direction
- Taking corrective action to bring beliefs, behaviors, and capabilities back into alignment with strategies required for competitive success

Too often, organizations in need of new leadership turn to "stars" from outside the organization who have been successful in other environments, only to find that success in one environment is no guarantee of success in another. On the other hand, "insider-outsiders" (such as those who have achieved success and established their credibility in a noncore portion of the business) have played significant roles in turning around strong, dysfunctional cultures in many organizations.

4

Culture in an Organization's Life Cycle

Cultures are formed at the earliest stages of an organization's life. They either are confirmed by successful performance as being effective or die along with a failed organization. They flourish, are diluted, and are renewed through methods we will explore in more detail later. But with the help of several examples, we'll take a quick tour of culture in an organization's life cycle.

How Cultures Are Formed

Whether or not they are defined early on, cultures often reflect the values and behaviors of an organization's founder long after the founder has departed the organization.

The ServiceMaster Story

Founder Marion Wade might have had more than an inkling that hard work and divine providence would play some part in the extraordinary success of the cleaning company he founded in 1929. Wade's early personal experience of surviving burns in a fire fueled by cleaning fluids he was using undoubtedly influenced his articulation of ServiceMaster's (for Service to the Master) values:

- To honor God in all we do
- To help people develop
- To pursue excellence
- To grow profitably

These values were confirmed by the organization's remarkable growth and success as the leading supplier of facility services (cleaning, catering, pest control, and landscaping) to institutions and homeowners in the U.S. and elsewhere. A later CEO, C. William Pollard, frequently pointed out that the first two objectives were "ends objectives" and the last two "means objectives." He commented on the link between the organization's values, behaviors, and strategy, built around a mandate for growth:

> The first (objective) is meant to provide a common starting point for all of us, not to convey a religious point of view. In combination with the second, it guides us by suggesting ways in which we treat people. The last two objectives not only provide the means for achieving the first two, they keep us in balance and provide a kind of creative tension for the management....[1]

The values were reflected in how ServiceMaster selected and developed new managers, rewarded and recognized people, and practiced what was called "servant leadership" starting with the CEO. Pollard himself provided a good illustration of servant leadership. I once observed him on his hands and knees cleaning up some coffee he had spilled on the rug during a board meeting. Remarkably, board members hardly noticed, seeming to take his actions for granted.

ServiceMaster's strong culture was reinforced even more by the organization's remarkable performance, which led all Standard & Poor's 500 companies in profit on equity during the period of 1975 to 1995. This provided a constant confirmation of the value of its culture to ServiceMaster's leadership. In 1998, ServiceMaster was named by the *Financial Times* as the "Sixth Most Respected Company in the World." But challenges to its leadership were already growing.

The IBM Story

The values that evolved at IBM under Thomas Watson, Sr. still influence how the company is managed.[2] They are "respect for the individual, the best customer service of any company in the world, and pursuit of all tasks with the idea that they can be accomplished in a superior fashion." (Of these, the first was cited by Watson as most important.) They've survived the ubiquitous artifacts such as white shirts and "THINK" signs that characterized IBM in the first several decades of its existence. They have fostered behaviors that change to reflect business practice. These continue to serve the company today. It's important to note that these values were articulated in 1963 by Watson's son 39 years after the founding of the company.[3] Had IBM not been wildly successful, there would have been little or no interest in taking the time to understand and articulate the values. By a process of natural selection, culture becomes intertwined with success. We know less about the process of IBM's less-successful competitors, in part because their cultures were not confirmed by success.

The Goldman Sachs Story

Founded in 1869, investment banking firm Goldman Sachs was run by the Goldman, Sachs, and Weinberg families for the next hundred years. It survived crises associated with both economic cycles and its partners' missteps. For example, the firm's partners became caught up in the mania surrounding the run-up to the market crash of 1929. They formed the Goldman Sachs Trading Corporation (GSTC) in December 1928 and invested half the partnership's capital in it, along with tens of millions of dollars of its clients' capital. In the process, they violated the long-held belief that all major decisions had to be based on the unanimous agreement of the partners. The result was the loss of 92% of GSTC's capital and much of the firm's good reputation. This fact was etched in the mind of Sidney Weinberg, who took over the chairmanship in 1930 and led the rebuilding of the firm's name over the next 39 years.

Among other things, Weinberg oversaw the sale of GSTC, ending the practice of trading for the firm's own account (to which the firm returned some years later). In 1931, senior partners who had been hired as much for their character, particularly their loyalty, as for their intelligence and who had devoted their careers to building the institution took a characteristic step. They bailed out junior partners who had acquired deficits in their capital accounts. It was not the last time this would happen. But it further cemented partners' loyalty to the firm, which, when extended to clients and their success, helped Goldman Sachs restore luster to its reputation and extraordinary returns to its bottom line.

The Process of Culture Formation

Effective cultures typically are formed with or without formal, organized effort. They are often shaped when early members of the organization observe the founder's assumptions, values, beliefs, and behaviors. This happens whether or not the founder takes the time to articulate them. They appear to produce success as they become first the lore and then the accepted wisdom of an organization until a successor to the founder typically codifies them.

Early on, the first members of an organization define its culture. At some point, however, the culture begins to define the people who are subsequently hired into the organization. If little effort is made to articulate the culture, little guidance is provided to those doing the hiring. As a result, new hires may have beliefs and exhibit behaviors that do not fit with those of employees already in the organization, thereby further diluting the existing culture. This is a strong argument for articulating an organization's culture relatively early in its development.

How Cultures Are Articulated and Institutionalized

Founders typically don't take the time to note the values and behaviors by which they expect their organizations to be run. They don't need to do so if they are the walking embodiment of the culture. At some point, however, a successor usually takes the time to do it.

This sometimes leads to efforts by dominant leaders to identify (and, in too many cases, manufacture) core values and behaviors that would seem to support good work habits and performance. Rarely does this kind of effort produce a strong, effective culture unless it reflects the ideas and inputs of the entire organization and is accompanied by clear communication, supportive behaviors, measurement, and corrective action.

It was Thomas Watson's son who articulated and institutionalized IBM's culture 39 years after the founding of the company. Similarly, it fell to John Whitehead to perform the task as cohead of his firm, Goldman Sachs, more than a hundred years after the founding of the company. According to one account:

> Because he worried that the ethos of the firm could be lost to rapid growth, Whitehead decided Goldman Sachs needed a clear set of business principles that all employees would adhere to in their business dealings. Working at home one Sunday afternoon, he drafted the...essential points that made Goldman Sachs distinctive [described later].... "With the exception of...principles added by the lawyers," he said, "Goldman Sachs today operates with the same business principles I wrote on that yellow pad."[4]

It is probably safe to say that the ideas Whitehead put down on that yellow pad were not his alone. Rather, they reflected what he had observed in his years with the organization. But they clearly have served the organization well. Recent events that have brought Goldman Sachs to the center of the debate over excesses in the financial community during the Great Recession suggest that the "principles" were more important than ever to the beleaguered financial services giant during that difficult time in its history.

As soon as a set of values, beliefs, and behaviors based on shared assumptions have been articulated, the hiring of those who subscribe to them can proceed more effectively. In every organization with a strong culture that I have observed, new employees are hired with substantial emphasis on their attitudes—that is, their willingness to live by the organization's culture—rather than just their skills.

Its business principles set Goldman Sachs apart from many other investment banking organizations. The company stresses the importance of attracting the best people, but only those who can thrive in teams and demonstrate selfless dedication to the firm rather than to their own fame. The principles are reinforced by leaders who believe in them and act them out.

Business Principles That Made Goldman Sachs Distinctive*

Our clients' interests always come first...

Our assets are our people, capital, and reputation. If any of these is ever diminished, the last is the most difficult to restore...

Our goal is to provide superior returns to our shareholders...

We take great pride in the professional quality of our work...

We stress creativity and imagination in everything we do.... While recognizing that the old way may still be the best way, we constantly strive to find a better solution to a client's problems...

We make an unusual effort to identify and recruit the very best person for every job...

We offer our people the opportunity to move ahead more rapidly than is possible at most other places...

We stress teamwork in everything we do.... We have no room for those who put their personal interests ahead of the interests of the firm and its clients.

The dedication of our people to the firm and the intense effort they give their jobs are greater than one finds in most other organizations...

We consider our size an asset that we try hard to preserve...

We constantly strive to anticipate the rapidly changing needs of our clients and to develop new services to meet those needs...

We regularly receive confidential information as part of our normal client relationships. To breach a confidence or to use confidential information improperly or carelessly would be unthinkable.

Our business is highly competitive, and we aggressively seek to expand our client relationships. However, we must always be fair competitors and must never denigrate other firms.

Integrity and honesty are at the heart of our business.

* Source: Based on John Whitehead's original principles. Excerpted in May 2010 from Goldman Sachs' web site.

How Cultures Are Diluted

If culture is to contribute to success, it has to be nurtured and reinforced by management action. Where this is not done, a culture becomes hard to describe and understand, political considerations often drive out attention to values and beliefs, and the organization is left to rely mainly on a good strategy for its success. The likelihood of this condition's remaining stable for long, however, is low. Reasons to associate with the organization become fewer, good talent leaves, and the ideas and behaviors critical to the organization's long-term success leave with them.

Back to ServiceMaster

An organization that regards itself as a "ministry" has no choice but to grow. As ServiceMaster's former chairman and CEO William Pollard has said, "Because this company is dedicated both to the development of the individual and our ministry to an increasing number of people, growth is an imperative."[5] As a result, the company, with about 120,000 people under its management in 1985, set for itself the objective of doubling its size every five years. This put substantial pressure for growth through acquisition on a company already dominant in providing its core group of customers, hospitals, with cleaning and other services. As a result, a vigorous effort was made to acquire companies offering related services such as pest control (Terminix), lawn care (TruGreen), and home cleaning (Merry Maids) to institutions as well as residences. Although a serious effort was made to ensure that these organizations had cultures with somewhat similar values, beliefs, and behaviors as those at the acquiring company, it was a difficult task, given the very strong culture of the acquirer. While managers of newly acquired companies at least gave lip service to ServiceMaster's corporate values, their behaviors sometimes called into question just how closely they were willing to be governed by them.

One who did fully embrace the values was Carlos Cantu, the CEO of Terminix, which was acquired by ServiceMaster in 1986. He assumed leadership of the entire company upon Pollard's retirement in 1994. However, health problems prevented Cantu from achieving his goal of implementing the ServiceMaster culture in its acquired subsidiaries. By the time Pollard stepped back in as an interim replacement in 1999, the company faced a combination of maturing markets, a dominant share with limited growth opportunity in nearly every market it served, a U.S. economy in recession, and a somewhat diluted culture. All of these factors contributed to the company's declining financial fortunes. As he prepared to leave for a second time, Pollard outlined strategic alternatives that someone else would have to implement.

As a result, upon Pollard's second retirement, the board recruited a successor who led management to rethink the growth goals and dispose of some of the company's properties, essentially putting aside the idea of practicing a "ministry through growth." Because he was brought in from the outside to turn around the company's financial fortunes, it's perhaps natural that he began with that as a primary goal. This was in distinct contrast to his predecessor's belief that the starting point for financial success was adherence to shared values.

Back to IBM

IBM has a parallel to the ServiceMaster story. At the time of our 1992 study of the impact of culture on performance, described in Chapter 3, we compared IBM's decline with Hewlett-Packard's success. IBM was one of our examples of the consequences of letting a strong culture founder. At that time, former IBM executives we interviewed questioned whether their successors could articulate IBM's values, even though they were often displayed in framed documents hanging on their office walls. In one meeting I attended away from IBM's headquarters, the CEO at the time, John Akers, fielded questions about the significance of the first layoff in the company's history, which he had just engineered. One questioner asked whether that action conflicted with IBM's shared value of lifetime employment. Akers replied that the layoff had to be carried out, even though lifetime employment had been one of the company's core values. He seemed unaware that lifetime employment appeared nowhere among IBM's core values. The relevant value was (and is) "respect for the individual," which produced a high priority on avoiding layoffs and a high degree of loyalty among its employees. This led to an assumption by many (apparently including its CEO at the time) that IBM embraced a core value of lifetime employment.

To the extent that an organization's culture helps attract and retain the talent and human capacity necessary to give freer reign to the execution of various strategies, it is an important enabler of success. The dilution of IBM's culture by neglect, not intent, may have accounted for its loss of talent prior to Louis Gerstner's arrival in 1998, described in the section "Renewal at IBM." It was one of the factors in IBM's declining performance in the years prior to his arrival.

The IBM and ServiceMaster examples suggest that an organization's culture, in concert with its strategies and leadership, can have a profound impact on performance. But when values and beliefs are either forgotten or not honored, there is little to suggest "how things are done around here" or to provide guidance in hiring those entrusted with an organization's future.

Enemies of an Effective Culture

Of the many influences on organization culture, eight stand out as being particularly lethal: inconsistent leadership behavior, arrogance born of pride and success, too-rapid growth, too little growth, non-organic growth, failure to maintain a small-company feel, "outsider" leadership, and ineffective measurement and action.

Inconsistent Leadership Behavior

Perceptions of the "fairness of my boss" were cited earlier as a primary factor influencing whether employees are satisfied with their jobs. This encompasses all kinds of behaviors, including the ability to determine the actions to take regarding people—particularly those unable to manage by the values and who need to be dismissed—and the willingness to take them in a timely manner.

This factor encompasses issues of compensation as well. An ill-timed bonus award to top management when wages in general are frozen can be perceived as putting self above the organization, damaging trust and effort on behalf of the organization. Its effects are not immediate and are impossible to quantify. But interviews in such organizations indicate that not only are the effects present but also will be felt when employees are asked to make their next sacrifice for the good of the organization.

Arrogance Born of Pride and Success

"We're number one" has become either the standard cry of winners or the goal of runners-up. When Avis employees subscribed to the mantra "We try harder (because we're number two)," they were not vowing to be a better number two. Leadership often encourages this behavior in the spirit of celebrating the achievement of something for which the organization has been working hard. The danger is that employees may come to believe they are number one, with an associated belief that they can't get much better.

Missions that foster causes can produce arrogance in the absence of conscious efforts by leadership to counter such attitudes and behaviors. In his study, Jim Collins identified this kind of behavior with early stages of decline. As he put it, "Whenever people begin to confuse the nobility of their cause with the goodness and wisdom of their actions ... they can perhaps more easily lead themselves astray."[6] One of the best indicators of such arrogance is how the organization's people treat those outside the organization, especially customers and suppliers. Collins calls this a "you must" attitude, as in Motorola's mid-1990s directive to Bell Atlantic, a retailer of its phones, that "You must promote our phones with stand-alone displays."[7] It was one signal of the early stages of decline at a company that had been identified just a few years earlier as a "Built to Last" organization, one of only 18 "visionary" companies that met a tough set of criteria for outstanding performance over many years.[8] Recall the Coors Brewing story from Chapter 3, where the assumption was that "We make the best beer; people will find a way to get to it." Or more recently, how about Steve Jobs' response to customer complaints that the Apple iPhone4's antenna couldn't receive cellular signals when the user's hand covered the phone's bottom-left corner? According to one report, Jobs urged customers to "alter the way they hold the phones."[9]

The line between pride and arrogance isn't as difficult to identify as you might imagine. There are a number of signs when organizations cross it. For example, one important indicator is the attitude toward learning. Do we worry more about what those outside the organization can learn from us than vice versa? Do we work for each other, or do we work for the customer and others we deal with? Are we the best, or are we still playing catch-up? Table 4-1 describes several indicators that I've found important.

Table 4-1 Indicators of Pride and Arrogance in an Organization

Pride	Arrogance
We work for the customer.	We work for each other.
We worry about what we can learn from others.	We worry about what others can learn from us.
We're open to the outside world.	We practice secrecy in dealing with the outside world.
We're still David.	We're Goliath, and we need to defend our position.
We hire selectively from outside.	We hire from within and sometimes isolate outsiders.
We spend time listening to, and hearing, outside views.	We spend time improving what we have and finding flaws in outside views.
We encourage innovation.	We encourage improving only what we do best.
Our planning starts with people.	Our planning starts with financial goals.
We emphasize results for employees, customers, and shareholders, in that order.	We primarily emphasize financial results.
We track and reward performance by a balanced scorecard of financial and nonfinancial measures.	We track and reward performance by financial measures.

Richard Tedlow has grouped several other behaviors associated with pride and arrogance under the rubric of "denial."[10] In other words, some people in an organization are conscious of creeping arrogance (leading to avoidable failure) and not only do nothing about it but also deny its seriousness. They observe such things as the selective use of information, the stifling of dissenting views, and the demeaning of competitors without acting to counter these behaviors.

It is at about this time that the "edifice complex," in Tedlow's words, sets in, leading to the construction of a new, shiny, larger head-quarters building that contributes little or nothing to financial performance but reinforces the image of invincibility.[11]

Too-Rapid Growth

The meteoric rise and fall of People Express in the 1980s is characteristic of the experiences of other organizations that have grown too fast. CEO Donald Burr attributed the company's demise to concerted efforts on the part of competitors to attack the company's pricing strategies on certain routes. But a more logical explanation is that the company outgrew its meager administrative organization and support systems as it sought to serve an ever-growing number of cities and customer segments through rapid route expansion and the acquisition of Frontier Airlines in 1985.

By comparison, the strategy employed by Southwest Airlines—on-time, frequent, fun service with low fares achieved by point-to-point service with fast turnaround of aircraft, all with a clear focus on the customer—could have allowed it to grow twice as fast as it did in an industry pursuing other strategies (and not too well at that). But throughout much of its first four decades in business, management chose to limit Southwest's growth to no more than 14% per year. Why? Because this was the rate of growth at which it was thought the company's culture could be maintained. Culture is, in effect, an element of the airline's strategy, so important that it is thought even today to be something that could bring the company's growth to a halt if neglected.

An important foundation for an effective culture is its hiring process. "Self-selection" is an important feature of the hiring process of companies with highly effective cultures. It results from the clear communication of what an organization stands for, what that means for the organization's work life, and what is expected of someone joining it. This, coupled with a carefully designed and implemented orientation process, often involving senior management, helps ensure that the right kind of "winners" are brought into the fold. Why is this so important? Richard Fairbank, CEO of Capital One, has put it this way: "At most companies, people spend 2% of their time recruiting and 75% managing their recruiting mistakes."[12] This is particularly likely to happen if an organization is growing so fast that there is little time to devote to less exciting activities such as recruiting and hiring.

Jim Collins describes the process of deterioration this way: "Any exceptional enterprise depends first and foremost upon having self-managed and self-motivated people—the #1 ingredient for a culture of discipline."[13] Companies outgrowing their capabilities for staffing and indoctrination expose themselves to the risks of hiring the wrong people and giving them the wrong assignments. This requires the introduction of more bureaucratic procedures to guide the misplaced newcomers, thus driving away the "right" people. As Collins puts it, "a culture of bureaucratic mediocrity gradually replaces a culture of disciplined excellence."[14]

Too-Little Growth

A healthy culture can thrive on the right amount of growth. However, when growth stalls—perhaps because an organization does not maintain its product line, has saturated its markets, or faces new competition—Edgar Schein has pointed out that shared assumptions developed earlier (say, during periods of high growth) can become liabilities. In his words, "Even if top management has insight, some new assumptions cannot be implemented down the line in the organization because people simply would not comprehend or accept the changes that might be required."[15] Stanley Davis has commented, "As business conditions worsen, a gap develops and grows ever larger between the rules they (organizations) set themselves to live by and the way they actually find themselves living."[16]

Early in an organization's life there is an implied shared assumption of "all for one, and one for all" in which employees put the organization's interests before their own. A high-growth strategy is centered around a "killer app" or breakthrough product or service, and compensation is based largely on the value of stock options and other incentive-based pay. It is a fun and heady time for those who can keep up with long hours and little traditional compensation.

Then growth slows. The new products come with decreasing frequency. Stock options as a significant part of a compensation package no longer make as much sense. People join the organization in part because of its past glory and an association with it. They are disappointed by what they find and lose their dedication to the culture. The organization takes on the hierarchy associated with a bureaucracy. The "fun" goes away. Acquisitions may follow—especially if the organization has amassed a cash horde—only adding to the loss of focus in strategy and culture. In short, the strategy and means of execution (organization, policies, incentives, controls) change, but the culture does not.

This scenario is typical of many high-tech start-ups. It used to occur more slowly. It probably didn't overtake Xerox until some 40 years after its founding in 1952. Some believe it has overtaken Microsoft just over 30 years after its founding in 1980. And some ask whether it will overtake Google in even less time after its founding.[17]

Nonorganic Growth: Acquiring Organizations with Different Cultures

In 2009, Chicago experienced a sharp increase in teenage deaths in several of its neighborhoods, many related to gang violence. Questions began to arise (too late) about whether there was a relationship between these incidents and the fact that the city's department of education had closed several high schools, merging their student populations into schools situated in other neighborhoods. This forced students to cross "boundaries" staked out by the city's gangs, bringing them into direct contact with both students and nonstudents from other cultures. The school administrators either failed to recognize or downplayed the importance of the fact that at least two different cultures were being merged in many of these cases. They were unprepared for the consequences. The same thing happens in the commercial world.

Organizations expected to grow rapidly, usually because of pressure from investors, often turn to acquisitions to meet expectations. This may dilute an organization's strategy by tempting it to extend its reach beyond its areas of expertise. At least one research study has called this practice "premature core abandonment," citing it as one of the primary reasons that an organization's growth stalls.[18]

If nonorganic growth can be detrimental to the health of a strategy, it may be especially toxic for an organization's culture. For example, the merger of Chase Manhattan Bank and J.P. Morgan in 2000 brought together two storied organizations with strong but very different cultures. As a result, the leadership of the surviving organization found itself with a dilemma. It had a desire to create a "one company" mentality among its employees. But this meant bringing together highly rewarded investment bankers who had a transactional deal mentality and less-handsomely rewarded bankers used to preserving assets while creating and maintaining long-standing relationships with clients. For some time after the merger, employees identified themselves by their "legacy" affiliations, Chase or J.P. Morgan. It wasn't until chairman and CEO William Harrison systematically began breaking down the walls that the "two-company" mentality began to disappear. He did so through management meetings, cross-cultural appointments, and seminars meant in large part to bring together managers from the two organizations. The effort has continued under current CEO Jamie Dimon. Even so, J.P. Morgan has had to "outgrow" this mentality over time. This occurred through the slow transformation of the makeup of its leadership as well as efforts to recognize and reward investment bankers and institutional bankers alike for both individual and overall organizational performance.

Nonorganic growth requires a basic decision to either try to integrate the acquired organization's culture into that of the acquirer's or allow it to stand as is. The decision typically is strongly influenced by the degree of diversification that the newly acquired company represents. A strategy involving the acquisition of companies close to the core of an organization's business may argue for integration of the cultures, whereas one representing clear diversification into new businesses may not. Whatever the decision, it also has important implications for other policies, such as measuring and rewarding the performance of employees of the new subsidiary. We'll return to this issue when we address the dynamics of subcultures in Chapter 10.

Failure to Maintain a Small-Company Feel

Cultures are fostered in small groups. They are reinforced and easier to sustain with the kind of peer pressure and transparency that are a part of such working environments. Growth tends to destroy the small-group feeling.

Leaders who recognize the importance of maintaining a small company organize around small groups with responsibility for the results they deliver. For example, at Nucor Steel, mini-mill steel-producing facilities are limited in size to what can be operated by roughly 200 employees. A similar limit is placed on the size of centers designed to serve customers of ING Direct, the direct-banking organization described in Chapter 2. For example, facilities performing the same functions are located side by side at the company's headquarters in Wilmington, Delaware. But they are separated by very thick walls, figuratively speaking.

Illinois Tool Works (ITW) is a manufacturing behemoth by most measures, with more than 50,000 employees generating $15.9 billion in revenues in 2010. It designs and manufactures a wide range of products such as industrial packaging, power systems and electronics, transportation components, construction tools and fasteners, food equipment, decorative surfaces such as countertops, and polymers such as adhesives and sealants.[19] The range is so wide that it may be hard to find a pattern or logic to this list, other than the fact that ITW is really good at running small businesses, or rather letting them run themselves. It may be one of the largest companies that few people have ever heard of. Its so-called "guiding principles" border on both strategies and shared assumptions. They include an emphasis on innovation, 80/20 process (with a focus for example, on 20% of products and customers producing 80% of the profit), and global growth (a recent substitution for the principle of decentralization).

Core values at ITW are as follows:

- Treating individuals with dignity and respect
- Encouraging open communications and trust
- Fairness and equity
- Encouraging employees to find an effective work-life balance
- Providing an inclusive environment by valuing diversity

You might reasonably ask how an organization as diversified and far-flung as this could ever hope to build an effective culture based on any set of values. That's because ITW's strategy has one more basic element. It has built its business by acquiring anchor businesses in each industry of interest and then giving managers of those businesses a great deal of latitude in how to run them and add smaller acquisitions to their respective portfolios. These sector managers haven't disappointed the home office. In all, they have played a key role in the company's acquisition of nearly 850 small subsidiaries. Thus, the average size of an operating unit at ITW is about $19 million in revenues produced by 70 employees or so. ITW creates a small-company feel by preserving small companies. As a result, it creates an atmosphere in which values and an effective culture can be preserved as well, often through the peer pressure typical of small work groups. This, along with its strong financial performance, helps explain why Illinois Tool Works can be found regularly on *Fortune* magazine's list of "Most Admired Companies."

"Outsider" Leadership and Thinking

The management succession process can be damaging to an effective culture. This risk is especially palpable if the successor is someone from outside the organization. In this context, a true "outsider" is not defined by an unrelated industry affiliation or a lack of understanding of the "business." Rather, it is someone who may have less than a fanatical commitment to the organization's existing values, beliefs, and behaviors. And yet, in carrying out their most important responsibility, how many board members take this into account when selecting a successor to a CEO? How often are specific questions posed to candidates to even assess their knowledge of, and interest in, the organization's values or the shared assumptions by which it is led and managed? This is not always easy to do.

Given its strong belief in the importance of ServiceMaster's culture in the company's prior success, I suspect that its board exercised extra care in selecting a successor to CEO William Pollard. As a sometime consultant to the company up to that time, I would have been surprised if the finalists were not questioned closely about their willingness to buy into the company's strong and somewhat unusual culture, described earlier. However, some board members argued for bringing in an "outsider" who could inspire the organization to meet some stiff challenges. Whatever the case, the person selected had broad leadership experience but no prior involvement with Service-Master, its businesses, or its somewhat unique culture. It may have been hard for the board to discern whether he would subscribe to the company's values in leading it forward in the face of more immediate pressures from shareholders for performance. As it turns out, the pressures won out. ServiceMaster's original core business containing most of its employees that provided an array of support services to hospitals was sold to ARAMARK. The focus was shifted to a franchising strategy rather than an operating strategy. A ministry to a congregation of franchisees is much different from one directed to employees.

Financial performance at ServiceMaster lagged, in part accounting for board decisions to first bring in yet another leader and then sell the company to a financial investor who took the company private in 2007. Although the core values (with one minor change) can still be found on the company's web site, they have been relegated to a back page.

Ineffective Measurement and Action

Measurement that focuses on the wrong indicators fails to alert an organization to the right impending problems. A management team that is unwilling to act on the basis of accurate and appropriate measures can produce the same result.

Early Indicators

As organizations approach their peak performance levels, managers typically wait for declines in financial performance before taking action to reverse the trend. Such widely read observers as Jim Collins have, for example, advised that the warning signs that managers should most closely track are "deterioration in gross margins, current ratio, or debt-to-equity ratio(s)."[20] But there is substantial evidence that by the time these measures peak, it may already be too late. Studies that several researchers have carried out, myself included, suggest that financial measures are at best lagging indicators of success or failure.

Warnings of impending problems begin when employee engagement, "ownership," and loyalty start to fall.[21] This triggers similar declines in customer engagement, ownership, and loyalty. And these phenomena contribute to stalled or declining financial measures, particularly revenues and profits.[22] Employee and customer engagement, ownership, and loyalty are predictors of future performance, financial and otherwise. Financial outcomes are history. This philosophy is captured in a comment by Marilyn Nelson, the highly regarded chairman and CEO of the successful travel-and-leisure provider Carlson Companies, who emphasized character, competence, and caring in the people she hired:

> I looked for people who had "a servant's heart." Servant leadership is an important driver of the culture we want to create. A satisfied employee delivers a satisfied customer. In the service business, customers understand very quickly whether you legitimately care about serving them.[23]

Behaviors

Whether or not they can make their numbers, some managers find it difficult to adhere to the organization's core values. They may think that their behaviors aren't observed. But research tells us that a jury of subordinates and peers observes and judges such behaviors. Failure to measure such failings (by asking subordinates) and take action based on the results leads the "jury" to conclude that making the numbers, particularly meeting financial goals, is all that really matters. A breakdown in organization values typically follows.

The most frequent failing cited by managers with whom I work is the unwillingness of leadership to act in a timely manner to rein in others, especially star performers, who fail to adhere to core values and accepted behaviors in their day-to-day managerial activities. This accounts for much of the decline of previously effective cultures.

How Cultures Are Renewed

As I said, employees define a good workplace in large part on the basis of whether "my boss is fair." Every decision and action regarding people in which a manager engages is watched by a jury of a manager's peers and those reporting to her. It also suggests that the best starting point for reviving a culture is not with changes in values but with agreement on the kinds of behaviors that will reflect the values and how managers will act on the behaviors. The Nike promotional slogan "Just do it" is appropriate here. That's the course that Louis Gerstner followed at IBM.

Renewal at IBM

IBM's decline led its board to seek new leadership from outside the industry. The choice of a new CEO, Louis Gerstner, turned out to be a good one. When questioned about his vision for the company, Gerstner said he didn't have one. Nor would he impose major change, beyond replacing several senior executives, until he had heard enough from others to understand how IBM's greatness might be restored. Instead, he set about to reemphasize the values that had made the company great and add to them the value of "restless self-renewal."[24] In meetings with employees, he emphasized the importance and relevance of the values to the company's future. Rather than convene a group to review the values, he reemphasized them in his own behaviors. For example, as one account put it:

> He made himself the role model for customer service. At the company's first customer conference after his appointment (an event that his predecessors never attended), Gerstner stayed for the entire two days. As his first step in changing IBM's culture (actually, reinforcing its existing values) he announced Operation Bear Hug, insisting that his top fifty executives each visit five of IBM's biggest customers within three months.[25]

As Gerstner said at the time, "If the CEO isn't living and preaching the culture and isn't doing it consistently, then it just doesn't happen."[26]

Toward the end of his association with IBM, Gerstner wrote:

In the end, an organization is nothing more than the collective capacity of its people to create value. Vision, strategy, marketing, financial management...can set you on the right path and can carry you for a while. But no enterprise...will succeed over the long haul if (cultural attributes)...aren't part of its DNA.[27]

This set the stage for the introduction of a strategy to become a provider of solutions (not just products or services) to customers managing their information. This strategy has contributed to IBM's success in recent years.

Renewal requires the reaffirmation of the values and beliefs shared by organization members as well as behaviors acceptable in their pursuit.

Renewal at Goldman Sachs

As soon as Goldman Sachs' business principles (described earlier) had been articulated, John Whitehead and Sidney Weinberg challenged department heads to review twice a year with their colleagues the firm's commitment to the business principles, any possible violations that had occurred, how the principles applied to their work, and possible challenges to them that might arise. Minutes of the meetings were then examined at higher levels of management to determine what changes, if any, needed to be made.[28]

These business principles continue to stand the test of time. The organization enjoyed the best financial performance in its history in 2009 and 2010 at the same time it became known as both a major survivor of, and an accessory to, the Great Recession. Goldman reluctantly participated in a government bailout program while being accused of having acted in ways that were alleged to have put its own interests ahead of its clients' and the country's.

Although it remains to be seen whether Goldman Sachs has seen its finest hour, many of its clients continue to express their satisfaction with the firm and its services. Few (mostly public entities sensitive to outcries from the citizenry) have taken their business elsewhere.

Recruiting talent in a tight job market following the Great Recession didn't seem to be a problem.

However, just as Richard Tedlow's "edifice complex," cited earlier, would predict, Goldman Sachs recently moved into a shiny new headquarters building in Manhattan. It even has the company's name on the entrance, in contrast to the anonymous "75" at its previous location. Significantly, the old cubicles without windows that were largely assigned without regard to rank have been replaced by more traditional offices with views of the New York Harbor for managers of a certain rank. Others are relegated to workstations in a common room.

As we saw earlier, the fallout from the Great Recession of 2008 is not the first major crisis that Goldman Sachs has faced. Time and time again, it has relied on the core values of its culture as a base on which to develop strategies that rescued the organization. It will have to do so again.

Reinforcing Effective Cultures

In the face of a lack of reliable evidence, I take it as a matter of faith that an effective culture can play a role in combating the effects of an organization's life cycle. Organizations described earlier that have survived the vicissitudes of time do exhibit common characteristics. Such cultures result from a clear mission; shared assumptions; the "right" values, beliefs, and behaviors; and a good fit with an organization's competitive strategy and how it is executed. They are reinforced first of all by leadership that believes in the power of culture, some amount of success, an effort to preserve pride without the accompanying arrogance, and the preservation of humility and an underdog mentality in the face of success. These are complemented by such things as rites and rituals; stories, heroes, and heroines; management policies such as promotion from within; care in hiring; and the "right" measures, profiled in the culture cycle discussed in Chapter 6, and actions to correct errant behavior on an ongoing basis. All of this is accompanied by a periodic reassessment of values and beliefs. But it all starts with leadership.

In organizations with proven cultures, periodic reaffirmation of values and beliefs may be all that's necessary. When he took over from Lou Gerstner at IBM, for example, Samuel Palmisano decided to revisit the IBM values. But instead of convening a small group to do it, in 2003 he solicited ideas from every IBMer in the world. His primary motive was to examine the company's long-held beliefs and the somewhat U.S.-centric way in which they were stated in the context of what had become a global company. This was done by means of a "values jam," two 72-hour chat sessions on the Internet in which 140,000 employees participated.[29] The result was three phrases (not unlike Thomas Watson's three originals, mentioned in Chapter 1), worded in ways intended to make them more globally universal:

- Dedication to every client's success
- Innovation that matters for customers and the world
- Trust and personal responsibility in all relationships

According to one report, "the values appeared everywhere...(and) were viewed as relevant everywhere."[30] Combined with the company's Business Conduct Guidelines, the values (and successful performance that gave them credibility) continue to guide behaviors at IBM.

Cultures require constant attention and periodic review, reaffirmation, and renewal. Experiences at ServiceMaster, IBM, and Goldman Sachs illustrate that it is important to do this on a timely basis, before a decline in belief in values sets in and long before financial performance begins to taper off. This is more easily said than done, because it may require top management attention at precisely those times when it least appears to be necessary.

Summary

Cultures are formed with or without formal, organized effort when early members of the organization observe the founder's assumptions, values, beliefs, and behaviors. This happens whether or not the founder takes the time to articulate them. Such a task often falls to a successor.

The "rightness" of an organization's culture is confirmed by the organization's success. This helps us understand why cultures are so difficult to change, given the absence of evidence of the need for change precisely when it may be needed most.

If culture is to contribute to success, it has to be nurtured and reinforced by management action. Where this is not done, a culture becomes hard to describe and understand, political considerations often drive out attention to values and beliefs, behaviors do not reflect the values, and the organization is left to rely mainly on a good strategy for its success. The likelihood of this condition remaining stable for long, however, is low.

Effective cultures result from the following:

- A clear mission
- Shared assumptions
- The "right" values and beliefs
- The "right" behaviors
- Rites and rituals
- A good fit with the organization's competitive strategy and how it is executed

Effective cultures are reinforced by the following:

- Leadership that believes in the power of culture
- Consistent, clear communication concerning values, beliefs, and behaviors
- The "right" management beliefs and behaviors
- Success combined with humility and an underdog mentality
- Stories, heroes, and heroines
- Management policies (such as promotion from within)
- Management practices (such as care in hiring to create a good fit with the culture)
- The "right" measures and actions to correct errant behavior
- Periodic reassessment and reinforcement of values and beliefs

Enemies of an effective culture include the following:

- Inconsistent leadership behavior
- Arrogance born of pride and success
- Too-rapid growth
- Too little growth
- Nonorganic growth that leads to the acquisition of organizations with different cultures
- Failure to maintain a small-company feel
- "Outsider" leadership and thinking
- Ineffective measurement and action

The decline of an organization's culture may well precede financial decline. To track the phenomenon, measures such as employee and customer engagement, loyalty, and "ownership" are much more relevant than financial measures.

Cultures are sustained by daily behaviors consistent with shared values. They are renewed through periodic reviews and reaffirmation of the assumptions, values, beliefs, and behaviors that members of the organization find important.

What's the payoff? It's substantial and can be measured, as shown in Chapter 5.

5

Economics of Culture: The "Four Rs"

Here's a familiar scenario. A CEO returns from a meeting of a board on which he sits, attends a seminar, or reads an article about the latest companies selected as the "best places to work." At his next board meeting, the CEO informs the board that efforts will be instituted to achieve a new goal: best place to work. The board members nod approvingly, and the meeting proceeds. There's only one problem. There is no periodic report of progress toward the goal. Board members forget to ask whatever happened to the initiative, even as year after year goes by and the company's name doesn't appear on any "best places to work" lists. Performance is up and down, and the board and management are preoccupied with making the quarterly numbers. The goal falls into the category of just one more "New Year's resolution." I've seen it happen too many times.

Fast-forward to a company like Procter & Gamble, lauded for its prowess in developing and marketing an array of products consumed daily around the world. P&G is very good at what it is regarded as doing best—building its organization and, some say, its success around product management. It's a strategy that puts individuals into management positions with profit responsibility at an early age. MBA students around the world regard P&G as a preferred place to work after receiving their degrees—a kind of postgraduate education. Many stay much longer than they had planned. But whether they stay or not, they are marked for life. Many "graduates" become very successful in other businesses. A number, like Scott Cook, founder and chairman of the Executive Committee of Intuit, the dominant provider of personal financial software, credit at least some of their success to their experiences at P&G. They remain members of the P&G "alumni association," one of the first and strongest of such groups that stay in touch after "members" leave their organizations.

Most credit P&G's long-term success to its marketing prowess. Too few people give sufficient credit to its culture. A notable exception is the *Built to Last* study.[1] Its authors note P&G's success over many decades and cite as one important reason its "cult-like culture." As they put it:

> Throughout most of its history, Procter & Gamble has preserved its core ideology through extensive use of indoctrination, tightness of fit, and elitism. P&G has long-standing practices of carefully screening potential new hires, hiring young people for entry-level jobs, rigorously molding them into P&G ways of thought and behavior, spitting out the misfits, and making middle and top slots available only to loyal P&Gers who grew up inside the company.[2]

My personal experience with this point of view was a lunch with then-CEO John Pepper. He tried to convince me that a policy of requiring three to four years of work experience to qualify for admittance to Harvard's MBA program, for which I was responsible at the time, was not in the best interests of his company. His view, not shared by many other potential employers, was that P&G preferred outstanding recruits who had MBAs but who had not yet worked at other companies. That way, they would not have to "unlearn" bad habits acquired in other organizations.

P&Gers like other P&Gers. I witnessed this firsthand as a board member of a small start-up led by two young P&G alumni who elected to establish their headquarters in Cincinnati near P&G's offices. On more than one occasion, P&G's senior officers would stop by our offices on their way to the parking lot just to relax and "shoot the bull."

In addition to psychic value, does P&G get anything else for its culture? What is it worth in economic terms? That's the question we address here.

Economic Advantages of an Effective Culture: The "Four Rs"

Organization culture is an abstract concept. No one argues against the value of an effective culture. But there is little hard evidence around which to rally in support of efforts to create one. However, some clues can be combined with a few assumptions to provide a convincing case for the economic value of an effective culture. It is based on four important sources of competitive advantage—the "Four Rs": *referrals* and *retention* of employees, *returns to labor*, and *relationships with customers* that foster customer referrals and retention.

Let's start with the assumptions and work backward with pieces of evidence.

Based on other research in which I have been involved over the years, it is logical to assume that organizations with effective cultures have the following advantages over their counterparts in which culture is not nurtured:

- They benefit from higher job satisfaction and employee "ownership" behaviors (such as help in recruiting potential employees).
- Their recruiting, hiring, and training costs are reduced because of a higher proportion of hires from the pool of people *referred* by current or former employees and higher retention rates.
- Their employee *retention* rates are higher because of two factors. Their careful hiring practices seek employees who subscribe to the organization's values. They also "self-select" into the organization people who are already attracted to the organization by its employees and their shared values.
- Their wage levels are not inflated by a large proportion of outside hires to fill new jobs or replace departing people. Hiring from the outside tends to inflate wage scales for everyone, particularly at higher levels of management.
- As a result, they benefit from higher productivity per dollar of compensation or, as economists would put it, *returns to labor*.

- Their higher employee continuity leads to better *relationships with customers*, which in turn produces higher sales levels. It also produces higher retention rates for customers and fewer customers who have to be replaced to sustain sales levels. Furthermore, it produces a higher proportion of customers obtained through customer word-of-mouth referrals, resulting in lower marketing costs.

It's important to note several things about these "assumptions." First, their benefits are not mutually exclusive. That is, some amount of double counting may result in calculating them, although I've tried to minimize this in the following example. Second, the assumptions have differing levels of importance for various organizations. They are the most important in labor-intensive businesses in which organizations have many frontline managers and a large proportion of employees interacting frequently with customers. Thus, these assumptions are particularly relevant for retailers as well as providers of professional, business, and consumer services making up as many as 70% of the jobs in a typical developed economy. They also apply to government agencies such as Social Security and the Internal Revenue Service in the U.S.—agencies offering "customer services." Here the benefits are primarily associated with creating better, more interesting jobs and places to work as well as the satisfaction that results from more positive interactions with satisfied "customers" (citizens).

Using the assumptions, I'll assess the importance of each of the competitive advantages they represent and then sum up their economic worth.

The First R: Referrals by Employees

Table 5-1 shows the basic assumptions used to estimate the impact of an effective culture on an organization's competitive advantage. Compared here are two competing organizations. Acme Corporation has an effective culture. Beta Corporation has a culture that has much less effect than Acme's on the organization and its performance. Both have profiles similar to retail or service organizations, with large numbers of customer-facing employees, and they have annual revenues of $3 billion. Acme's pay scales are about 10% higher than those of Beta. But because of higher productivity in Acme, whose benefits we'll estimate later, Beta employs 20% more managers and employees than its competitor. Furthermore, Acme's employee turnover rates are lower.

Table 5-1 The First Advantage of an Effective Culture: Employee Referrals (Reduced Cost of Recruiting People Recommended by Current or Former Employees)

Assumptions	Acme (Effective Culture)	Beta (Ineffective Culture)
Annual revenue	$3,000,000,000	$3,000,000,000
Number of employees:		
Managerial	2,000	2,400
Nonmanagerial	18,000	21,600
Turnover of employees per year:		
Managerial	10%	20%
Nonmanagerial	30%	50%
Number of new hires per year:		
Managerial	200	480
Nonmanagerial	5,400	10,800
Percentage of hires referred by employees	40%	10%
Total compensation of each person replaced:		
Managerial	$110,000	$100,000
Nonmanagerial	$33,000	$30,000
Employee turnover costs as a percentage of annual compensation for each person replaced:		
Managerial	200%	200%
Nonmanagerial	50%	50%
Reduction in normal cost of employee turnover through employee referrals	25%	25%
Value of 25% reduction in cost of turnover through referrals:		
Managerial	$4,400,000	$2,400,000
Nonmanagerial	$8,910,000	$4,050,000
Total	$13,310,000	$6,450,000
Savings as a percentage of annual revenue	.44%	.22%
Advantage to Acme as a percentage of annual revenue	.22 percentage points	

Employee engagement results from an effective culture. It has a significant influence on performance. A significant indicator of an employee's engagement is his willingness to recommend his organization to a good friend as a place to work. Going a step further, employee "ownership" is measured by whether he has actually made such a recommendation and whether his friends followed up with an interview and joined the organization.[3] Rather than track these behaviors, however, many organizations simply document the proportion of new hires recommended by current employees.

In the case of our two hypothetical organizations, high employee engagement at Acme results in 40% of its new hires coming from employee referrals, four times greater than for Beta. It's assumed that the cost of hiring a referral is 75% that of someone recruited and hired without such referrals. This is a very conservative estimate in the opinion of human resources managers with whom I've talked.

One estimate of recruiting, hiring, and training costs for employees is that they represent anywhere from 41% of annual compensation for frontline employees up to 241% of annual compensation for middle managers and above.[4] This includes allowances for losses of productivity or sales resulting from turnover, especially in critical jobs, and this is consistent with the experiences of organizations that I have observed. As shown in Table 5-1, I've assumed that such costs are twice the annual compensation for managerial employees and one-half the annual compensation for nonmanagerial employees.

Applying the turnover rates shown in Table 5-1, we obtain figures for the number of new employees who must be hired each year by the two organizations, with no allowance for growth. As you can see, the differential in costs associated with new hires recommended by employees produces a cost "discount" of .44% of revenues for Acme, roughly twice that of its competitor, or an advantage of .22 percentage points. These numbers represent savings in operating costs as a percentage of annual revenue for each organization.

The Second R: Retention

A Corporate Leadership Council study estimates that more highly engaged employees, likely to be found in an organization with an effective culture, are 87% less likely to leave their jobs than those who profess a low level of engagement.[5] We also know that turnover rates decline the longer an employee remains with an organization and becomes more senior. In particular, turnover rates among managers are much lower than among frontline employees. The gap is typically lower in manufacturing and higher in such businesses as fast food chains. Also, the costs of recruiting, hiring, and training a frontline employee are much lower than those for a manager.

Let's scale down our assumptions for Acme and Beta from the evidence just presented, as shown in Table 5-2. Here, we assume that managerial employees turn over at the rate of 10% per year at Acme and twice as fast at Beta. That's the case for "top five" executives as well. High rates of leadership turnover (along with the reasons for it) can demoralize an organization. They are associated with relatively weak cultures.

Table 5-2 The Second Advantage of an Effective Culture: Retention (Lower Employee Turnover)

Assumptions	Acme (Effective Culture)	Beta (Ineffective Culture)
Annual revenue	$3,000,000,000	$3,000,000,000
Number of employees:		
Managerial	2,000	2,400
Nonmanagerial	18,000	21,600
Turnover of employees per year:		
Top five	10%	20%
Managerial	10%	20%
Nonmanagerial	30%	50%
Cost of turnover (recruiting, hiring, training, lost productivity) as a percentage of annual compensation:		
Top five	200%	200%
Managerial	200%	200%
Nonmanagerial	50%	50%
Compensation per year:		
Top five	$2,000,000	$4,000,000
Managerial	$110,000	$100,000
Nonmanagerial	$33,000	$30,000

continued

Assumptions	Acme (Effective Culture)	Beta (Ineffective Culture)
Number of replacements per year:		
Top five	.5	1.0
Managerial	200	480
Nonmanagerial	5,400	10,800
Cost of turnover:		
Top five	$2,000,000	$8,000,000
Managerial	$44,000,000	$96,000,000
Nonmanagerial	$89,000,000	$162,000,000
Total	$135,100,000	$266,000,000
Cost of turnover as a percentage of annual revenue	4.50%	8.87%
Advantage to Acme as a percentage of annual revenue	4.37 percentage points	

Again the costs of replacing managers and employees are assumed to be 200% and 50% of annual compensation, respectively. This is assumed to cover the cost of recruiting, hiring, training, and lost productivity.

This calculation introduces assumptions for the five most highly paid executives—the "top five." They are assumed to make twice as much at Beta than at Acme, but their turnover rate is twice as high. This too characterizes organizations with ineffective versus effective cultures.

Working through the numbers presented in Table 5-2, the result is a total cost of turnover of about $135 million per year at Acme as compared to $266 million for its competitor. This is an advantage of about 4.37 percentage points (when compared to the firms' respective revenues) for Acme.

This analysis does not reflect an implicit cost of low employee retention—the damage it does to efforts to sustain a culture. It's the effect of losing what are known at Goldman Sachs as "culture carriers"—the people who would have trained the next generation of partners.[6] This was a particular cause of concern when the firm, having experienced significant trading losses, lost 30% of its partners in 1994.

It took years for the firm's culture to recover from such a loss of talent. Some speculate on whether it ever did.

The Third R: Returns to Labor

If Southwest Airlines operated with the same productivity per dollar of compensation as other airlines, it would face severe economic difficulties or even bankruptcy in a few short years. For years Southwest Airlines has boarded at least 50% more passengers per employee than the average of the other major airlines. If its ratio had been the same as that of the industry, Southwest would have added more than a billion dollars per year to its expense base between 2005 and 2009, producing operating deficits in four of these five years.[7]

Note that we're not necessarily talking about paying low wages here. In fact, Southwest pays its employees at least as well as other airlines, if not a bit more. But because of a combination of the way its employees are organized to work (in teams with joint responsibility for performance under peer pressure and unusually great latitude due to favorable labor agreements with the company's unions) and their dedication to the company (putting the organization before themselves), they achieve remarkable results. Clearly, some of this is due to the company's strategy, particularly its on-time performance, fast turnaround of flights, frequent departures, and team organization. People work harder and smarter at Southwest than at other airlines. But they do so willingly (if the company's relatively high employee loyalty is any indication) in large part because of management's close attention to maintaining the organization's strong culture. As David Glass, then-CEO of Wal-Mart Stores, Inc., once put it: "Give me fewer, better trained, better paid people, and they'll win every time."[8]

A more general estimate of the impact of culture on productivity is provided by a study of the benefits of employee engagement (that is, those who respond favorably to questions such as "Do you like your job, manager, peers, etc.?" or "Would you recommend your organization to a friend as a place to work?"). It estimates that engaged employees are perceived as performing 20 percentile points better than those not so engaged.[9] One large study of more than 2,900 Danish manufacturing firms concluded that employee turnover affects productivity negatively, an effect that can be reversed only with heavy capital investment.[10]

Let's try to estimate the possible impact of an effective culture on productivity more concretely, using the assumptions shown in Table 5-3 for our two organizations. Again, compensation levels for those below the top five are assumed to be about 10% higher at Acme. But because of lower productivity at Beta, it employs about 20% more managerial and nonmanagerial people than its competitor. I believe these are conservative assumptions. Based on the assumptions shown in Table 5-1, Acme obtains $3.64 in revenue for every dollar spent for compensation (including benefits) compared to $3.30 for Beta. Factoring in the payroll for the top five executives in each case, the total payroll is 27.47% of revenue for Acme and 30.27% for Beta, a 2.80 percentage point advantage for the former. Note that this applies even assuming 10% higher compensation per manager and employee at Acme. This assumption is in line with results at organizations that employ some form of profit sharing, for example. All other things being equal (which they never are), Acme would make more money than its competitor, thus paying more in the form of profit sharing, assuming it has such a program. Profit sharing may account for some of the higher per-person compensation levels at Acme.

Table 5-3 The Third Competitive Advantage of an Effective Culture: Returns to Labor (Higher Revenue Per Dollar of Compensation)*

Assumptions	Acme (Effective Culture)	Beta (Ineffective Culture)
Annual revenue	$3,000,000,000	$3,000,000,000
Average total compensation per employee:		
Top five	$2,000,000	$4,000,000
Managerial	$110,000	$100,000
Nonmanagerial	$33,000	$30,000
Number of employees:		
Managerial	2,000	2,400
Nonmanagerial	18,000	21,600
Revenue per employee:		
Managerial	$1.5 million	$1.25 million
Nonmanagerial	$166,670	$138,890
Average for all	$150,000	$125,000

Assumptions	Acme (Effective Culture)	Beta (Ineffective Culture)
Revenue per dollar of compensation:		
Managerial	$13.63	$12.50
Nonmanagerial	5.05	4.63
Average for all	3.64	3.30
Total compensation costs (including top five)	$824,000,000	$908,000,000
Compensation costs as a percentage of revenue	27.47%	30.27%
Advantage to Acme as a percentage of revenue	2.80 percentage points	

* Note that under these assumptions, the ratio of the average compensation of the top five executives to everyone else is 60:1 for Acme and 109:1 for Beta. This, I believe, is typical of comparisons of organizations with relatively effective and ineffective cultures. It is, however, a hypothesis that has yet to be proven.

The Fourth R: Relationships with Customers

The fourth R addresses the economics of customer retention and acquisition.

Customer Retention

No amount of marketing effort can offset the long-term negative effects of poor customer retention. On the other hand, high retention rates reduce the pressures on marketing to grow revenue by attracting new customers. The long-term benefits from sales efforts are preserved, and the resulting continuing relationships with current customers set the stage for the organization's organic growth. Culture's effect on customer retention grows with the importance of customer-facing activities and the proportion of employees engaged in customer-facing activities.

As shown in Table 5-4, the number of customers for Acme and Beta at the end of the year is the result of beginning customers minus lost customers plus new ones. Both ended with one million customers, but Beta's turnover rate for the year was much higher. It lost 500,000 of the customers with which it began the year. The loss of operating profit per customer (assuming on average the loss of half the year's revenue and operating profit with a 20% defection rate due to the effects of culture in Acme's case and a 30% rate in Beta's case) is equivalent to $63.20 for Acme and $94.80 for Beta. When multiplied by the number of customers lost and compared to the sales for the year, the loss in operating profit is .63% of sales for Acme and 1.53% for Beta.

Table 5-4 The Fourth Advantage of an Effective Culture: Relationships with Customers (Reduced Customer Acquisition/Retention Costs Through Customer Referrals)

Assumptions	Acme (Effective Culture)	Beta (Ineffective Culture)
Number of customers:		
Beginning	900,000	900,000
Lost	300,000	500,000
Retained	600,000	400,000
New	400,000	600,000
Ending	1,000,000	1,000,000
Cost of lost customers:		
Revenue per customer (average for year)*	$3,158	$3,158
Cost of lost customer due to culture (50% of revenue for year × 20% of loss due to culture for Acme and 30% for Beta)	$316	$474
Lost operating profit (20% of lost revenue)	$63.20	$94.80
Number of customers lost	300,000	500,000
Lost operating profit due to culture	$18,960,000	$47,400,000
Lost operating profit due to culture as a percentage of revenue	.63%	1.53%
Savings from customer referrals:		
Cost per customer referred	$50	$50
Cost per customer not referred	$200	$200
Percentage of new customers obtained through referrals	40%	10%
Number of new customers obtained through referrals	160,000	60,000

Assumptions	Acme (Effective Culture)	Beta (Ineffective Culture)
Percentage of referrals attributable to culture	20%	10%
Number of new customers attributable to culture	32,000	6,000
Savings from referrals attributable to culture ($150 per customer)	$4,800,000	$900,000
Customer acquisition cost savings attributable to culture (as a percentage of revenue)	.16%	.03%
Operating profit on new customers:		
Operating profit on new customers attributable to culture[**]	$10,105,600	$1,894,800
Operating profit on new customers (as a percentage of revenue)	.34%	.06%
Total net operating profit effect (cost of lost customers offset by savings from customer referrals and operating profit on new customers attributed to culture)	(.13%)	(1.44%)
Total advantage to Acme from relationships with customers	1.31 percentage points	

* Calculated as annual revenue divided by beginning plus ending customers divided by 2.
** Calculated as the number of new customers attributable to culture × $3,158 average revenue per year per customer × 50% (for a half year) × 20% operating profit.

Customer Acquisition

Table 5-4 compares customer acquisition costs for Acme and Beta. Here it's assumed that Acme, because of the superior customer relationships that accrue because of the quality of its frontline employees, retained 600,000 of its 1,000,000-customer base compared to 400,000 for Beta.

In our example, the assumption is that customers obtained through referrals (word of mouth) from employees or other customers cost an organization one-fourth as much as those obtained through typical marketing methods. This reflects, for example, ING Direct's experience (reported in Chapter 2) of spending about $100 to attract a new customer, as opposed to roughly four times that amount for its more traditional banking competitors. This may understate the actual comparative costs of the two sources, because a relatively small proportion of ING Direct customers are still recruited by conventional advertising. At Acme, 40% of customers come through the referral route, compared with 10% for its competitor. Of these, 20% are attributable to Acme's culture, as opposed to 10% for Beta. At a savings rate per referral of $150, Acme's savings from referrals attributed to its more effective culture are .16% of revenue, as opposed to .03% for Beta.

New customers produce added operating profit as well. If assumptions similar to those made earlier are applied here, such operating profit attributable to culture produces over $10 million in new profit for Acme, or about .34% of sales, more than five times the number for Beta.

In total, these three sources of benefits associated with customer relationships result in cost or benefit differences for the two organizations that represent an advantage of 1.31 percentage points in operating profit for Acme.

Other Competitive Advantages: The Economics of "Identity"

These are only four of the competitive advantages of an effective culture. Others may be more difficult to document. For example, higher continuity in staffing is associated with high productivity. Not all of this may have been captured in the calculations just shown.

Because revenues are held constant in this example, no effort has been made here to estimate revenue increases resulting from the quality of relationships between engaged employees and the customers they serve. But research has shown that customer loyalty is directly related to sales per customer. The longer a customer remains with an organization, the more he purchases, and the higher the customer's lifetime value.[11]

Organizations with strong cultures tend to be more likely to promote from inside the organization.[12] They don't suffer from the wage escalation effects associated with hiring from outside. This phenomenon has not been captured here; it may be one of several factors determining compensation levels. For example, in Table 5-1 we assume higher, not lower, compensation levels for the organization with the most effective culture. This is primarily because of better profit performance and the assumption that employees are included in profit sharing.

Identity economics, a concept introduced in Chapter 1, would argue just the reverse. Economists, including Nobel Prize winner George Ackerlof, have concluded that something important is missing from the vast body of economic theory that assumes that people act rationally. They label it "identity." That is, out of a desire to "belong" to a group, people make decisions—get a tattoo, wear unusual garments, or go to work for an organization paying below market wages—that appear not to be in their best interests.[13] This helps explain why "intrinsic" motivators are often more important than money in a job, and why salaries in "great places to work" or prestigious organizations (such as universities) are often lower than in others at which their employees easily could get a job.

Summing Up

Summing up the "Four Rs" (measurable sources of advantage) for Acme in our example, as shown in Table 5-5, we see that its effective culture accounts for all or most of an 8.70 percentage point advantage in margin over its competitor. This is significant. In some industries with slim operating margins of 10% or less, this can mean the difference between profit or loss. Even in industries where operating margins are as much as 40%, it can represent roughly 20% of all profit before or after tax.

This example may raise several questions. Can you count on the differentials shown here between a highly regarded culture and one that gains no plaudits? No. The size of the advantage depends on the importance of these costs in the cost structure of a particular industry. In the two organizations in our example, the cost of talent is 27% to 30% of revenue. This would be found in industries such as professional services and retailing, but it could be quite different in others, ranging from 65% in educational institutions to less than 10% in some mining and manufacturing businesses.

Table 5-5 Sum of the Four Rs (Measurable Competitive Advantages) of an Effective Culture, Hypothetical Example, in Percentage Points Related to Sales

	Acme (Effective Culture)	Beta (Ineffective Culture)	Competitive Advantage for Acme (in Percentage Points of Revenue)
Costs as percentages of revenue:			
Referrals: Cost savings from referrals of new employees by existing ones	(.44)	(.22)	.22
Retention: Lower labor turnover	4.50	8.87	4.37
Returns to labor: Lower costs resulting from higher productivity	27.47	30.27	2.80
Relationships with customers: Sum of operating profit on customer retention, referrals by existing customers, and operating profit on new customers*	(.13)	(1.44)	1.31
Total cost advantage for Acme			8.70

* These costs represent a mix of gains and reduced losses, as shown in Table 5-4.

Are these comparisons directionally correct? Yes. Are they sufficiently documented? No. Are they fair in that they give the advantage to Acme on every dimension? Probably, because an advantage for Beta on any one of the dimensions would be an aberration. It just doesn't happen very often unless the quality of two competing cultures is quite similar, against which we've controlled here.

One such real-world example can be found at SAS Institute, the privately owned North Carolina-based software systems developer that has enjoyed double-digit revenue growth since its founding in 1976. In an industry that has endured high rates of employee turnover, SAS has sought to provide an outstanding work environment for systems developers. As one manager we interviewed at SAS told us, "We do everything in our power to make SAS the place you spend the rest of your career."[14] Vice president Jim Davis said:

(SAS founder) Jim Goodnight is responsible for this culture. He was a visionary upfront in terms of recognizing if I spend an extraordinary amount of money on making sure my employees have a good work-life balance, then it's going to pay off for me in terms of returns for my customers, quality of software, et cetera. So we're running a turnover rate of around 4 percent on an annual basis, where the industry is 18 percent to 22 percent.[15]

In 2000, Charles O'Reilly and Jeffrey Pfeffer attempted to estimate what that differential is worth. As they put it:

> If the average turnover (of employees) in software is 20 percent, a conservative estimate, and the SAS workforce (turns over at about 4%, it)...means that about 925 fewer people per year leave SAS than other companies. What does it cost to replace someone? Most estimates range from one to two times the annual salary. Even with a conservative salary estimate of $60,000 per year and an estimate of 1.5 times salary as the replacement cost, SAS Institute is saving more than $100 million per year from its lower turnover—from a revenue base of about $800 million.[16]

Of much greater importance than a comparison at one point in time is tracking trends in such comparisons in an effort to gauge the importance of the competitive advantage afforded by an effective culture. This exercise is critical for a disadvantaged competitor where culture is not a high management priority and in which leadership may be unaware of its negative competitive "culture gap." The Acmes of the world are much more likely to have a general sense of the advantages their effective cultures afford them, whether or not they've documented them. They don't have to be convinced of the importance of maintaining such advantages.

To what extent do senior managers regularly track the comparisons shown in Tables 5-1 through 5-5? Many managers track indicators such as employee loyalty and the percentage of business from existing customers. But I'm often surprised at how often questions about these statistics draw blank looks from executives who should be able to recite them. Rarely do managers track all of them. And even more rarely are all measurements assembled in one place, as suggested by responses to an informal, unscientific survey of several human resources managers that I carried out recently (shown next). It indicated that human resources managers actually have direct access to very few of the 35 pieces of information listed here. Of the 35, 13 were regarded by most respondents as either being in their possession or easy to get from others in the organization, another 10 existed in the organization but would be difficult to obtain, and 11 were thought not to exist. In other words, such analyses are difficult at best and next to impossible at worst, at least not without a lot of effort.

Ease of Access to "Four R" Data for Human Resource Managers

"I have the data; it's easy to get."

1. Year-ending and year-beginning number of associates
2. Number of associates applying for jobs
3. Number of associates hired
4. Year-ending and year-beginning number of managers
5. Number of managers hired
6. Measurement of employee engagement with the job and company
7. Annual revenues
8. Annual operating profit
9. Total annual compensation costs, including benefits
10. Total annual compensation costs for the top five executives
11. Company reputation as a place to work

"Others have the data; it's easy to get."

12. Year-ending number of customers
13. Number of customers lost during the year

"Others have the data; it's difficult to get."

14. Total all-in cost of employing associates
15. Total all-in cost of employing managers

16. Number of associates leaving voluntarily in the past 12 months

17. Number of associates asked to leave in the past 12 months

18. Number of managers leaving voluntarily in the past 12 months

19. Number of managers asked to leave in the past 12 months

20. Total cost of recruiting an associate

21. Total cost of recruiting a manager

22. Number of customers added during the year

23. Estimated revenue represented by new customers

"I don't think the data exists."

24. Number of associates hired who were recommended by employees

25. Amount by which costs of recruiting associates are reduced by employee referrals

26. Estimated cost of associate replacement due to lost productivity

27. Number of managers applying for jobs

28. Number of offers made to fill managerial positions

29. Number of managers hired who were recommended by employees

30. Amount by which costs of recruiting managers are reduced by employee referrals

31. Total cost to train a manager

32. Estimated cost of productivity loss in replacing a manager

33. Approximate number of individual customers

34. Number of new customers recommended by existing customers

35. Estimated cost of obtaining a new customer with and without a referral

This explains why, to my knowledge, no organization has attempted an analysis of the "Four R" advantages of an effective culture shown here, other than in an effort to humor me. And none are in a position to do so for any important competitor. But businesses with multiple operating sites can develop measurements for two or more sites to test the importance of effective cultures. That's what I did in one especially cooperative organization in an effort to test the hypotheses implied by the comparisons shown in Table 5-5, a project described in Chapter 7. In that analysis, nearly half the differences in operating income for three offices was explained by the Four Rs.

Culture Impact Model

The economic advantages of an effective culture are diagrammed in the Culture Impact Model shown in Figure 5-1 with numbers from our hypothetical example. It shows how the advantages are related to each other as well as to revenue and cost. Here we see that high job satisfaction, loyalty, productivity, and customer "ownership" lead to high employee and customer engagement levels that produce more employee and customer referrals; lower costs of recruitment, selection, training and lost productivity; higher revenue/compensation ratios; and ultimately higher profit.

Numbers shown in the figure are drawn from Tables 5-1 through 5-5.

Several Caveats

In making the assumptions and presenting the analyses shown here, I run the risk of criticism from several directions. This is a simplified example designed to illustrate the importance of relationships. Some people (I trust not too many) may regard it as simplistic. Others will criticize the impression of precision in the calculations. These are valid criticisms. The estimates are directionally correct, but not to hundredths of a percentage point. But perhaps the most significant criticism will concern the importance attached to culture. In the assumptions, for example, the economic impact of higher productivity is attributed to culture, something that accounts for more than 30% of the total benefits. Other contributors could be superior technology, a different mix of product, or better processes. But the argument is complicated even further by my conviction that in an organization with a learning culture, superior processes and even superior technology often result from greater employee and customer "ownership," a direct result of culture.

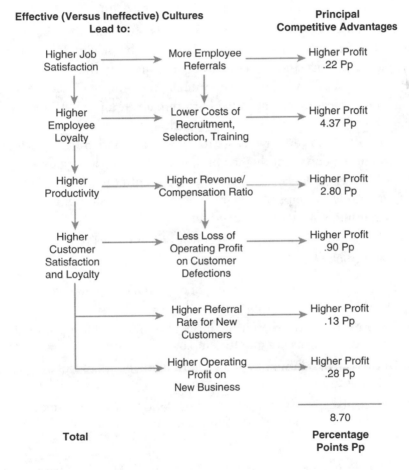

Figure 5-1 Culture Impact Model

You should draw no conclusions about how good or bad, respectively, the profiles for Acme and Beta are. They should not be used as benchmarks. My only point here is to show the importance of the impact that a quality workplace can have on competitive advantage.

The assumptions and analyses may be open to criticism, but they serve the purpose of triggering a useful debate.

Summary

Few would argue that an organization's culture is unimportant, but there is little hard evidence of the value of an effective culture. Few efforts have been made to quantify it. It is often forgotten in the press of short-term business concerns. However, by piecing together the results of various studies, we can begin to quantify the value and "make the soft hard." We know, for example, that engaged managers and employees are much more likely to remain in an organization, leading directly to fewer hires from outside the organization. This, in turn, results in lower wage costs for talent; lower recruiting, hiring, and training costs; and higher productivity (fewer lost sales and higher sales per employee). Higher employee continuity leads to better customer relationships that contribute to greater customer loyalty, lower marketing costs, and enhanced sales.

"Four Rs" of an effective culture can be (but rarely are) documented and tracked:

- **Referrals:** A higher proportion of potential employees recommended by current or former employees
- **Retention:** Lower recruiting, hiring, training, and lost productivity costs because of greater employee loyalty
- **Returns to labor:** Greater productivity per dollar of compensation
- **Relationships:** Better customer relationships, resulting in greater loyalty, lower customer acquisition costs, and more sales

Another indicator that is more difficult to track is the effect of wage escalation resulting from extensive hiring from outside the organization. This effect is especially important at middle to top management levels.

In total, these competitive advantages can spell the difference between competitive advantage or disadvantage, profit or loss. A small, informal survey of those responsible for human resources, however, shows that relatively little of the information needed for such analyses is readily available to them. Some of it is not even believed to exist. And much of what is available would, they estimate, require considerable effort to collect.

An explanation of causes of differences in performance due to an organization's culture can be obtained only through a deeper exploration of individual employee reactions to management, their jobs, and the quality of their working environment. We focus on that next.

6

The Culture Cycle: Measuring Effectiveness

Why should you worry about measuring and tracking the effectiveness of an organization's culture? Because it is a predictor of future success.

An effective culture is the product of a set of strongly held shared values. But just as important, it also depends on the way in which members of the organization perceive how (and how well) those values are interpreted and administered by leadership and how they help leadership execute a chosen strategy.

One sign of an effective culture is the organization's longevity. James Collins and Jerry Porras captured this idea in describing "cult-like cultures" in their book *Built to Last*.[1] These are cultures that both "preserve the core" (by means of "fervently held ideology, indoctrination, tightness of fit, and elitism) and "stimulate progress." They remind us that the things that preserve the core produce an early demise unless offset by values that stimulate progress. In their words, "it's important to understand that you can have a cult-like culture of innovation, or a cult-like culture of competition, or a cult-like culture of change."[2] The implication is that you can't just have a cult-like culture that preserves the status quo if longevity is a goal. They conclude that strong, deeply held core values can actually provide a basis for trust and common understanding on which organizations can allow their members to act creatively in administering by the values. This ensures adaptability and agility necessary for organizational "learning" and long-term survival.

Observations built on a retrospective look at a small number of long-lived, successful organizations—in this case just 18 meeting stringent conditions over more than 180 years—are one thing. Measuring the effectiveness of today's cultures to predict those that are "built to last" into the future—a particular concern of today's leaders—is something else.

By now it should be clear that it's the health as well as the strength of a culture that matters. Too often, we talk about the importance of strong cultures and ignore their health. I speak from experience, having fallen victim to this error in the study described in Chapter 3. When we asked executives whether "there is a (company name) way of doing things" in their respective industries, we were actually measuring strength, whether or not it was beneficial to performance. Organizations named in response to the question displayed both good and poor performance.

A healthy culture must be both strong and centered around the "right" assumptions and values—those most appropriate for an organization's mission, people, and strategy. The "right" assumptions and values don't mean much if they are not widely known, shared, and used as guides for decision-making and action. As well, a strong culture that rallies people around an outmoded set of basic assumptions or no-longer-appropriate values for the strategy it is trying to pursue—or that, for example, shuts out the outside world in the continued pursuit of success in the same old time-tested ways—may be equally unhealthy.

An exploration of several examples will help illustrate these points. More important, they provide insights that help clarify important elements of effective cultures that can be organized into what might be called a culture cycle. The culture cycle is a concept that helps us understand the kinds of measurements—a "dashboard" of indicators of effective cultures—that support organization success.

The following vignettes about USAA, Nucor Steel, and Toyota also raise the question of whether, at the beginning of 2009, we could have predicted which of these three organizations would face a culture-driven crisis.

USAA: Effectiveness Through Trust

A visitor to USAA's headquarters in San Antonio, Texas walks just a bit taller than normal. Why? The company's leadership probably has the best posture of any American corporation. It is comprised of former military officers.

The first impression is of USAA's headquarters itself, reputed to be the second-largest office building (next to the Pentagon, an appropriate comparison) in the United States devoted to one organization, housing 10,000 employees. The second impression is of employees intent on what they are doing, but willing to take time to talk about why USAA is a great place to work. The visitor quickly learns that USAA's management has an edge in understanding the needs of its customers. They share military service experiences with them.

USAA was formed by 25 military officers in 1922 who decided to insure each other's vehicles. As time passed and the founding officers reentered civilian life, they continued to sense the special needs of military officers. Members of the military often were rejected or charged higher premiums when they applied for life insurance because of the perceived risks in their occupations. USAA's founders shared an important assumption that escaped the company's competitors. They saw their potential military clients differently. They were a group of honest, honorable, healthy, even risk-averse people who could be served quite profitably by an organization that understood their changing needs and was willing to develop financial products that met these needs. This assumption has served USAA well.

Over the years, the organization has grown to provide an array of financial services to 7.7 million members (customers), many of whom who are active and retired U.S. military officers and their families who qualify as members. USAA seeks to "facilitate the financial security of its members."[3]

Even though it operates somewhat under the radar as a company mutually owned by its policyholders, USAA regularly is cited as a great place to work and a provider of exceptional customer service. *Computerworld* magazine recently named it one of the "100 best places to work in IT." *Latina Style* magazine cited it as one of the "50 best employers for Hispanic women." *MSN Money* magazine rated USAA number one in the United States in 2009 as the "company that treats customers the best." And *Businessweek* in recent years repeatedly has named it one of the top two "customer service champs." So USAA apparently meets two of the criteria for an effective culture. Not only is it a great place to work, but that work apparently produces something valued highly by its customers.[4]

It takes just a few conversations to impress even an uninformed visitor to USAA that this organization's culture gains its strength from its shared values drawn from the military ("service, loyalty, honesty, and integrity") and that the majority of its senior managers are former military officers. USAA's leadership bought into its values years before joining the organization. A visitor begins to realize that he is in the middle of an organization whose culture is so strong that you, as they say, can "cut it with a knife."

So far, so good. But how about the health of a culture shared by managers whose personal values all led them to do the same thing—serve in the military, many for multiple tours of duty? The secret lies in the first of the values, "service." It is practiced in dealings with employees, many of whom perform relatively boring jobs, who are given the opportunity to develop themselves. This is possible through such things as the provision of time and facilities to allow employees to pursue personal fitness and education, a four-day workweek that enables them to lead more balanced lives, and latitude to carry out their various responsibilities at USAA and produce results for members. This latitude is given freely to people at all levels who were hired for their "loyalty, honesty, and integrity." These qualities provide the foundation for a powerful value—trust—that underlies much of this organization's success.

"Service" also refers to a set of policies and behaviors that add up to a fanatical focus on the rather special needs of a highly focused group of customers in an effort to "be the provider of choice for the military community."[5] Operating from a base of strongly shared values, participants in this "cult-like culture" are then given the latitude to serve USAA's membership in ways that make sense to the employee. For example, a soldier being sent to a theater of war may be advised to increase his or her life insurance.

Other service processes are more carefully scripted. A service representative fielding a call from a member involved in an auto accident is instructed to first ask, "Are you hurt?" This is empathetic and at the same time yields important information about the seriousness and complexity of the accident. It enables the representative to determine whether he or she can handle the matter immediately (including authorization to determine the amount of reimbursement to be sent to the member) or whether other USAA specialists will have to be involved. For auto damage only, the policyholder is advised either to take the car to a USAA-approved garage to get it fixed or to just get it fixed and send the company a bill—without the inconvenience of getting multiple estimates, approvals, and the like. This is what is most frequently mentioned when USAA members tell me about the organization's service. It is evidence that the company trusts its customer-members.

How can the company afford to do this? Remember, customers come preselected by the military. And this saves so much money that USAA offers some of the lowest rates of all insurers.

Instead of working at boring jobs, service representatives at USAA repeatedly get satisfaction from delivering remarkable service resulting in part from the trust placed in them. At the same time, they collect ideas for new services from customers behaving like USAA "owners."

The operative value here may be service. But what is really practiced is a complete and intensive identification with the needs of the organization's customers. This produces a continuing awareness of their changing needs for new products and services and fuels continuing success. It's little wonder that USAA has realized this kind of success for nearly nine decades.

It would be easy to overlook the health of this organization's culture by examining only its rather unremarkable set of values and failing to measure what they really reflect—trust, meeting expectations, "safety" (in implementing new ideas, for example), and continuous innovation. These lead to such things as high employee and customer "ownership," low costs, high service levels, and continuing innovation.

It requires an assessment not only of shared assumptions, values, and behaviors but also the following:

- The degree to which they fit with strategies, organizational arrangements, and even the backgrounds of individual managers
- The way in which the values facilitate a strategy, as well as how it is executed
- The degree to which employee expectations are met, especially on the organization's front lines
- The way in which what is delivered and how it is delivered are perceived by customers
- The extent to which the culture encourages behaviors that generate new ideas for future business

Using these criteria, values by which USAA is led fit with a strategy of serving an underserved market, an organization that has for years been staffed with leaders who subscribe to the values, and a hiring policy that creates a clear set of expectations that are then met. Judging from employee surveys and customer service ratings, the result is valued highly by employees and customers alike.

Nucor Steel: A Study in Learning, Accountability, Self-Direction, and Innovation

Nucor Steel gives us a different perspective on the effectiveness of cultures. It operates minimills and even micromills and has grown to become the largest producer of steel in the United States and the largest recycler of steel in the world. It has been lauded many times for its extrinsic methods of motivation through a combination of below-market wages and the opportunity to triple those wages through productivity-based incentives. This makes it sound like a company that Frederick Taylor could only dream about. But in reality it has successfully transformed some of his thinking in ways that he would neither recognize nor approve of.

Nucor has seen more than 150 consecutive quarters of dividends and the highest return to shareholders of any company in the Standard & Poor's 500 between 2004 and 2009. Its success is due in large part to the successful application of technology resulting from innovative ideas generated by both employees and customers. Ken Iverson, who led the company until 2002 and still serves as an inspiration to the organization, attributes 30% of the company's success to technology and industry-leading innovation. What about the other 70%? He attributes that to culture.[6]

There is something special about the culture. For one thing, after declaring in its mission statement that the goal of Nucor's employees is "to take care of our customers," its statements of "responsibilities" and "basic principles" don't mention customers. Responsibilities are to a safer workplace, a cleaner environment, and a stronger community, period. The four basic principles are as follows:

1. Our employees, neighbors, and shareholders should always be treated fairly, honestly, and respectfully.

2. Our decisions should be based on securing long-term survival, not a short-term gain.

3. Management should always be accessible and accountable.

4. Everyone in our company should conduct themselves according to the highest ethical standards.[7i]

The notion these statements convey is that Nucor Steel's leadership's first concern is about employees, the environment, and the communities in which Nucor operates—the nonnegotiables in its business. This isn't a bad set of priorities for a steel company offering some inherently dangerous jobs in an industry in which pollution is a major concern.

Nucor has pioneered the development of several important processes that are the headlines for a learning organization. These include thin-slab technology, "Castrip" micromill processes for making steel with 95% less energy and pollution, and HIsmelt technology that bypasses coke production. Just as important are the day-to-day improvements that result from internal best-practice exchanges fostered by intermill visits by managers. They are supplemented by a flood of ideas from people on the mill floor about how to do things faster, more productively, and for less money. This wouldn't happen if Nucor's people were afraid to fail. The philosophy is expressed in terms of quotes from managers such as "At Nucor, workers excel because they are allowed to fail." In Iverson's words, "if something's worth doing, it's worth doing wrong.... Get on with it and see if it works."

Nucor practices a strategy of self-direction and accountability. It does so through its organization, with just five levels from the bottom to the CEO, and with less than one-half of 1% of its employees at its Charlotte, North Carolina headquarters. It does so through its staffing, with 20,000 employees spread over 200 facilities. In the words of one Nucor executive, "Ironically, we've gotten big by thinking small." And it does so through its compensation policies, reflected in below-market wages with outsized incentive pay based on the amount of prime steel (up to quality standards) produced *each day*. Ironically, this helped Nucor survive the 2008–2009 recession, requiring that it cut its use of available steel-making capacity from 95% to 50% without laying anyone off. Given the compensation policies tied to output, employee compensation declined by as much as 40%, although the company tried to soften the blow with modest year-end bonuses. But people kept their jobs, and Nucor kept its people for the recovery to come.[8i]

Thus, the managers and employees of each small facility (typically no more than 200) are responsible for running their own facilities and addressing their customers' needs. In fact, during a recession prior to the big one, several mills, facing a need for orders, sent some of their steelmakers out onto the road to sell steel to astounded customers who had never met a steelworker. The steelmakers were so successful that they were soon back in their mills trying to catch up with demand. This experience has led to the practice of regularly sending steelmakers into the field to sensitize them to customer needs and produce ideas for new products that thereby become "presold" to the workforce.

Another story concerns three electricians who were informed that the electrical grid at Nucor's Hickman, Arkansas minimill had failed.

Not long after they arrived at the plant, a fourth electrician from another mill drove in from an Indiana facility he had been visiting. Two others assigned to Nucor's mill in Hertford Country, North Carolina flew into Memphis and drove from there to Hickman. Together, working 20-hour shifts, they were able to get the mill up and running in three days instead of seven.

According to the account: "No supervisor had asked them to make the trip.... They went on their own.... There wasn't any direct financial incentive for them." What's most amazing about this story is that at Nucor it's not considered particularly remarkable. According to an officer of the company, "It happens daily."[9] The mill not only regained its production capability, it went on to break its record for shipments for the quarter.

At Nucor, these kinds of stories are told frequently. Their subjects are the heroes and heroines of the organization. Are these stories entirely accurate? Possibly not. Have they been exaggerated over time? Probably. But that's not the point. These stories fit with and reinforce (rather than detract from) the company's values of treating people with respect and giving them power to influence results.

The culture's values include "granting trust and freedom, giving all workers a stake in the company, and turning everyone into a decision-maker." As you might expect, Nucor uses neither job descriptions nor formal performance appraisals. As Iverson puts it, "We let our employees define their own jobs as they search for ways to optimize their productivity safely." What the values, policies, and practices really signal is self-direction in work, decision-making, compensation, and the generation of innovative ideas. Iverson has been quoted as saying that "employees—not managers—are the engines of progress."

Self-direction and accountability in the workplace and the learning and innovation they foster explain why Nucor's employees earn the highest compensation in the U.S. steelmaking industry and use their ingenuity to achieve the lowest cost per ton of steel "produced safely" in the industry.

Like USAA, Nucor Steel's values are reflected in accepted behaviors. A careful employee selection process helps ensure that Nucor people can be trusted to do what they say. The organization emphasizes safety in the traditional way. But it also makes it safe to fail in an effort to innovate. The reward, more tons of lower-cost steel and steel products, is reflected in everyone's compensation. So everyone succeeds or fails together. Collectively they decide, control the outcomes, and reap the reward or suffer the losses.

A wide range of responsibilities are delegated to the lowest level of the organization, with a minimum of controls on such things as staffing, the division of labor, and performance reviews. Why does this work? In part, it works because a large organization has purposely been made small. It's much harder to underperform in an organization of 200 than in one of 20,000, especially if each unit is responsible for its own hiring, training, and problem-solving. So the strategy and ways in which it is executed are well aligned with the organization's values and accepted behaviors. As a result, people self-select themselves into not only an organization, but its values and behaviors as well. It's little surprise, then, that their work experiences meet or exceed their expectations, an important measure of the health of a culture. Nucor and its culture are not for everyone, but for the right people, it is perennially ranked as one of the best places to work in the United States.

Cultures both facilitate and impose limits on strategies and how they are executed, as Toyota has found to its regret recently.

Toyota and the Importance of Alignment and Agility

Those examining Toyota's culture as recently as 2008 praised it for how its credo, The Toyota Way, embodies a clear statement of values, provides alignment with the execution of its "lean manufacturing" strategy, includes behaviors that delegate authority to the lowest levels of its manufacturing operations, supports continuous improvement, and encourages employee "ownership" behaviors. The Toyota Way, described next, is a comprehensive set of statements that prescribes ways of solving problems through continuous improvement and learning; respecting, challenging, and growing people and partners; executing processes that eliminate waste; and thinking and acting in the firm's longer-term interests. It is also a statement of "the way things are done around here" at Toyota. It has been lauded around the world for both its value in practice (particularly in a manufacturing setting) and the systematic way in which Toyota managers have used it to produce automotive products of good value with high quality and performance for the price. Systematic is the operative word here. The key to The Toyota Way is the manner in which it is implemented. Toyota executives would not say it in so many words, but they are quite confident that no other company could implement The Toyota Way as successfully as Toyota itself. The Toyota Way reflects both the Japanese culture and a firmly held set of principles comprising a culture that has produced phenomenal success over many years. To implement it would require that a competitor completely rethink both its strategy and culture. This helps explain why, in the words of one observer, "Toyota has been remarkably open in sharing its source of competitive advantage with the rest of the world."[10]

The Toyota Way

The Toyota Way comprises the following elements*:

Philosophy (Long-Term Thinking)

> Base management decisions on a long-term philosophy, even at the expense of short-term financial gain.

Problem-Solving (Continuous Improvement and Learning)

> Continual organizational learning through Kaizen

> Go see for yourself to thoroughly understand the situation (Genchi Genbutsu).

> Make decisions slowly by consensus, thoroughly considering all operations; implement rapidly.

People and Partners (Respect, Challenge, and Grow Them)

> Grow leaders who live the philosophy.

> Respect, develop, and challenge your people and teams.

> Respect, challenge, and help your suppliers.

continued

---

* Adapted from Jeffrey K. Liker, *The Toyota Way: 14 Management Principles from the World's Greatest Manufacturer* (New York: McGraw-Hill, 2004), p. 6.

Process (Eliminate Waste)

Create process "flow" to surface problems.

Use pull systems (of inventory control) to avoid overproduction.

Level out the workload (Heijunka).

Stop when there is a quality problem (Jidoka).

Standardize tasks for continuous improvement.

Use visual control so that no problems are hidden.

Use only reliable, thoroughly tested technology.

The Toyota Way has been driven so deeply into the psyche of employees at all levels that it has morphed from a strategy into an important element of the company's culture—the very assumptions, shared values, and accepted behaviors on which the company operates. It is lauded because it works, having enabled Toyota to become the largest and most profitable auto manufacturer in the world. That is, it worked until it didn't.

In 2008, allegations of defects in Toyota cars began making news. Most were linked to unexpected acceleration in its vehicles that was alleged to have led to crashes, injuries, and deaths. Product defects bedevil all automakers. But coming from "the world's greatest manufacturer," this was unexpected. It was so shocking that it may have led to some amount of denial on the part of Toyota's leadership, as well as many loyal customers.

In testimony before a U.S. Congressional committee, the CEO of Toyota, Akio Toyoda, provided a better explanation: "We grew too rapidly." In fact, manufacturing data shows that Toyota did indeed increase its output significantly in 2007 in the United States as its competitors there faltered. This was not the case in the rest of the world. Toyoda cited, as an example, the fact that Toyota had increased the number of suppliers to meet its increasingly voracious manufacturing needs. In doing so, it may have challenged a precept of The Toyota Way to "respect, challenge, and help your suppliers." This assumes a long-lasting relationship with a small, preferred set of suppliers rather than recruiting anyone who can make a particular part. In addition, demands were placed on Toyota to hire new employees in unprecedented numbers. This in turn burdened the indoctrination process, the very vehicle by which The Toyota Way was inculcated into every employee. This had to dilute the strength of the company's culture.

Something even more basic occurred. In a rush to increase output to meet demand, Toyota violated an important principle that the company should never manufacture new products in a new plant with new people. Traditionally, the company had populated its new manufacturing facilities with a sizeable contingent of veterans from other Toyota plants. That apparently was not done in one or more new plants. In a sentence, Toyota's strategy may have outrun the capabilities of its culture in an organization where culture matters a great deal. Putting it another way, the culture and its importance to Toyota's success imposed limits on the company's growth that were violated. Students of management would term this a loss of alignment in the Seven S's described in Chapter 1—particularly between the "hardware" of strategy and the "software" of systems, staff, skills, and, most important, shared values.

Ironically, after all of this analysis and self-analysis, it turns out that many of the accidents involving Toyota autos were due to driver error, not the product. This raises the question of whether Toyota's primary problem was in the company's products or in how management responded to allegations of defects. To what degree was the nature of the response triggered by The Toyota Way?

A principle in The Toyota Way admonishes managers to "make decisions slowly by consensus, thoroughly considering all operations." Another—Jidoka—advises managers to "stop when there is a quality problem." Yet another, Genchi Genbutsu, suggests a method of problem-solving that requires that managers "go see for yourself." Did this account for Toyoda's perhaps unnecessary admission to the U.S. Congressional committee that Toyota had grown too fast? Given the quest for information about a quality problem and decision-making by consensus, is it possible that Toyota's investigation was incomplete at the time of Toyoda's testimony, and later accounted for the continued delays in Toyota's response?

To this day it can be debated whether the cause of Toyota's problem was a strategy that outran its culture, a culture that failed Toyota, or human error in the implementation of both.

Fortunately for Toyota, its culture encompasses values other than those cited that may allow it to thrive for many more decades. But Toyota reminds us that strong, healthy cultures, if they fall out of alignment with strategy or if they are unable to accommodate rapidly developing events, can still fail to achieve their promise.

These three examples carry with them a warning that we may have difficulty predicting which of today's cultures are designed and executed in ways that will enable their organizations to be "built to last." But surely the task begins with an assessment of the strength and health of a culture.

Measuring a Culture's Strength

Based on their intensive study of a sample of organization cultures, Terrence Deal and Allan Kennedy concluded, in a comment cited previously, that "a strong culture has almost always been the driving force behind continuing success in American business."[11] There may be a few exceptions, such as firms with monopolistic market positions or a dominant product (as in big pharma) with patent protection. But over time, the conditions change in such firms, the weak cultures are exposed, and performance declines.

The problem with strong cultures, as we saw in Chapter 3, is that they can also be the driving force behind decline and obscurity. Nevertheless, the first step in assessing a culture is to appraise its strength.

Anyone studying the strength of an organization's culture has to figure out how to measure it. Measurement has challenged leaders and researchers alike. The following sections describe some of the methods and questions that have been used.

Articulation of Mission, Basic Assumptions, Values, Beliefs, and Behaviors

First and most basic, have the organization's mission, basic assumptions, shared values, and beliefs been articulated? We said earlier that they develop naturally, whether nurtured or not. But has anyone taken the trouble to identify them? When Deal and Kennedy studied 80 large organizations some years ago, they found that only 25 had clearly articulated beliefs.[12] Of these, roughly two-thirds had what they called "qualitative beliefs," such as "IBM means service." The other third had widely understood financial goals, which I would argue neither qualify as values or beliefs nor constitute important elements of an organization's culture. And this work speaks not at all to the question of whether these organizations had examined the basic assumptions behind their shared beliefs, something that is rarely found in organizations today. That's why ING's Orange Code, described in Chapter 2, is so unusual. It is an amalgam of mission ("to help people take care of the wealth they make"), values (fairness, truthfulness), and beliefs. But it also includes some basic assumptions such as "We are new here," "We will be here for everyone," "We are not here to destroy; we are here to create," and "We will never be finished."

The mission, assumptions, values, and beliefs are important only if they are shared throughout an organization. As Peter Senge has commented, "You cannot have a learning organization (the importance of which we will note later) without a shared vision."[13] That's why the process by which mission, assumptions, values, and beliefs are articulated matters. Too often, it involves a few senior members of the organization closeted in a room, sometimes with a consultant, engaged in an exercise designed to produce one or more lists of values. If time permits, the group may spend whatever time remains trying to associate behaviors with the values and beliefs. Alternatively, as we saw earlier, organizations such as IBM have followed a multiphase strategy of having senior executives draft some values, beliefs, and even behaviors and then test and revise them based on widespread discussions of values and/or behaviors throughout the organization. This process not only engages the organization in the task but also facilitates communication, the next step.

Communication of Mission, Shared Assumptions, Values, Beliefs, and Behaviors

Are members of the organization at all levels aware of the mission, shared assumptions, values, and beliefs? Do they know what they stand for? The mission ("know why") may be of special interest to potential employees, for example. It will contribute later to their level of engagement and "ownership," core phenomena critical to an effective culture and the strategies it supports.

Communication requires more than the distribution of an e-mail or sheet of paper. It requires discussions between managers and their direct reports about the kinds of behaviors on the job that are associated with each of the values. If necessary, it suggests the need for conversations about what happens when behaviors fall out of line with values. It is a good time for "management by story."

Effective efforts to communicate mission, shared assumptions and values, beliefs, and behaviors seek to answer two questions for others in the organization: What's in it for the organization?—and— What's in it for you (or me)?

Acceptance and Practice of Values and Beliefs

Do you subscribe to the values and beliefs? Do they make a difference in how you carry out your work? More important, do you think they work for you and the organization? Do they make you a more effective manager or worker?

Positive responses to these questions suggest that people at all levels in an organization are willing to try to work within the culture to produce successful results.

What people say is important. What they do is even more important. Thus, a telltale measure of strength is whether or not the values and beliefs articulated in a credo or other statement of culture are used regularly in making important decisions.

As these questions suggest, measuring a culture's strength is a comparatively straightforward exercise. The same cannot be said for measuring its health. But the case examples described earlier help us in this respect.

Measuring a Culture's Health: The Culture Cycle

There are a number of theories about how an organization's culture affects performance. These seem to cluster around a few dominant ideas. Like the magic word uttered by the executive to the recent college graduate in the film *The Graduate*—plastics—secrets of success such as accountability, engagement, ownership, transparency, teamwork, and delegation of authority are trumpeted widely.[14] Each contains useful ideas, but only when they are organized as part of a wider view do they really begin to make sense, as suggested by the USAA, Nucor Steel, Toyota, and other examples described elsewhere in the book. One such wider view is shown in Figure 6-1, a map of the culture cycle, encompassing elements of a healthy culture.

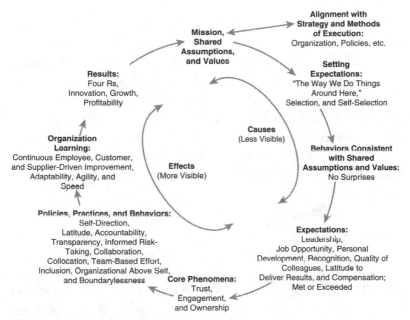

Figure 6-1 The culture cycle

At the top of the map, of course, are the mission ("know why") and shared assumptions and values ("know how"). They help establish expectations for people who are selected (and who self-select themselves) into the organization.

Meeting Expectations

When individual behaviors and actions are consistent with the values, this sets the stage for a culture in which expectations are met or exceeded regarding things most important to employees—the "fairness" of my boss, recognition for work done well, opportunity for personal development, the quality of my colleagues, the latitude I have to deliver results, and reasonable compensation. The process of establishing and meeting expectations has been characterized elsewhere as "the deal."[15] Expectations that consistently are met or exceeded on the job contribute to three core phenomena: trust, engagement, and ownership.

Trust, Engagement, and Ownership

When an organization and its people do what they say they will do, this produces trust in the ranks, making possible other qualities such as speed and agility in how an organization's strategy is carried out. Trust is reciprocal. USAA provides a good illustration of this. Here leadership's trust in both customers (members) and employees produces the fastest and lowest-cost claims adjustment process in the property insurance industry. On the other hand, distrust in colleagues or the "system" leads to such questionable behaviors as "workarounds" that subvert policies and procedures, hoarding, slower decisions, and even reduced initiative.[16]

Trust also leads to engagement in, or loyalty to, an organization—a phenomenon with significant value, as discussed in Chapter 5. One study concludes that loyalty to an organization is highly correlated with an individual's perceptions of an organization's loyalty to the individual.[17] According to the authors, the phenomenon is global in scope. Of particular interest here is that data shows that employees' perceptions of reciprocal loyalty are higher, for example, in nations of the Middle East and South America than in Europe and the United States.

Engagement, associated with a willingness to recommend the organization to others as a good place to work, can in turn result in ownership. This mentality encourages employees to take the initiative in advancing ideas, solving problems, and growing business relationships—in short, to act as owners. This may involve actual ownership, as at Goldman Sachs or Southwest Airlines. Or it may be an attitude fostered by a strong culture, as at Toyota. It requires the highest level of engagement, evidenced by an employee's willingness to engage in continuous-improvement activities as well as recommend her organization as a place to work and to influence and recruit others to join it. For example, teams of "Racksters" at Rackspace, Inc., a web site design and management service, develop goals for growing the customer accounts to which they are assigned. But no one tells them how to meet those goals once they are established. It's up to the team to figure that out. And figure it out they do. In an industry that has come to be regarded as operating in the "backwater" of the Internet, Rackspace's growth has, at times, had to be capped at 60% per year to enable the organization to staff itself to meet its high standards for premium customer service.

Ownership among employees tends to foster ownership behaviors among customers. And a customer who is also an "owner" can have a value to a business that is many times that of a typical customer.[18]

Both engagement and ownership are encouraged by such things as the organization's mission; its policies, products, or services; the kinds of jobs it offers; and the quality of people it hires. But above all else, the quality of leadership may have the greatest influence on all three core phenomena, as shown in the trust–engagement–ownership "pyramid" in Figure 6-2.

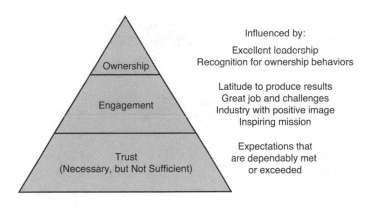

Figure 6-2 Influences on the trust-engagement-ownership pyramid

Policies, Practices, and Behaviors

Trust, engagement, and ownership make possible a number of useful policies, practices, and behaviors, such as self-direction and latitude, accountability, transparency, informed risk-taking, collabo-ration, collocation, inclusion, organization above self, and boundary-lessness. Many or all of these may be reflected in the core values, and they are often the subject of "single issue" self-help books and articles. They are symptoms of healthy cultures.

Self-Direction, Latitude, and Accountability

These are cornerstones of success at Nucor Steel. They often go hand in hand. Control over one's job, how it is done, and how much it earns are the order of the day at Nucor. The emphasis is on the result, not how it was achieved, as long as the effort reflects the organization's values. This philosophy is also true of other remarkable organizations such as Google and W. L. Gore & Associates. The basic assumption is that personal control over one's work leads directly to higher engage-ment and responsibility for success. In the case of Nucor, it encour-ages employees to drop their work to help others and, by extension, the organization without explicit permission from above. Self-direction may vary greatly from one job to another. In some organizations, the employees have much more discretion in some jobs (headquarters) than in others (the distribution center). Nevertheless, self-direction has been demonstrated successfully in all types of jobs and organiza-tions. For example, the hundreds of small subsidiaries of the Illinois Tool Works, as we saw in Chapter 4, represent the method by which the company delegates decisions and holds managers accountable in each of their small manufacturing businesses.

Transparency

Transparency is a popular theme in management circles. But it cannot succeed without trust that managers will distribute and share only information that is in the organization's best interests. Need to know is a good criterion for practicing transparency. For example, operating information, if shared across business units, may stimulate the sharing of best-practice ideas, as we saw in years past at Banc One. However, this makes sense only if managers feel that performance measures reward such behaviors. On the other hand, there may be little reason to distribute compensation data if it does not contribute to informed decision-making.

Transparency often fosters innovation. It helps explain why Google makes available information about current projects that have yet to be commercialized through its web site, googlelabs.com. Reasons for this practice are that it will facilitate the work of people developing related ideas across its organization as well as attract ideas from interested outsiders.

Informed Risk-Taking

New ideas can fail. How organizations react to that goes a long way in determining whether new ideas will be advanced, particularly from the front line. One recent study found that, particularly in organizations heavily dependent on "high reliability," there is a strong tendency to "encourage the reporting of errors and near misses, exploiting these incidents to improve their operative processes."[19] Recall Ken Iverson's comment at Nucor: "If something's worth doing, it's worth doing wrong...." A similar attitude exists at USAA as well. And at Toyota, there may be more deliberation about the implementation of the idea, but all are acknowledged and recognized. This helps explain why hundreds of thousands of such ideas have been advanced in recent years at the automaker as part of the continuous improvement associated with The Toyota Way.

Collaboration, Collocation, and Team-Based Effort

Teams, especially those made up of people from a variety of backgrounds or who have different responsibilities but are located in close proximity to one another, invite the kind of interaction that can lead to such things as outstanding, "seamless" customer service; solutions to complex problems; continuous improvement; and innovation. Learning, at least according to some people, goes hand in hand with team-based effort. As Douglas McGregor pointed out some years ago, "An effective managerial group provides the best possible environment for individual development."[20] At the Harvard Business School, for example, new instructors are often assigned to groups of faculty teaching large, required MBA courses because of the unique opportunity to learn about the craft of teaching that takes place within such groups.

Team-based effort is often linked closely to self-direction, latitude, and accountability. Accountability, when combined with team-based recognition and rewards and the latitude to deliver results, encourages teams to select the right people, ensure behaviors that are consistent with the culture, and meet or exceed their operating goals. This is characteristic of what has happened at Rackspace, Inc., the previously mentioned company that designs and manages web sites for clients. Increasingly, it found itself operating in what many regard as a portion of the Internet beset by modest growth and limited profit. As a result, the company repositioned itself to serve only customers who had complex web site design and operating challenges and were willing to pay a premium for support services. Rackspace reorganized into teams of "Racksters" with the array of interests and capabilities necessary to solve complex customer problems. Employees are located together in "pods" and are given full responsibility for serving and developing business relationships with small portfolios of customers.[21] The company selects people who can work together to do this. It then entrusts them with managing their teams, from hiring to firing, as well as building Rackspace's business with their assigned customers. The self-managed teams have come up with so many innovative ideas for customers that Rackspace's growth and profitability have soared in an Internet neighborhood that other high-tech firms find uninteresting. Appropriately, Rackspace's innovative team-based organizational arrangement was suggested by one of the firm's customers. It literally saved the company.

Richard Hackman has pointed out that, based on his research, teams get into trouble when the following occurs:

- They don't have a clear and compelling direction.
- Members aren't sure who is on and off the team.
- Tasks are poorly designed, and norms are unenforced.
- Members are not rewarded for team effort.
- They aren't coached in team process.[22]

For example, when the Toyota Production System, focused on team-based effort, was introduced at NUMMI, the joint venture between Toyota and General Motors, initial efforts didn't work well because GM team leaders didn't understand their jobs. One observer commented: "The lesson was clear: don't implement work teams before you do the hard work of implementing the system and culture to support them."[23]

In my experience, teams function best when they have specific ongoing responsibilities for such things as solving customer problems or turning around a commercial aircraft on schedule—tasks that are repeated many times. This is particularly true in cases where teams have relatively wide responsibility for such things as hiring, training, assignments, problem-solving, and business development. Teams help "shrink" the workplace, injecting self-control into an organization in the form of peer pressure. Hackman suggests that smaller teams are more effective, but if the workforce at a given facility is relatively small and jobs are well defined, team-based effort may extend to nearly every member of the organization and even beyond, as we saw with Nucor's minimills.

Feedback from employees about the quality of their workplaces tells us that the quality of team members matters greatly. Everyone likes to work with "winners." The better the team members, the lower the turnover, according to one study of securities analysts in 24 securities firms over a nine-year period. It concludes that "...analysts working with higher quality colleagues are less likely to turn over."[24]

Teams flourish when authority with accountability is delegated to them. They also benefit from team-based incentives, recognition, and rewards, and the collocation of those encouraged to collaborate. They benefit as well from inclusion.

Inclusion

Inclusion is used here to mean many things, including people with diverse backgrounds, training, interests, and ideas. Studies have shown that these kinds of diversity are related to success in innovation when a conscious effort is made to bring them together both organizationally and through collocation. We will examine this topic in more detail in Chapter 8.[25]

Team members' diverse backgrounds may enhance learning. An analysis of 108 empirical studies of performance in more than 10,000 teams has concluded that "cultural diversity (in teams is associated with)...increased creativity and satisfaction."[26] This same study, however, noted that "cultural diversity (in teams)...leads to process losses through task conflict and decreased social integration."

Organization Before Self

At Goldman Sachs, Nucor, and Toyota, we have seen examples of organizations in which employees go out of their way to help colleagues solve problems of importance to their companies. This is often done without regard for extra compensation or recognition. But extraordinary examples of these efforts become the subject of organization lore and the stuff of legends that are told repeatedly.

Boundarylessness

Boundaryless behaviors include visits to centers of excellence found in outside organizations; efforts to assist others in one's own organization, regardless of functional boundaries; and the sharing of resources. It requires such things as encouragement from leadership, rewards for sharing resources, budgets for travel, and recognition of how these efforts can support continuous improvement.

The prime purpose of many of these policies, practices, and behaviors is to support the organization learning critical to innovation as well as adaptive and agile organization strategies and actions.

Organization Learning: Continuous Improvement, Adaptability, Speed, and Agility

As we saw in Chapter 3, a healthy culture must support constant change that reflects responses to a changing competitive, social, and legal environment. The policies, practices, and behaviors just described provide a basis for maintaining such a culture. But it requires devices—"listening posts"—for the transfer of ideas and suggestions from customers, employees, and suppliers. For example, this is the lifeblood of the software development and improvement processes at Intuit, the developer and marketer of personal finance software. It means that some of the most talented people at Intuit are assigned responsibility for what might be called "customer service" but is in fact a major contributor to product development.

Best-practice information sharing is one of the best vehicles for continuous improvement, especially in organizations with multiple operating sites. So why is it so often overlooked or underutilized? The most frequent cause is a set of performance measures and incentives that ignore or even discourage the activity. This leads managers to believe that what is a gain for one has to be a loss for another—a "zero-sum" result that discourages the sharing of ideas.

Benchmarking and other "boundaryless" behaviors provide rich sources of ideas from outside the organization. Although they are most effective in the transfer of processes and practices, they can even lead to the development of new product ideas. This helps explain why it has been standard practice, recognized and rewarded, in innovative organizations such as GE for years.

Speed and agility are particularly important in industries competing in the fast-moving worlds of fashion and high technology. They require delegation and informed risk-taking, as well as the assurance that mistakes made in the name of agility or speed will not be unduly criticized. Speed and agility are linked to the core phenomena of the culture cycle. When I asked a head of human resources how her company was able to act with unusual speed and agility in a fashion business, she replied with one word: "Trust."

Organizations with strong cultures sometimes have curious ideas about the acceptance of new ideas. There is a fear that new ideas (and even their bearers) may somehow disrupt something that is working now. By way of contrast, learning organizations are frequently found engaging in benchmarking, internal best-practice initiatives, information and personnel exchanges of various kinds, and boundaryless behaviors that lead to cross-functional, cross-business, and other kinds of developmental assignments.

The effects of employee turnover on learning are unclear. The value of ideas brought by new employees may be offset by a lack of continuity in innovative effort. But one of the more extensive studies of a large longitudinal database of Danish manufacturing firms led to a conclusion that, at least in those firms, "in- and outflows of human resources...(affect) organizational learning negatively."[27]

Assessing the Payoff and the Need for Change

The final "station" of the culture cycle comprises the measurement of results, as shown in Figure 6-1. A strong and healthy culture in synch with an organization's strategy and how it is executed should have a significant payoff. This can be expressed variously in terms of the Four Rs, introduced in Chapter 5, as well as others included in the following list:

- Relative measures of employee trust, engagement, and "ownership" (such as the percentage of new employees recruited by existing employees) (referrals)
- Employee loyalty (retention)
- Returns to labor or productivity (cost per unit of activity)
- Relations with customers (resulting in both retention and referrals)
- Innovation (the rate of new-product development or the proportion of total revenues produced by new products)
- Value (the ratio of results to costs) for customers
- Ultimately, growth and profitability

The relationships shown in Figure 6-1 are reflected in comments by executives such as Stephen Sadove, chairman and CEO of Saks, Inc., who said:

> I have a very simple model to run a company. It starts with leadership at the top, which drives a culture. Culture drives innovation and whatever else you're trying to drive within a company. And that then drives results. When I talk to Wall Street, people really want to know your results, what are your strategies, what are the issues. Never do you get people asking about the culture, about leadership, about the people in the organization. Yet, it's the reverse, because those are what ultimately drive the numbers and the results.[28]

It may require some time for the effects of culture to appear on the bottom line. Measures of payoff begin to show the effects of the behaviors and decisions generated by a culture some time after the actions themselves. Thus, careful measurement requires longitudinal observation followed by analyses that "lag" outputs from inputs to establish such relationships. One such analysis was performed at Sears in the 1990s. It concluded that an effort to raise employee engagement in a sample of stores produced a 5-unit improvement in employee satisfaction, a 1.3-unit improvement in customer satisfaction, and a store-level revenue growth rate of 0.5% above the average of stores in a control group. This provided the evidence needed to suggest ways of turning the company around, at least for a while. However, it was found that this chain of cause-and-effect required about 18 months, testing the patience of Sears' managers who perhaps needed faster, more dramatic results.[29]

Matters of time lags and the like may be of more interest to academics than to managers, who are more concerned with how such measures can help their organizations produce both short-term and long-term results.

Practical application of the relationships shown in Figure 6-1 is more likely to involve snapshot measures of the practices and performance of an organization against a peer group. In some cases, the peer group may include competitors. Gaps in both effort (causes) and performance (effects) can be identified and used as a means of taking corrective action. This is a version of benchmarking that generally involves comparing one organization's practices and accomplishments against another's.

For operators of multiple-unit businesses, such measurements can be used to fuel best-practice initiatives on the part of unit managers. For years, the Banc One organization (which eventually was merged into what is now J.P. Morgan) was run on a best-practice system that calculated and circulated to all of its bank managers a common set of cost ratios and other operating results. The CEO, John B. McCoy, had to call an unprepared poor performer only once before that manager began making sure that he checked out best practice with at least one other strong performer before McCoy called again to inquire about the actions being taken to improve performance. Before long, proactive calls among managers on at least a monthly basis became habit. Chapter 7 presents an example of best-practice analysis applied to three offices of the same organization.

Persistent failure to meet targets set for the Four Rs, innovation, growth, and profitability may trigger inquiries into the need for change in the organization's culture, its strategy, methods of execution, or all three in an effort to produce a self-reinforcing fit between them. We'll return to this matter in Chapter 13.

Measuring a Culture's Fit

A healthy culture, if it "fits" with an organization strategy and how that strategy is executed, produces remarkable results. It is characterized by a high degree of employee and customer satisfaction, loyalty, engagement, and ownership that in time produce growth and profit. In addition, it confirms and reinforces the "rightness" of a set of shared assumptions and values, triggering another turn of the culture cycle.

By now, it should be clear that managers who begin their planning processes by setting goals for growth and profitability—or who plan strategic moves without considering their impact on culture— are putting the cart before a horse that has many working parts. They are pursuing risky practices at best—practices that inevitably, over time, put the entire organization at risk.

The culture cycle map is not simple. It comprises both proven and unproven relationships. It could occupy the efforts of researchers for years. But it provides the specifications for efforts necessary to measure the health of cultures. Some questions used to provide such measurements, keyed to elements of the culture cycle, are suggested in Appendix A. But in applying them, it is important to keep in mind that not all are of equal importance for all organizations. They have to be adapted to a particular set of values and expected behaviors. Furthermore, experience suggests that the consistent application of the questions and an analysis of trends in the information they produce are of greater importance than the particular set of questions used. In other words, there is room for error; a search for perfection shouldn't drive out the good in measurement efforts.

Earlier we addressed the issue of a culture's fit with strategy, how it is executed, and the competitive environment, implied in the illustration of the culture cycle shown in Figure 6-1. Circumstances may require different values and behaviors. But a set of basic questions can help you determine whether fit is being achieved. The following are some examples that characterize the nature of these questions (although they are by no means a complete list):

- How much growth does a strategy require? Can the culture—particularly the staffing and orientation mechanisms—support that kind of growth?

- What demands are placed on the organization by the nature of the business in which it is engaged? For example, what premium is placed on speed of decision-making and action, generally referred to as agility? To what degree can the culture deal with this need?

- How important are innovation and new-product development to the success of a strategy? Do the values of the organization's culture place sufficient emphasis on them? Do behaviors reflect these needs? Do often-repeated stories feature heroes characterized by their willingness to persist in the face of disinterest or opposition?

- To what degree does continuous improvement lead to superior processes and the higher quality and/or lower cost they produce that are central to the strategy? Is it similarly reflected in elements of the organization's culture?

Caveats

The culture cycle is derived from a personal, subjective appraisal of a number of observations and anecdotal case studies that have appeared in print. Its elements are not meant to be a complete list of drivers of success. Instead, they represent an interpretation of what has worked for a number of organizations, each with its own set of needs.

This presents a measurement challenge. Does it mean that an organization has to achieve high values on every dimension, particularly "policies, practices, and behaviors," to achieve success? Probably not. There may be different profiles for sustained competitive performance, depending on an industry's rapidity of change and need for innovation, among others. It's up to each organization to define its own culture cycle.

Summary

An effective culture is a predictor of an organization's future success. That's why it's important to measure and track both its strength and health.

Based on a number of examples described throughout this book, a strong culture can be indicated by the following:

- Efforts to articulate and communicate assumptions, values, beliefs, and behaviors.
- Knowledge and acceptance of the assumptions, values, beliefs, and behaviors on the part of members of an organization.

Measuring the health of a culture is more complex but doable. It requires exploring employees' perceptions of the degree to which:

- Their expectations are met by their actual experiences for things important to them in affiliating with an organization.
- They trust that people do what they say they will do on the job and feel safe in taking informed risks (thereby innovating) and coming forth with ideas and constructive suggestions (measures of engagement and "ownership").
- They have control over how they do things on the job.
- They are held accountable for what they do.
- They have sufficient shared information (transparency) with which to bring insight to their jobs.
- They are encouraged to search for new ideas and methods outside the organization (transparency and boundarylessness).
- Collaboration and team-based effort often are important to their success and job satisfaction.
- Inclusiveness and diverse inputs contribute to innovative products and methods.
- They are willing to put the organization's interests before their own.

A systematic way of measuring the health of a culture can be keyed to the culture cycle. It is centered on shared values that provide a basis for the selection and self-selection of employees who will exhibit behaviors consistent with the values. This raises the probability that expectations of employees for such things as "fairness" of treatment, job opportunity, feedback and personal development, the quality of colleagues, latitude to deliver results, and reasonable compensation will be met. Expectations that are met foster trust, engagement, and "ownership", important drivers of "policies, practices, and behaviors" such as self-direction, accountability, transparency, informed risk-taking, collaboration and teamwork, innovation, inclusion, organization above self, and boundarylessness. These, in turn, support continuous customer-, employee-, and supplier-driven improvement, adaptability, agility, and speed, all directly related to the "organizational learning" that is so critical to the long-term success of organizations and their cultures that are "built to last." Favorable trends in measures such as the Four Rs—referrals, retention, returns to labor, and relationships with customers; the rate of innovation; and growth and profitability suggest success, again confirming the usefulness of the culture (and fueling another turn of the cycle).

Cultures both facilitate and pose limits on strategies and how they are implemented. No matter how strong or healthy it is, an effective culture has to fit with a strategy and how it is executed. This requires a subjective appraisal involving the question of whether a culture can support such things as the growth rate; particular business demands for speed, agility, innovation, and new-product development; and continuous improvement called for in the strategy.

Strong and healthy cultures that fit with an organization's strategy and how it is executed produce employee and customer behaviors that lead to high productivity, good value in products and services, innovation, and ultimately growth and profitability. These behaviors include assistance in recruiting new employees and customers and providing recommendations for ways to improve products, services, and processes. That's why the strength and health of cultures are important predictors of future success and why it is so important to measure and track them over time and employ this information in the day-to-day management of an organization.

To show how the health of cultures affects performance, I went into the field to apply the ideas from Chapters 5 and 6 to a functioning organization. What I found is next.

7

The Four R Model: A Field Test

Even the most comprehensive appraisals of the effects of culture on performance have garnered a lot of criticism. Chief among the complaints are that so many things—particularly involving strategy and how it is executed—influence performance that the effects of culture are diluted at best and completely washed out at worst. Another concern is that it is impossible to examine enough organizations to draw valid conclusions regarding hypotheses. Some argue for larger organizational samples. Others argue for a smaller number of in-depth analyses. Still others argue for examinations of a single organization from multiple perspectives.[1] These arguments, although useful and often valid, should not be so daunting that they allow perfection to drive out the good among efforts to examine just why and how cultures affect performance.

Any study of this kind requires extraordinary access to an organization. Fortunately, I was provided that access by managers in a subsidiary of a very large global firm offering a range of marketing services. I will call it RTL, Inc.

The Setting: RTL, Inc.

RTL, Inc. is a large, Chicago-based multinational provider of B2B marketing services through offices worldwide. All competitors in this business seek to provide extraordinary client service. Professionals typically allow themselves to be consumed by the work. This often creates intense pressures for client-facing professionals. Sometimes they have to work odd hours and make difficult decisions regarding their responsibilities to the organization and to their loved ones.

Professionals comprise nearly all the staff in individual offices. As indicated in the survey data in Appendix C, they are typically devoted to and proud of their work and their closest associates. However, as is often the case in many organizations, they sense that they work harder than others.

RTL's leadership faced the same challenges confronting most providers of marketing services during the Great Recession of 2008–2009. Many clients decided to cut back on budgets for marketing services. In some cases, they severed their relationships with service providers. Leadership, reluctant to reduce head count in early 2009, began to see what was happening as an opportunity to better serve a smaller number of more valuable clients. This required fewer, more productive professionals and led to a large turnover in talent and associated turmoil in many of its offices in late 2009 and 2010.

My choice of RTL as a site for testing the hypotheses described in Chapters 5 and 6 was based on several factors. First, of course, was access to the organization and its data. Second, instead of comparing companies with different challenges and cultures, I could gather data from three (or more) offices in the same organization with the same strategy. Thus, I could control for at least one major influence on performance. Third, I could work with a senior leadership team that was willing to reflect on and provide interpretations of my findings.

The Research and Findings

Data for three of RTL's offices—Chicago, Baltimore, and Minneapolis (names all disguised)—was made available. As in other professional services firms, nearly all the personnel of the organization are client-facing, in total commanding a relatively high average compensation. The organization's and an office's culture have a strong influence on employee and client loyalty as well as financial performance—much more so than in, say, a coal mining company. So you would expect culture to play a significant role in explaining financial performance. And in this case it did.

My access to a large set of data resulted in part from a gambit I designed to catch the attention of some very busy executives. Here was the "deal": Managers agreed to provide me with data for 2009 and 2010 from three U.S. offices of their choice. The offices were to have very different levels of performance in these years. Performance levels were not to be shared with me until I had computed the effect of culture on performance using the Four Rs—referrals, retention, returns to labor, and relationships with clients. I would base my findings solely on data of the kind discussed in Chapter 5 that was supplied by management. In exchange, I offered to identify the best-performing office and estimate how much of the difference in performance between the three offices was due to culture-related factors analyzed in Chapter 5.

Each of the three offices—Chicago, Baltimore, and Minneapolis—provides the same mix of marketing services. Each has a somewhat different clientele, however. Chicago's business mix includes a large proportion of global clients, reflecting the heavy influence of corporate headquarters there. Baltimore's clientele tends toward a relatively large proportion of government-related business. The Minneapolis office commands a relatively high share of a base of more regional or even local clients.

Table 7-1 shows the data I received for these three offices. Not all data needed for the study existed in the subject company. Where this was the case, management had to make estimates.

Table 7-1 Data for Three Offices of RTL, Inc., 2009 and 2010 (and Assumptions Used in Its Analysis)

Data	Chicago	Baltimore	Minneapolis
Annual revenue:			
2009	$22,608,000	$16,617,000	$8,203,000
2010	22,403,000	14,379,000	9,644,000
Number of client-facing employees, beginning and end of year:			
2009	90/91	57/46	37/35
2010	91/81	46/48	35/38
Number of new hires (with referrals):			
2009	5(?)*	0(?)*	1(?)*
2010	40(15)	11(2)	11(3)
Number of voluntary terminations:			
2009	4	1	3
2010	39	10	7

continued

Data	Chicago	Baltimore	Minneapolis
Number of involuntary terminations:			
2009	0	10	0
2010	8	0	4
Turnover of employees per year:[**]			
2009	4.4%	21.4%	8.3%
2010	54.7	21.3	30.1
Average total compensation per employee:[***]			
2009	$102,350	$158,700	$100,960
2010	116,000	135,000	114,470
Revenue per employee:[****]			
2009	$249,810	$322,660	$227,860
2010	260,500	305,940	264,220
Total compensation costs as a percentage of annual revenue:			
2009	45.53%	51.78%	46.64%
2010	49.39	46.44	45.60
Number of clients (beginning + new − lost = ending number):			
2009	$54 + 5 − 24 = 35$	$64 + 7 − 36 = 35$	$33 + 3 − 13 = 23$
2010	$36 + 7 − 15 = 28$	$42 + 7 − 24 = 25$	$26 + 7 − 9 = 24$
Rate of client turnover:[*****]			
2009	39.0%	40.8%	27.8%
2010	34.9	49.0	27.3
Average revenue per client:[******]			
2009	$502,400	$313,530	$278,070
2010	700,090	429,220	385,760
Percentage of new clients obtained through referrals (no data available)	?	?	?

Assumptions			
Turnover costs as a percentage of annual compensation for people replaced:[*******]			
Voluntary departures	100%	100%	100%
Involuntary terminations	75%	75%	75%

Data	Chicago	Baltimore	Minneapolis
Costs of recruiting and training for net new additions, as a percentage of annual compensation:			
New hires without employee referrals	50%	50%	50%
New hires with employee referrals	25%	25%	25%
Estimated revenue loss per lost client, as a percentage of annual revenue	25%	25%	25%
Estimated operating margin on lost clients	30%	30%	30%
Cost per new client (equals one employee year of compensation):			
2009	$102,350	$158,000	$100,960
2010	116,000	135,000	114,470

* Calculated on the basis of voluntary and involuntary terminations compared to the average number of employees for the year

** Excluding 10% of total compensation costs in Chicago and 5% of total compensation costs in both Baltimore and Minneapolis for "management."

*** Data for employee referrals was unavailable for 2009.

**** Revenue for the year divided by the beginning and ending number of employees divided by two

***** Rate of client turnover equals the number of clients lost divided by the sum of beginning clients and those added during the year

****** Average revenue per client equals the total revenue divided by the average number of clients during the year

******* Assuming that losses of productivity (revenues/employee) were significantly less for those terminated involuntarily as opposed to those leaving voluntarily, but that termination costs for involuntary departures are higher than for voluntary departures

The data in Table 7-1 suggests that all three offices had significant client losses during this two-year period. Either the company was hit hard by the recession or was pursuing a general strategy during this two-year period of shedding less-attractive clients to achieve higher revenue per client. As I found out later, it was a combination of both. The loss of clients was especially great in Chicago and Baltimore. This was accompanied by significant numbers of voluntary departures of employees in both Chicago and Baltimore in 2010, not a favorable sign. Both achieved modest reductions in head count for client-facing employees. But Baltimore's did not equal its loss of revenue, resulting in lower productivity (revenue per employee) for that office during what was a challenging time in the economy and the industry. This was especially the case in the Chicago and Baltimore offices, but less so in the case of the Minneapolis office, where there was lower churn of both employees and clients. Without any more information, this would lead you to expect better economic performance for Minneapolis than the other two offices. And it turns out that that was the case.

The Blind Results

Using the data and assumptions shown in Table 7-1, I calculated on a "blind" basis (without knowing the actual operating profit for each office) the differences due to culture-related matters that I would expect in operating profit for each pair of offices. The method employed for doing this is described in Appendix B, along with assumptions employed in the analysis. The results are shown in Table 7-2.

Table 7-2 Blind Estimates of Performance Attributed to Culture (in Percentage Points of Operating Profit) Using Four R Analysis Compared to Actual Differences from All Causes in Three Offices of a Large Marketing Services Firm*

Four R Dimensions	Blind Estimates by Office**		
	Chicago	Baltimore	Minneapolis
2009:			
Employee referrals		.1	.1
Employee retention (defections)		2.0	
Returns to labor (productivity)		1.6	.3
Client relationships:			
Retention	1.9	6.6	
Referrals***	N.A.	N.A.	N.A.
Total	1.9	10.3	.4
Differential from best	1.5	9.9	

Four R Dimensions	Blind Estimates by Office**		
	Chicago	Baltimore	Minneapolis
2010:			
Employee referrals		1.4	1.0
Employee retention (defections)	6.4		.6
Returns to labor (productivity)	.9	.2	
Client relationships			
Retention	2.7	8.9	
Referrals***	N.A.	N.A.	N.A.
Total	10.0	10.5	1.6
Differential from best	8.4	8.9	
Actual operating profit (in 000s):			
2009	$3,813	($341)	$1,673
2010	2,216	1,362	2,376
Operating profit as a percentage of revenue:			
2009	16.9%	(2.0%)	20.4%
2010	9.9%	8.3%	24.6%

* Detailed assumptions and calculations are shown in Appendix B.

** This should be read as follows: On each dimension, differences are measured in percentage points (in costs or cost savings to revenue) from the best performance. Therefore, the best performance equals 0 on each dimension.

*** Data unavailable.

Here we see the predicted differences due to culture, expressed in percentage points of operating profit, between each pair of offices. These are compared to actual differences due to all causes. Thus, shown as the "differential from best" in Table 7-2, the culture in the Minneapolis office was estimated to account for 1.5 and 9.9 percentage point advantages in operating profit over Chicago and Baltimore, respectively, in 2009. Chicago enjoyed an 8.4 percentage point advantage over Baltimore due to culture that year. For 2010, Minneapolis again was estimated to outperform Chicago and Baltimore by 8.4 and 8.9 percentage points, respectively, with Chicago again outperforming Baltimore, but by only .5 percentage points.

Clearly, this was a period of substantial volatility in the Chicago and Baltimore offices, with both experiencing relatively high rates of employee turnover and client defections. In terms of the blind estimates, this fact imposed substantial penalties on the operating performance of both.

Blind Result Comparisons

After the blind results for each office and the differences between offices were calculated and communicated by e-mail to the company's management, I accessed actual operating profit outcomes for the three offices for the years 2009 and 2010. This data is also presented in Table 7-3. The numbers show that the performance at Minneapolis was substantially better than at either Chicago or Baltimore for both 2009 and 2010. It actually exceeded the rule of thumb for excellence (operating profit of 20% of revenue) throughout the company. Also, Baltimore experienced a significant turnaround from a losing performance in 2009. Chicago's performance declined substantially in 2010 in both dollars of operating profit and as a percentage of revenue.

Table 7-3 Comparison of Blind Estimates of Differences Due to Culture to Actual Differences in Operating Profit (in Percentage Points of Operating Profit to Revenue)

		Blind Estimate	Actual
2009	Chicago versus Baltimore*	+8.4	+18.9
	Chicago versus Minneapolis	–1.5	–3.5
	Minneapolis versus Baltimore	+9.9	+22.4
2010	Chicago versus Baltimore	+.5	+1.6
	Chicago versus Minneapolis	–8.4	–14.7
	Minneapolis versus Baltimore	+8.9	+16.3

* This should be read as follows: Chicago was estimated to have an 8.4 percentage point advantage in operating profit as a percentage of revenue over Baltimore due to differences in culture in 2009. The actual differential from all sources was 18.9 percentage points.

Most important for our purposes, the actual numbers for both years were directionally the same as the blind estimates.

These are admittedly crude estimates, but a look at the comparisons of blind estimates (based on Four R analysis) with actual performance, also shown in Table 7-3, tells us that *culture accounted for about half of the differences in operating income as a percentage of revenues for both years*. Thus, culture has a relatively high impact on

operating income at RTL. This is the kind of business in which referrals, retention, returns to labor, and relationships with customers are
of paramount importance. They are not just interesting elements of
the business; they are the core of the business.

Caveats Regarding the Blind Estimates

The method used to arrive at the blind estimates, presented in
Appendix B, will raise questions. The first will concern the time frame
for the study. This is a snapshot of a two-year window in the business. Many will argue that these were not two "normal" years. My
only defense is that the analytic approach is not meant to provide
estimates only for normal years, whatever that means.

Some will question the small size of the offices examined. This
produced wide swings in raw data and potentially wide swings in blind
estimates. However, when such swings were calculated over the Four
R dimensions, they tended to modulate. Nevertheless, it is a valid
question that would benefit from comparison with comparable studies in larger organizations.

The numbers are not lagged in any way, even though you could
argue that employee turnover in one year could lead to client turnover and an attendant effect on operating profit in a following year.
A look at the data on a lagged basis did not provide any additional
accuracy or insights into this particular analysis.

Not all the desired information was available. For example, it was
just not possible to come up with realistic estimates of the number
of new clients that were engaged at the recommendation of existing clients, an element in estimating the effects of culture on client
relationships.

Perhaps most of all, there will be arguments about the assumptions regarding the portion of differences in performance attributed
to differences in culture. A range of estimates could have been used.
For example, in a manufacturing organization with less impact of customer-facing employees, lower loadings for culture would have been
appropriate. Given the information in Appendix B, others are free to
substitute their own estimates.

There is no claim for precision here. The assumptions used in the calculations, for which there is full disclosure in Appendix B, may raise arguments. If so, they should trigger a useful discussion of a complex topic.

Finally, familiarity and access may come at the price of bruised objectivity. But at every step of the way in designing and carrying out the research, I attempted to overcompensate for this.

Comparisons of Culture Cycle Elements

My application of the Four Rs to data provided by RTL raised questions that begged for more data. Fortunately, in addition to financial data, I received the results of an employee survey that RTL had conducted in all its offices in mid-2010. All three offices in the RTL network used the same method to measure employee engagement. The 2010 survey evoked a rate of response of over 90% of employees company-wide. It was reviewed carefully by management and is intended to serve as the basis for decisions to make changes in policy to deal with weaknesses suggested by the responses. Selected data from the survey for the three offices is shown in Table 7-4. (A complete set of data from the survey is presented in Appendix C.) The data both reflect and help explain differences in financial performance examined earlier.

Table 7-4 Culture Cycle Measurements of Selected Data from the 2010 RTL Employee Survey of the Chicago, Baltimore, and Minneapolis Offices

	Chicago	Baltimore	Minneapolis
Employee defection rate:[*]			
2009	10.0%	21.4%	8.3%
2010	54.7%	21.3%	30.1%
Client defection rate:[**]			
2009	40.7%	50.7%	36.1%
2010	34.9%	46.2%	27.3%
Operating profit as a percentage of revenue:			
2009	16.8%	(2.1%)	20.4%
2010	9.9%	9.5%	24.6%
Survey response rate	70%	80%	75%
Employee engagement index[***]	3.93	3.53	4.17

	Chicago	Baltimore	Minneapolis
Agreement with statements:[****]			
I intend to stay with RTL for another 12 months.	70%	46%	72%
I am highly satisfied with my job.	53%	32%	61%
I get a great sense of accomplishment from my work.	61%	46%	75%
I am proud to work for my company.	67%	39%	77%
I would recommend my company as a great place to work.	58%	27%	77%
The amount of work I have keeps me challenged, but not overwhelmed.	44%	17%	33%
In my office, management is trusted.	46%	30%	69%
In my office, management gets the best out of everyone.	34%	23%	65%
Here you are required, not just encouraged, to learn and develop new skills.	57%	33%	72%
We have high-quality training opportunities to improve skills.	35%	21%	47%
Those who contribute the most to the overall success of the office are the most highly rewarded.	31%	11%	34%
We invest a significant amount of time in things that will pay off in the future.	55%	19%	56%
My company has a strong culture.	44%	39%	81%

[*] Calculated as the sum of voluntary and involuntary employee departures as a percentage of the average number of employees for the year.

[**] Calculated as the number of client losses as a percentage of the beginning number of clients plus those added during the year.

[***] This comprises a combination of responses to these statements: (1) I would recommend my company as a place to work, (2) I intend to stay with my company for at least another 12 months, (3) My colleagues are willing to go beyond what is expected for the success of my company, (4) I am proud to work for my company, (5) My colleagues are passionate about providing exceptional customer service, (6) I understand how my job (role) contributes to the success of my company.

[****] Percentages reflect the top two of six levels of agreement with each statement.

The data tell very different stories, even while RTL management (as I found out later) was pursuing a common strategy of winnowing clients to focus on its highest-potential clients across the network.

Compare Baltimore with Minneapolis, for example. At Baltimore, over the two-year period, relationships with 60 clients were severed or lost. This represented fully 77% of those on board at the beginning of 2009 and added during the following 24 months. This probably accounted for the 13% decline in revenue from 2009 to 2010. The comparable client departure rate for Minneapolis was 51%. During the same period, there were 21 employee departures from a Baltimore office that employed an average of 49, a two-year turnover rate of 43%. The comparable two-year defection rate for Minneapolis was 39%. (For Chicago, the number was 58%.) Yet both Minneapolis and Chicago were able to maintain cultures that were perceived as being stronger than Baltimore and organizations that employees were much more proud of and more willing to recommend to others. There had to be differences in how turmoil, including reduction in head counts, was managed in the three offices. Compare Baltimore and Chicago, for example.

Baltimore's employee engagement index in 2010 (comprising responses to six questions noted in a footnote to Table 7-4) was 3.53 as opposed to 3.93 for Chicago (on a scale of 0 to 5, with 5 being the best). Although the difference may not appear to be large, it was associated with significant differences in responses to other questions. For example, employees in Baltimore, compared to those in Chicago, exhibited a lack of trust in the management of their office, apparently resulting from perceptions of management's inability or unwillingness to "reward people in relation to their contribution," provide training opportunities, "invest in the long-term success of the business," or "get the best out of everybody." The results? Low job satisfaction, low intent to stay with RTL, and a high rate of voluntary departures (following a year with a high rate of involuntary departures) in the Baltimore office. New hires to replace those departing in 2010 undoubtedly added to a workload that apparently was perceived as being "overwhelming" by many.

Worse yet, Baltimore's culture suffered at a time when it was most needed. This was reflected in low scores for pride in the organization and a willingness to recommend RTL Baltimore as a place to work.[2]

This may have resulted in part from a concerted effort to turn around economic performance in ways that increased perceived workloads.

Minneapolis' superior performance on the employee survey was consistent with its bottom line relative to the other two offices for both 2009 and 2010. Similarly, the data from the study helps us understand why Chicago was able to perform as well as it did in 2010, although it suffered revenue declines. Data in Table 7-1 shows a significant advantage for Baltimore over Chicago in 2010, given the huge turnover in personnel in the Chicago office. However, survey data in Table 7-3 suggests that how change was managed in the Baltimore office may have dissipated any advantage that Baltimore was predicted to have over Chicago. In fact, given the information from the employee survey, it's perhaps surprising that Baltimore performed as well as it did, in fact turning a loss in 2009 into a profit in 2010. More about that later.

In fact, there is evidence that the effort to increase client focus and increase the productivity of staff was managed much more effectively in both Minneapolis and Chicago than in Baltimore. Consider Chicago, where the organization experienced a mass exodus of professionals, including 45% *who left voluntarily* in 2010 alone—not a good sign. Yet expressions of pride, a sense of accomplishment, and intent to stay at RTL remained relatively high among those who did not leave. Many more remained willing to recommend RTL Chicago as a place to work than at the Baltimore office.

All this led me to conclude—before any exchange of views with RTL's management—that the variable unaccounted for in my calculations was not some element of culture . It was leadership. Leadership accounted for Chicago's unexpectedly good economic performance and extraordinarily favorable employee perceptions in the face of turmoil and uncertainty. If strategies in the three offices were substantially the same, the high quality of Chicago's leadership must have created an atmosphere in which employees favorably viewed how it was being executed.

Management's Interpretation of What Happened

Having exhausted ways of interpreting the data, I shared my interpretation with RTL's corporate management and asked for its views of what happened in these three offices.

As expected, RTL's leadership adopted a strategy in 2009 and 2010 to discontinue relationships with less important clients—those occupying what was described as "the long tail." At the same time, RTL lost clients that it didn't intend to lose during a time of economic cutbacks.

For the reasons just cited, the Minneapolis office is held up as one of the best in the RTL network. It has a culture that allows it to maintain a relatively constant talent base and superior client relationships.

The more interesting information is about what was going on in the Chicago and Baltimore offices during these two years. By 2010, Baltimore was seen as an office in distress, with a greater client loss than planned, actual monetary losses in 2009, and a performance on track to produce another loss in 2010. The office was being led by someone described by management as "a top-down, heavy-handed" leader who was "spending too little time with associates." He was replaced in mid-2010 at about the time of the employee survey, a low point in the morale of the office. His replacement was someone whose leadership traits were much the opposite. Her efforts to turn around the culture of the office coincided with several big "wins" of new clients that helped bolster the economic performance and save the year. But, given its timing, none of this is reflected in the results of the employee survey.

Chicago, on the other hand, according to RTL's leadership, has a manager who is "reasonably effective with his people." But it views the Chicago office as having performed beneath its potential in 2010, with declining revenues and operating profit. In spite of higher employee survey results than Baltimore, it is seen as "coasting on past accomplishments," led by someone who is "terrific with clients, but not a strategic thinker."

In contrast, Minneapolis is seen by the company's leadership as having a collegial group of associates with a leader who is "focused on talent." Because its management has been successful in establishing client expectations that discourage unreasonable demands on its employees, there is perhaps less pressure on associates to disrupt their lifestyles in order to maintain a superior level of client service.

Conclusions

Based on this field test, we can conclude that performance on the Four Rs that describe the impact of culture on performance—referrals, retention, returns to labor, and relationships with customers—explained up to half of the differences in bottom-line economic performance. But that's only part of a story supplemented by noneconomic indicators of the effectiveness of an organization's culture. An effective culture can reinforce positive trends in the Four Rs and mitigate negative ones. When combined, these two types of information can provide a reliable snapshot of what is going on among comparable businesses.

Culture, however, is only one leg of the three-legged stool also comprising strategy and execution. Although the test described here controlled for strategy differences, it did not anticipate the importance of how the strategy was executed by the leadership in three offices of the same company. It suggests that the relative importance of the effects of strategy, execution, and culture on performance varies from time to time, particularly with substantial change in the economic environment. It underscores the importance of leadership in any study of this kind.

The perceived effectiveness of a culture does not correlate with perceptions of its strength. Note in Table 7-3 that perceptions of culture strength were low in both the Chicago and Baltimore offices. But perceptions of the quality and effectiveness of the culture in Chicago were much higher than in Baltimore, as shown in favorable ratings for training and learning, personal development, reasonableness of the workload, and job satisfaction. This was accompanied by higher levels of trust in management and pride in the organization, leading in turn to a higher intent to stay with the organization and to recommend it to others as a place to work. All this contributed to a relative level of performance that was higher than predicted by culture-related measures.

The effectiveness of culture undoubtedly contributed to very different economic performance levels. But what is cause and effect over what time period is unclear. Furthermore, the first effects of a turnaround such as the one apparently under way at Baltimore in 2010 are often perceptions of overwork, the turnover of associates, and too much time spent dealing with distractions from the day-to-day job to train newcomers. Even if handled well, this can foster a sense of unfairness and distrust of management, at least until the process brings to bear evidence of success—new clients, fewer employees departing voluntarily, more bonuses. How management builds on the early success may well determine whether the turnaround succeeds. At Baltimore, it is probably too early to tell. But for some months, economic performance might appear to be out of sync with improvements in perceptions of the effectiveness of the organization's culture. At least another year of data will be needed to substantiate any interpretation.

The study described here provided information leading to a sharper picture of why and how culture matters. But it covered a group of organizations engaged in a narrow range of activities. To what extent do the observations reported here apply to other types of businesses and activities? And what does this mean for leaders of those organizations? These questions will have to be left to another time.

Summary

A test of the power of the Four R model (described in Chapter 5) to predict the effect of culture on performance was carried out in three offices of a large, multinational marketing services organization RTL, Inc. It produced results that were directionally correct in all six office pairings for 2009 and 2010. From it we can conclude that culture is a major influence on relative economic performance among offices offering professional services where talent is expensive, relationships between associates are critical, and nearly everyone is a client-facing employee. *In the organization studied, culture accounted for roughly half of the differences in performance between three offices of the subject company.*

Inaccuracies in predicting the effects of the Four Rs were related to differences in the effectiveness of leadership, as demonstrated by the impact of a midyear change of leadership in one of the offices studied. Differences in the quality of office leadership appeared to explain why one office was able to equal the 2010 performance of another despite problems in 2009.

The data for economic performance, when combined with that for employee engagement, suggests that the timing of engagement surveys can be critical to their accuracy. Perceptions related to employee engagement require time to reflect new leadership and economic accomplishments.

Management of RTL characterized the performance of its office in Chicago as being on the way down and that in Baltimore as being on the way up. Given the impracticality of running employee surveys more often than every year, it may be difficult for such surveys to provide information that is sufficiently accurate and timely to influence quantitative assessments of the importance of the effect that culture has on performance. However, trends in such measures are of real importance in knowing what to expect in the future and in deciding whether to make changes in leadership.

All this suggests that it is possible to assess the effect of culture on performance quantitatively as well as qualitatively. It illustrates both the importance and complexity of the task.

8

Culture and Innovation

What does culture have to do with success or failure in the design of strategies based on innovation? We could do worse than to turn to 3M, an organization that has been decades ahead of its time.

In the age of Internet innovation and the dramatic innovations brought to us by Google, Apple, and others, we've nearly forgotten about pioneers such as 3M. It quietly continues to turn out new abrasives, adhesives, medical supplies, and other products based on ideas spawned in its laboratories. In fact, 3M has undoubtedly had a strong influence on today's most publicized innovators. For example, its practice of allocating 15% of a scientist's time to devote to projects of personal interest likely influenced Google's allocation of 20% of a professional's time for such activities. In both cases, the practice works largely without close supervision but with a great deal of trust in knowledge workers. They are joined in a mission and subscribe to a set of values that place the organization's goals above their own. At both 3M and Google, it is assumed that they will make good use of their time.

Chairman William L. McKnight has outlined 3M's corporate culture of self-direction as a "basic rule of management" this way:

As our business grows, it becomes increasingly necessary to delegate responsibility and to encourage *men and women* to exercise their initiative. This requires considerable tolerance. Those men and women, to whom we delegate authority and responsibility, if they are good people, *are going to want to do their jobs in their own way*. Mistakes will be made. But if a person is essentially right, *the mistakes he or she makes are not as serious in the long run as the mistakes management will make if it undertakes to tell those in authority exactly how they must do their jobs.* Management that is destructively critical when mistakes are made kills initiative. And it's essential that we have many people with initiative if we are to continue to grow.[1]

The date of McKnight's statement? 1948.

At its birth in 1902, 3M was one of the most unfortunately named companies in existence. Known as Minnesota Mining & Manufacturing Company, it was named for a mining venture based on the acquisition of land that contained abrasive material with which to make sandpaper. There was only one problem. The mine contained the wrong abrasive material. The mining venture lasted about two years, which may help explain the organization's tolerance for "educated mistakes" (which has risen to the level of a shared basic assumption in 3M's culture) to this day. Using imported material, it then took today's 3M Company 12 years to make any money selling sandpaper. This was the first of several ventures that required a decade or more to prove themselves, giving new meaning to the term "patient capital," another shared assumption. (Some have argued that at 3M capital is too patient; however, evidence suggests otherwise.)

3M is an organization decades ahead of its time in many respects. For example, several features of 3M's philosophy and strategy stand out. They include bringing together people with diverse scientific backgrounds (jokingly called "misfits" at 3M), assigning them to the same laboratory (originally called Central Research, or "the funny farm"), and creating the "15% rule" to allow people to spend up to 15% of their time working unsupervised on their own ideas. All of this, combined with patient capital, can result in what may appear like new-product development through serendipity. But a closer look, provided by stories of the real heroes of this organization, suggests that the serendipity happens because of curious and persistent "heroes" who were relentless in their efforts to assemble resources in any way possible, even when told to stop their activities. One such story is presented in the following sidebar.

Stories and Heroes at 3M Feature Innovators

In innovative organizations, the stories and lore typically are associated with persistence leading to new inventions. One of the most common stories told at 3M, for example, is that of the lab scientist who was told to turn to more promising assignments or risk losing his job. He persevered "in classic 3M style" and invented a context-changing product or process. At 3M people tell again and again how Spencer Silver, a chemist, in 1968 made an adhesive he had never seen before. It didn't stick very well, but it allowed an item to be removed without damaging the paper to which it was stuck, and it could be restuck several times. Five years later, a colleague from another part of the lab, Art Fry, thought of Silver's adhesive when his hymnal bookmark fell out during choir rehearsal. He remembered it because sample bottles had been distributed in hopes that someone could come up with a use for the product; he had seen them lying around the lab. As he began using his "15% time" working on it, he concluded that "It wasn't a bookmark at all, but a note." It took seven more years for Fry and his colleagues to come up with a product that could be tested (with Lee Iacocca, chairman of Chrysler, personally writing to find out how he could get more Post-it Notes) and finally placed on the market. Why seven years? Many problems arose, including how to get just the right degree of adhesiveness, how to make sure it behaved properly on paper, and how to get manufacturing to come up with a process to coat the paper properly. As Gifford Pinchot describes it:

> "It takes patience to locate all the different kinds of coaters and paper handlers available at 3M and then find out when they have open time," says Art. "It can't be done through formal channels."... Designing the production process was not Art's job.... Manufacturing told him it was impossible.... He invented a machine that looked like it might just do the job.... The manufacturing engineering function said the machine he had designed would take six months to build and cost a small fortune.... The next morning when people came to work they

> found Art's new process up and running. He had built a crude
> version of the machine overnight in his basement, brought it
> to work, and installed it. It was working.[2]
>
> Was this a product of serendipity? Sure. But it was also a prod-
> uct of perseverance. Twelve years in development is a long time.
> It wasn't the first such product in a company that has produced
> Scotch Tape, new reflecting technologies, pharmaceuticals, basi-
> cally improved coatings, and thermography. The bet at 3M is that
> by bringing together people with different talents and interests,
> giving them time to interact, and not telling them exactly what to
> do, serendipity can be engineered frequently enough to power a
> $23 billion-plus organization that obtains 31% of its annual rev-
> enues from products developed in the previous five years.[3]

In addition to stimulating highly engaged employees to work at
the sometimes-lonely late-night pursuit of new ideas, 3M fosters
cross-disciplinary exchanges in a company with 14 division laboratories through a Technology Forum and a number of initiatives to provide "grants" outside the corporate budget to people with ideas to
work on. As one newspaper columnist summed up 3M's culture and
its impact on innovation: "Most big businesses are run like grade
schools. 3M is college."

The Culture Cycle and 3M Innovation

Just what we know here is loaded with clues to 3M's success
at innovation, as outlined in the culture cycle shown in Figure 8-1.
McKnight's statement emphasizes the basic assumptions and values
that include a tolerance for informed failure, delegation of authority
and responsibility that let people do jobs their own way, and patient
support and capital for innovative efforts. Emphasis is placed on hiring people with diverse backgrounds ("misfits") for whom those things
are important and then making sure that their expectations are met
through such means as latitude on the job, "free time" for exploration,

and the freedom to fail. It is backed up by a leadership cadre that practices what is regarded as a management style that assumes that responsible, "best in class" adults have been hired who want to learn, develop themselves, get frequent feedback and support, and have the latitude (within limits) to determine how their work is to be performed in return for reasonable compensation.

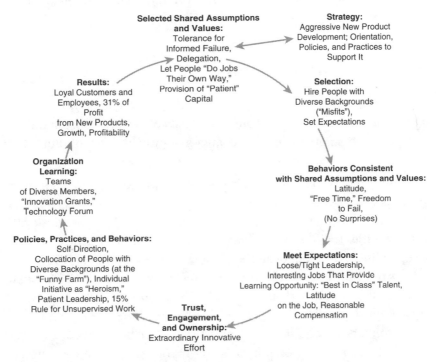

Selected Shared Assumptions and Values:
Tolerance for Informed Failure, Delegation, Let People "Do Jobs Their Own Way," Provision of "Patient" Capital

Strategy:
Aggressive New Product Development; Orientation, Policies, and Practices to Support It

Results:
Loyal Customers and Employees, 31% of Profit from New Products, Growth, Profitability

Selection:
Hire People with Diverse Backgrounds ("Misfits"), Set Expectations

Organization Learning:
Teams of Diverse Members, "Innovation Grants," Technology Forum

Behaviors Consistent with Shared Assumptions and Values:
Latitude, "Free Time," Freedom to Fail, (No Surprises)

Policies, Practices, and Behaviors:
Self-Direction, Collocation of People with Diverse Backgrounds (at the "Funny Farm"), Individual Initiative as "Heroism," Patient Leadership, 15% Rule for Unsupervised Work

Meet Expectations:
Loose/Tight Leadership, Interesting Jobs That Provide Learning Opportunity: "Best in Class" Talent, Latitude on the Job, Reasonable Compensation

Trust, Engagement, and Ownership:
Extraordinary Innovative Effort

Figure 8-1 The culture cycle and innovation at 3M

This fosters the trust and engagement that are essential to encouraging innovative activities and outcomes characterized by such things as transparency in sharing ideas, collaboration resulting from the collocation of people with diverse backgrounds in what was once (respectfully) called "the funny farm," a sense of individual initiative against the "system" as "heroism," the freedom to fail as well as the time (through the 15% rule) to accomplish innovation, and a leadership cadre that understands the importance of these things. The result is an organization in which individuals and the organization as a whole constantly learn, both on the job (through "innovation grants") and in planned activities and colloquia (such as Technology Forums).

Results achieved include an engaged group of employees who provide the continuity that progressively more successful innovation requires. Customers and others contribute to the process. Innovation thrives, judging from the fact that 3M generated 31% of its sales in 2010 from products developed in the past five years.[4] This fact, as well as the company's growth and profitability, confirm the rightness of the shared assumptions and values. And the cycle turns once more.

Levels of Innovation

Innovation is generally regarded as the combination of invention plus commercialization. As Tom May, CEO of NStar, a Boston utility, has put it, "It's not an idea that changes the world. It's a product that gets manufactured and used that changes the world."[5]

Innovation is part of an entrepreneurial process. Students of that process describe a simple model often used by venture capitalists weighing investment opportunities (see Figure 8-2). It begins with opportunities that result from changes in the "context"—the competitive, technological, political, social, and legal environments. Think of a big wave (a change in context) that uncovers treasure that has been buried on a beach, perhaps for a long time. The size of the opportunity often depends on the size of the change in context. The major determinants of whether the opportunity can be realized are first people (with a strong emphasis on their track record in other start-ups) and then their business model (not plan) for achieving an "edge" over competitors in meeting the needs that comprise the opportunity. This helps explain how venture capitalists view business proposals by hopeful entrepreneurs. And it also helps explain levels of innovation.

Tactical Innovation

Changes in products, services, and processes are critical to sustained success in the marketplace. They take place continually and result from suggestions by customers, employees, and others who have become what we have elsewhere termed "owners."[6] They often are the product of marketing research followed up with effective research and development. Or they may result from formal or informal continuous-improvement initiatives in which employees are recognized and rewarded for suggestions for new products and process improvements. They rarely are stimulated by changes in context or support new ventures.

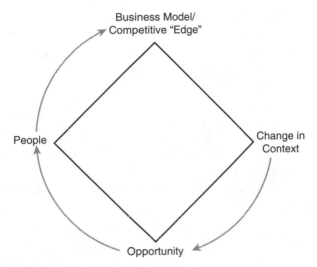

Figure 8-2 A venture capital view of new ventures

Source: Adapted from concepts presented by William A. Sahlman in "Some Thoughts on Business Plans," Note No. 9-897-101 (Boston: Harvard Business School Publishing, 1996) which was in turn derived from unpublished work by Howard H. Stevenson.

Intuit and other software makers regularly put 1.0 software on the market and rely on users to suggest improvements for future versions, either through marketing research or customer calls for help. At Intuit, this is often done by software engineers carefully selected in part for their devotion to making things simple (not a common trait among software engineers) for users of Intuit's Quicken, QuickBooks, and tax-preparation software. On a more routine basis, Intuit's service representatives are carefully selected and trained to field user concerns and help software engineers convert them into product improvements. In a similar manner, Toyota elicited more than half a million suggestions, largely from employees, for process improvement in a recent four-year period. Most of them were small but, when added up, provided significant product and process improvements.

Such initiatives are often embodied in elements of an organization's credo about how things are done, as in The Toyota Way.

Strategic Innovation

Strategic innovation influences the direction of the innovating organization. It typically results from a response to economic, social, or regulatory changes in the environment. For example, "green" solutions to a number of problems have resulted from changes in customer attitudes toward the environment fueled by the scientific community, governments, and social peer pressure. They represent opportunities for new products and processes resulting from a basic change in context, using the language of Figure 8-2.

Strategic innovation is characteristic of both start-ups and established organizations. The former have the benefit of a small organization made up of people with diverse talents and interests interacting closely with one another and operating without the bureaucratic "baggage" of a large organization. The latter have the primary benefit of money to conduct the research needed to identify and size up opportunities as well as test new ideas in the marketplace. The most successful among them have taken steps to create a well-networked organization, incentives for cooperation, and physical or mental proximity of innovators to one another to overcome bureaucratic behaviors that often overwhelm innovation.

For example, CEMEX, the world's second-largest producer of cement and concrete products, has organized itself around a "one company" culture (described more fully in Chapter 10). It fosters transnational innovation, with ideas filtered through an Innovation Committee serving managers in more than 30 countries.

As just one example of an innovation requiring transnational coordination, CEMEX managers have developed a way of serving Mexican immigrants in the United States who want to repatriate savings to their families in Mexico while ensuring that the money is spent as intended. Its Construmex initiative allows immigrants to select plans for new additions to their families' homes in Mexico and purchase construction materials at CEMEX's "retail" stores in the United

States for delivery in Mexico at a small surcharge to the purchaser. The surcharge is a fraction of the cost of sending a money order for the same amount of money. This would be impossible without close coordination between the United States and Mexican subsidiaries of CEMEX fostered by its "one company" approach to global business and a leadership that is organized to systematically bring innovation (based on creating results versus just products) to a somewhat mundane industry. It is strategic innovation at its best.

Transformational or Context-Changing Innovation

The third and most significant level of innovation results from products and services that literally change the context. They open the way for numerous opportunities for strategic innovations and the new products and services they spawn. These kinds of changes are sometimes called disruptive, altering basic behaviors and the rules of the game for competition in entire industries, often by simplifying products or processes in ways that provide effective solutions at much lower costs.[7]

Context-changing innovations include Xerox's 940 copier, Microsoft's Windows operating platform, the Internet itself, and the iPhone. They do not occur with great frequency. They may not be birthed in a commercial organization. For example, the Internet's origins can be traced to university campuses and the U.S. government. They are not always immediately recognized. The new science of xerography, on which not only Xerox but a number of other businesses were built, was turned down by IBM, 3M, and Kodak. This happened in part because of market estimates based on the limited use of mimeograph machines at the time. What they failed to realize was that xerography itself might change office behaviors and the nature of demand for copying equipment and materials.

It is hard to achieve transformational change repeatedly. Microsoft's investors may never see anything that matches Windows. Benetton's innovative manufacturing- and retailing-based business model has served it well, first in Europe and then on other continents. It has essentially undergone few changes since its introduction, even in the face of emulation from competitors such as Zara and H&M. Although Amazon has rapidly introduced its model to the online retailing of an increasing range of products, the basic model and operating philosophy remain the same. Twenty20's "reinvention" of the game of cricket, resulting in a three-hour format to shorten notoriously long matches to accommodate TV and handheld devices, is probably a one-off effort. Some regard transformational innovation as a "once in a company's lifetime" phenomenon. Only a few exceptional organizations such as Apple have defied the rule.

Few organizations in the world are truly innovative. Most just can't or don't want to "Think different," to use Apple's tagline. This is especially true if you exclude the large number of organizations engaged in continuous-improvement efforts encompassing many small ideas, many of them conceived by emulating the best of what other organizations do.[8]

Much of the important innovation that has taken place over time has occurred in small start-up entrepreneurial ventures, characterized by Hewlett-Packard's birth in William Hewlett's famous garage in Palo Alto, California or Cisco Systems' genesis in the laboratories of Stanford University. Most have been funded by venture capitalists who place many small bets, typically expecting one in five to pay out significantly enough to more than finance the other four and produce a return on investors' funds. All the companies just cited except Apple achieved their biggest innovation at or shortly after their founding. If that's the case, clearly the availability of vast amounts of money is not critical to innovation. In fact, many would argue that the riches and success that big ideas produce stifle rather than stimulate other big ideas. Although organizations such as Google and Microsoft are attempting to prove that thesis wrong, so far they haven't been able to. Even Facebook, a child of the intersection of the Internet with a generation craving social networking, had trouble figuring out how to profit from its disruptive breakthrough without alienating the hundreds of millions of regular users attracted to its site.

The question of interest here is: What can we learn from stories of success and failure about what culture has to do with success, or the lack thereof, in the design and implementation of strategies based on innovation?

Adaptability and Innovation

In Chapter 3, I outlined research findings suggesting that organizations with merely strong cultures produce much poorer long-term performance than those that contain elements that provide both strength and adaptability. A growing body of detailed anecdotal evidence illustrates the point. It suggests the nature of the shared values and behaviors that are particularly supportive of important innovation. It also suggests that it is not enough to say "We value innovation and those who achieve it." This claim has to be backed up with other values and behaviors as well as acted on. Tim Brown, president of IDEO, a consulting firm that seeks to transform organizations through "design thinking," and Barry Katz relate an example from Procter & Gamble that illustrates the point:

> All the innovation workshops in the world would not have transformed P&G if (then CEO) A. G. Lafley had not increased the number of design managers by more than 500 percent, built the P&G Innovation Gym, created a new approach to partnering with the outside world ("Connect and Develop"), and elevated innovation and design to core strategies of the company.[9]

Value "Clusters" That Foster Innovation

There has been no mention of the influence of the product development budget on innovation. Innovative organizations allocate substantial amounts of money to innovation, but they often achieve more "bang for their buck" than their competitors. Experiences of successful innovators suggest that a subset of the conditions and behaviors shown as part of the culture cycle depicted in Figure 6-1 have particular relevance for success in encouraging entrepreneurial behavior and innovation. They are illustrated in 3M's profile, shown in Figure 8-1, and include related "clusters" such as the following:

- Trust that results from careful selection and hiring of people who believe in and are engaged by the organization's shared assumptions and values

- The careful selection of people who will pursue individual initiative (when that is called for) and can be trusted to make good use of the latitude, time, and money given them to carry out their work, combined with policies that enable them to do so.
- An inclusive strategy encouraging the collocation of people with diverse backgrounds who are encouraged to practice transparency and share ideas often as part of a team-based effort (when that is called for)
- Learning that results from tolerance for "useful failure" as well as support for "boundaryless" behaviors
- A leadership cadre that understands the value of these behaviors and knows how to facilitate them

Policies, practices, and behaviors individually don't account for the success in innovation that these organizations have achieved. They are often found grouped in what we might call value "clusters." And they have to support and be supported by reinforcing strategies and organization. None of this would happen without leadership devoted to the notion of a strategy based on organic growth through innovation.

Trust, Engagement, and Ownership Through Careful Hiring, Training, and Expectations That Are Met

Innovative organizations demonstrate high levels of trust, engagement, and ownership. These are often in short supply, given basic assumptions spawned during the era of Taylorism described in Chapter 1 as Theory X management. By way of contrast, innovative organizations give employees wide latitude (within limits) to deliver results to customers, a practice that often produces surprising results. However, this practice must be preceded by careful hiring and training.

Trust relies on sophisticated hiring practices that are designed to select people on the basis of their attitude as well as skill, at the same time setting expectations that are then met. At W. L. Gore, associates understand that they are required to find their own spot and tasks in the organization by selling their ideas to others. They are granted 10% of their time to work on projects of interest to themselves. This happens without supervision.[10] As a result, the company has developed a versatile polymer, expanded PTFE—branded as Gore-Tex—and a myriad of related products.

A culture of trust assumes that adults with integrity are being hired into the organization. This combination is not confined to the high-tech or scientific community. My colleagues and I first encountered it at Taco Bell, where it was discovered that "adults with integrity" come in many ages, even late teens.[11] At the time, the 1990s, Taco Bell was led by an ambitious CEO, John Martin. Martin envisioned "Taco Bell ubiquity," a world in which the United States would be blanketed with more than a hundred thousand "points of access" offering Taco Bell products. The number was so large that Martin quickly realized that a traditional hierarchy of division managers responsible for ten stores would result in an organization with thousands of managers. To increase the "span of control" (a notion out of the management dark ages) from ten to one to at least 60 units to one, the job of store manager was essentially changed to include responsibility for six units (or was eliminated, depending on how you look at it). This required changing the entire model of policies and practices by which individual Taco Bell stores were operated. Selection and training had to assume that self-managed, customer-facing teams would be responsible for such things as interviewing and staffing, training, problem-solving (including disciplining and/or firing deviants), and cash management.

Even though the practice has largely been abandoned with changes in leadership and strategy, Martin learned some surprising things from the initiative. Perhaps the most remarkable was that self-managed teams were quite innovative in developing new approaches to their work. Several teams assigned two jobs to team members, one (at which they were really good) for peak hours and another (at which they needed training) for off-peak hours. This system was comparable to the Navy's "call to battle stations" and became known at Taco Bell as "Aces in Your Places." By shifting associates' assignments from training to "battle" mode, service capacity was increased 60% during peak business hours with no change in personnel. As a result, training was achieved on the same days that peak demand was served most effectively.

Collaboration, Inclusion, Collocation, and Transparency

By now you are probably struck by how many of our examples have been characterized by collaboration and teamwork. They have special significance for activities associated with innovation. This is particularly true for activities that have become so complex that no one person can possibly have the knowledge necessary for innovation that transcends traditional bounds of knowledge.

Collaboration and Team-Based Effort

Collaboration and team-based effort are important to the workings of the Mayo Clinic. Many leading medical organizations seek the kind of integrated problem-solving that leads to medical innovation. However, few can achieve it, because there is no basis for dependably bringing together "free agent" doctors who develop their particular specialties in their individual practices. As employees at Mayo, they buy into the concept that teams on salary are more innovative in diagnosing and treating especially complex ailments than a group of sole-proprietor entrepreneurs. Of course, to make this happen, team members have to be collocated and supported by highly sophisticated communication technology.

Inclusion and Diversity

Can diversity of knowledge, skills, and interests brought together in one place foster innovation? Thomas Edison believed so.[12] And research has shed some light on this question. One mega-study of 108 empirical studies of the effects of cultural diversity in teams concluded that "cultural diversity leads to process losses through task conflict and decreased social integration, but to process gains through increased creativity and satisfaction."[13]

Nearly all organizations say they practice diversity, but few reach the critical mass needed to make diverse ideas heard. Those that do achieve diversity are more interesting places in which to work, in part because they foster personal learning and development. As a result, they are more likely to produce innovative ideas.

Collocation

Diversity is not enough. It has to be supplemented with a healthy dose of communication and accessibility. This accounts for the frequency with which innovative organizations are found to have campuses intended to bring people together. For example, the Mayo Clinic grew organically from an increasing number of medical disciplines "clustered" over several blocks in Rochester, Minnesota with a central value or strategy (depending on how you look at it) of "putting patients first." This required that the clinic attract physicians and medical researchers with a broad range of specialties and interests to address patients' needs.

Collocation is a feature of innovative organizations such as Microsoft, Apple, Google, Amazon, and Cisco Systems. But collocation as a strategy is meaningless without values that foster the exchange of ideas. These values include the importance of teaming, transparency, communication, and sharing (of both ideas and results), and putting the interests of the organization (and therefore the organization's customers) above one's own.

When the Mayo Clinic decided to expand to other locations, the decision consisted of much more than just locating a research and clinical hospital in some other city. It had to accommodate what you might call "the Mayo Effect." "The Mayo Effect" (my term) is based on an innovative diagnostic process. It consists of sequential examinations and tests that take place over a short period of time in close proximity to one another with a lot of collaboration among medical professionals with different backgrounds and interests. It is supported by technology that provides everything from timely medical information to schedule preparation and routing centered around patients' needs. It has produced better diagnoses and treatments as well as a superior (effective and efficient) service to clients.[14] When applied to research at Mayo, it has also produced medical breakthroughs such as the Nobel Prize-winning development of cortisone. It required re-creating Mayo's facilities and offerings in another city comparable to those found at its main campus in Rochester, Minnesota, not just establishing a hospital with one or two specialties.

Transparency

Google is noted for hiring people for their problem-solving abilities, regardless of their educational or other backgrounds. When organized into teams, they have proven to be effective in sharing and combining widely different sources of knowledge in the search for solutions to problems that have defied solution.

Google's Google Labs web site is especially useful to employees developing ideas of their own or contributing to the efforts of teams. Remarkably, outsiders and potential competitors can access it as well to track what is going on inside the company and even assist in its development. In some organizations this might lead to fear that one's ideas might be stolen. But Google encourages a confidence born of trust that ideas won't be stolen by insiders. If they are, appropriate credit will be bestowed internally. As for theft by outsiders, the assumption is that Google will have an inherent advantage in capitalizing on new ideas first. A particular value of transparency in this setting is that it speeds innovation by allowing teams of innovators to remain connected whether or not they are collocated.

Latitude, Individual Initiative, and Informed Risk-Taking

W. L. Gore founder Bill Gore, who was strongly influenced by Douglas McGregor's Theory Y view of management, discussed in Chapter 1, set out to create a bureaucracy-free organization in which no one had the authority to tell someone else what to do. As a result, the company had to hire individuals who could work in that kind of environment. It's not for everyone—particularly not for someone who requires structure and stability in his or her work life. The chemical engineering and other skills of those hired are, of course, carefully examined and tested. But care is taken to screen out those who do not have the emotional makeup and attitude to work independently or in teams in an environment that is often highly collaborative, infused with a great deal of peer pressure created by team-based appraisals and incentives, and intensified by the knowledge that all teams will know how every other team is doing. Other high-tech organizations have gained some notoriety in the past decade by utilizing the same values, strategies, and methods of execution. But W. L. Gore began doing this shortly after its founding in 1958.

Useful Failure, Boundarylessness, and Learning

Formal learning and development achieved by means of research centers and the kinds of "innovation gyms" that P&G has established capture the headlines in the business press. But much more important are the less visible elements of a culture that tolerates useful failure, develops clear but achievable standards for the acceptance of new ideas as well as a "test, then invest" attitude, and exhibits the patience needed to develop important innovations.

Tolerance for useful failure encourages innovative activities. Even though the term "useful failure" provides some standard of accountability, it is still very difficult for most managers to exhibit the tolerance needed to enable an organization to learn and benefit from its creative failures.

One important indicator of such tolerance is whether an organization's "lore," characterized by stories told and retold, includes a celebration of failures that eventually led to progress. You hear it at Nucor, the minimill steel producer mentioned in Chapter 6. And you hear it at 3M, as just described. Of course, if the stories are to live on, they must be accompanied by success. But the humility of the failures leading to that success must not be forgotten if an organization's innovative edge is to be maintained.

Learning organizations find ways to exchange information and ideas through interactions with others by means of such practices as benchmarking . And they manage to propagate what they learn on the outside through "boundaryless" behaviors that lead to frequent sharing of the talent that possesses the ideas.

Leadership, Policies, and Practices that Support Entrepreneurship

Innovation at the Mayo Clinic is fortified by policies and practices designed to deliver patient-centered service. For example, one reason that these values are effective is that all professionals are on salary plus bonuses for extraordinary performance. They don't operate as individual entrepreneurs with their own interests, competing with those of their colleagues and patients. Mayo selects professionals for whom intrinsic rewards (such as recognition, personal relationships, and organization success) are more important than extrinsic rewards (money). According to research by Teresa Amabile, this approach contributes to creativity. As she puts it, "It appears that when people are primarily motivated to do some creative activity by their own interest in and enjoyment of that activity, they may be more creative than they are when primarily motivated by some goal imposed on them by others."[15]

Such policies and practices not only support strategies based on innovation but in the process also foster a great deal of entrepreneurial behavior.

Entrepreneurship

Entrepreneurs don't like to be told what to do. That's why they leave conventional organizations and form their own. (Of course, many then begin telling others what to do.) But the challenge for a large organization seeking to be innovative is how to accommodate entrepreneurial behaviors (or "intrapreneurship," as it was popularly called for a time in the 1980s) in its ranks.[16] This challenge has been met in a number of ways.

One approach has been to encourage entrepreneurs with great ideas to start their own organizations with funding provided and some ownership assumed by their former employer. This strategy has been employed with some success, but risks are involved. It requires that boundaries be set on the number of employees an entrepreneur can recruit from the "mother" company. Conflicts may arise when the two companies compete for the same customers. Hoped-for cooperation on product development and marketing may not result. And there is often a strong incentive for the entrepreneur to "buy" his organization free from the "mother ship" at the first opportunity, thus mitigating the intent of the process.

Another approach has been to retain talent by offering large rewards for entrepreneurial wins. At Google, for example, "Founders Awards" have been created for those coming up with ideas that have a large impact on the company's financial performance. They have been as large as $10 million in stock grants. (This was for the development of "Smart Ads," an algorithm that predicts the number of visitors that will view an ad. It allows Google to identify ads that will best serve the advertiser and produce the most revenue for Google.) Typically, the awards are much smaller. But every software developer in the organization remembers $10 million, not some lesser amount. And this has proven to be an effective way for Google to retain associates who have an entrepreneurial inclination.

Monetary rewards can be much more effective when they are given along with significant long-term recognition. The inventors of Scotch tape, Post-it Notes, and Tartan Turf at 3M are still celebrated in person and in story decades after their accomplishments.

Of course, the most effective way to retain creative and entrepreneurial talent is by creating a working environment that such people find comfortable. At 3M and W. L. Gore, for example, a basic assumption is that those who make it a habit of telling others what to do are presumed to drive away talent and thus cannot complete their projects. Eventually they will be asked to leave the organization.

Strategies designed to retain entrepreneurs rather than spinning them off require mechanisms for funding their work. Several successful approaches have involved the creation of internal markets for both talent and money. People with ideas at Google, for example, are free to convince others to join them. The ability to attract a team is an important indicator of a high-potential investment. Projects earn financial support based on their ability to attract interest among those in the firm responsible for allocating capital. In a sense, this is an effort to create a venture capital market, described earlier, inside the organization. It is often characterized by many small investments rather than a few large ones. Just as with venture capital, the philosophy is to bet on the law of large numbers in seeking successes, managing risk by holding off substantial investments until the entrepreneur has proven that an idea has good potential—in short, a "test, then invest" philosophy.

Innovation "Value Clusters" at Apple

At this point you may be wondering how these relationships work at Apple, arguably one of the few organizations that has been able to develop more than one "context-changing" innovation in its relatively short history. Apple has changed how we use computing for personal matters; how we access and listen to music; and how we use handheld devices to access information, play games, and communicate. For that reason alone, it's appropriate to examine how several "Apple-watchers" think the relationships shown in Figure 6-1 work at Apple, Inc.

Reams of materials have been written about Apple. Surprisingly little of it provides insight into how Apple's culture contributes to its enviable record of innovation. On the surface, innovation at Apple appears to be a product of paradoxes. Its success was achieved in spite of early disorganization and leadership that, at least in the company's first nine years, violated many of the principles of good management. But a deeper look suggests parallels between Apple and its forerunners (see the following sidebar). Furthermore, the Apple experience illustrates many of the innovation "value clusters" just discussed.

From 3M to Apple

At 3M they were known as "misfits" working at the "funny farm." At Apple, those who had developed the Apple II were regarded by recent arrivals from HP and National Semiconductor as "talented backyard hackers...working for a game company."[17] Those who have teamed up in both organizations to create a steady stream of innovations come from diverse backgrounds and have attracted their share of measured scorn from their more conventional colleagues. Their champion at Apple, Steve Jobs, is a direct descendant of William L. McKnight at 3M. The ironic thing is that McKnight's strength was in the commercial side of 3M's business. Jobs' higher educational experience lasted a bit more than a year at Reed College, where the closest he got to science and electronics apparently was in a job "maintaining electronic equipment used by the psychology department for animal-behavior experiments."[18] His real interest was in the design and functionality of high-tech hardware. He teamed up with a software geek, Steve Wozniak, to create a company. Had Wozniak prevailed, Apple would have been a very different company, led with a very different philosophy (if it would have survived at all). But instead, the cofounders' backgrounds complemented one another, leading to highly functional and beautiful products developed for individuals, not large organizations, who could appreciate their attractiveness and logic.

McKnight at 3M believed that "the most important innovations respond to unarticulated needs." Unarticulated needs could be realized through the "organized serendipity" that results when people with different interests and skills are brought into close contact and encouraged to think constantly about the possible. That's what Art Fry was doing in his church choir when he began to articulate the need for Post-it Notes, as we saw earlier. That's what Jobs refers to in saying about Apple, "The system is, there is no system. That doesn't mean we don't have process. Apple is a very disciplined company, and we have great processes. But that's not what it's about. Process makes you more efficient. But innovation comes from people meeting up in the hallways or calling each other at 10:30 at night with a new idea...."[19] This helps explain why Apple has done relatively little formal marketing research other than testing for functionality in product use over the years. Instead, it has relied on the interests and needs of its employees, who listen to music constantly. They took what might have been regarded in another organization as a strategic detour to invent and introduce the life-changing iPod and supplement it with an iTunes system.

Innovation in both organizations is based on platforms, albeit very different ones. At Apple it is the operating system—most recently, the OS X operating system, adapted from one developed at Jobs' NeXT company, which Apple acquired in 1997. At 3M, it is, among other things, technologies such as adhesives, which have provided the basis for everything from sandpaper to Scotch Tape. In a sense, it is the platform that brings together people from different backgrounds to work together.

3M scientists have been very good at combining ideas developed by others to come up with new applications and products. Jobs is known to have gotten the inspiration for features later appearing on the Apple II from a visit to Xerox's famed PARC laboratories in California in the 1980s. Ironically, some of PARC's fame resulted from its inability to sell its often brilliant ideas at Xerox's Rochester headquarters. Given the leadership at 3M and Apple, moving ideas from invention to commercialization, the true mark of innovation, has not proven to be as much of a problem as at Xerox.

As is usually the case, there is nothing new under the sun, even Apple. Although the parallels aren't perfect, two of the most innovative organizations in the past century competing in two very different arenas share common ideals, philosophies, and practices. In its 2010 special issue on innovation, *Fast Company* magazine listed Apple along with Amazon and Google just behind Facebook as the most innovative companies. But, ironically, 3M was nowhere to be found among the 184 companies mentioned in the piece.[20] This was in spite of the fact that more than a hundred years after its founding, 3M's innovation machine was still churning out new products at roughly the same rate as ever.[21]

The immediate success of Apple's first full-blown product, the Apple II, in 1978 produced so much profit that it gave the company room to organize itself for more systematic innovation. This required massive hiring, providing the opportunity to bring together people of diverse backgrounds, selected in part for their interest in creating simpler, more logical products. This effort produced what was described as "relentless pressure" of Apple's own making in an atmosphere that was "almost inhuman"[22] to meet the demand for the product. At this time, several years after the founding of the company, former Hewlett-Packard transplants made a rather ineffective, textbookish attempt to form a culture committee and define nine values for the company:

1. Empathy for customers/users

2. Achievement/aggressiveness

3. Positive social contribution

4. Innovation/vision

5. Individual performance

6. Team spirit

7. Quality/excellence

8. Individual reward (psychological as well as financial)

9. Good management

None of this seems to have made much impact, particularly on cofounder Steve Jobs, who may or may not have been involved in the process.

At Apple, the culture is instead influenced by basic assumptions that are derived from the organization's lifelong emphasis on hardware, not software. This has produced several behaviors related to the innovative process:

- The company does not release products until they have been thoroughly tested and proven in use.
- The assumption is that potential users are not good at defining their needs but do serve a useful function in testing already-designed products.
- The real creativity comes from inside Apple, not through conventional marketing research.
- There is a firm belief that simplicity is the ultimate sophistication.

In addition, employees, suppliers, and dealers alike understand that Apple is a secretive company when it comes to innovation. Surprise is part of a strategy that influences its culture. The extensive exchange of ideas that takes place inside Apple doesn't extend to its relationships with the outside world. Jobs may borrow ideas for product features from Xerox's PARC (see the earlier sidebar "From 3M to Apple") or retailing ideas from The Gap, on whose board he sits, but those organizations may learn little from Apple other than what they can observe in the marketplace.

Apple houses people with diverse backgrounds in close proximity to one another on its Cupertino, California campus. They have an unusual amount of freedom to "free associate," exchange ideas, and cocreate (fostering internal transparency and collaboration). They are driven to make products that are simple, elegant, and easy to use. They are organized into teams with at least generally described goals, working on a campus and in an atmosphere that fosters the exchange of ideas at any time of the day or night.

Teams are funded through a process in which ideas brought forth from the organization are reviewed by a group of senior executives and revised and reviewed through an iterative process. This ensures, for example, that work will make use of a common platform. As soon as it was under way, according to "a major architect of the Mac OS X operating system," the subsequent work first made sure that the design was right. Then "We...figured out how to achieve it technically.... It was great because we were applying a lot of creativity and ingenuity on the design side and then pushing the engineers to use the same kind of creativity and innovation to make that happen."[23] As one commentator put it:

> The iPhone was a glorious expression of Apple's approach to product design. It did not start with laborious research, focus groups or the acquisition of another company with a hot product. It began with a few people trying to design a product they would want to use and be proud to own.... (It involved)... taking a close look at the shortcomings of existing products, adapting ideas from others and melding them into something that, by 2007, could only have come from Apple...(an exquisite refinement)...of the half-baked ideas and products full of compromises and shortcomings that other companies had prematurely rushed onto store shelves.[24]

Apple is known for its innovation, its marketing, and particularly its design capabilities. It's not known for manufacturing (which it outsources) or component development (which it leaves to its suppliers), or even for the development of applications that appear on its products. For these, it relies on individual software developers, many of whom seek intrinsic, not necessarily extrinsic (monetary), rewards. It was (and apparently still is) an exciting place to be for the right kind of creative people. Personal development is the order of the day. As one former Apple employee put it, "When I was there (at Apple) in the late 1980s and early 1990s, people were given amazing opportunities to stretch themselves and grow and do amazing things."[25]

An important reason why Apple is so exciting for designers is its design-oriented culture. A visitor to both Apple and Microsoft on the same day provided this contrast, according to John Sculley, former Apple CEO:

He went into the Apple meeting...and as soon as the designers walked in the room, everyone stopped talking because the designers are the most respected people in the organization. Everyone knows the designers speak for Steve because they have direct reporting to him.... Later in the day, he was at Microsoft...everybody was talking and then the meeting starts and no designers ever walk into the room. All the technical people are sitting there trying to add their ideas of what ought to be in the design....[26]

External secrecy combined with collaboration and a certain degree of internal transparency have fostered high levels of "ownership" among employees at Apple, especially those involved in product development, as well as suppliers and manufacturers. This is reinforced by a mission to create easy-to-use, aesthetically pleasing products that change the lives of individuals. The mission is led by Steve Jobs, who cares intensely about the work of Apple's creatives and wants to be involved in nearly every detail of the process before personally signing off on the aesthetics of a product's or retail store's appearance and feel.

Given Apple's rise with Jobs' presence (1976 to 1985 and 1997 to 2011) and its fall with his long-term absence (1985 to 1997), it is tempting and necessary to view the organization's culture for innovation in a somewhat personalized way. This view is accurate, given Jobs' influence on innovation at Apple. Jobs' early bias toward the design of hardware (as opposed to his cofounder's primary interest in software), combined with his eye for design and bias toward simplicity of use, have been hallmarks of Apple's products. John Sculley's views on Jobs' interests are instructive:

Steve...always loved beautiful products...even things like how the (internal circuit) boards were laid out.... (He) had this perspective that always started with the user's experience.... He always believed the most important decisions you make are...the things that you decide not to do. He's a minimalist... constantly reducing things to their simplest level. It's not simplistic. It's simplified.... He simplifies complexity.[27]

Jobs' public image is of a leader who influences the most minute features of final product designs, repeatedly turning back designs containing questionable features and holding the organization to a policy of avoiding products that are not worthy of Apple's reputation. One Apple dealer with whom I talked recently claimed that his dealership (an unsuccessful Apple experiment) had to delay its opening until Jobs personally passed on it. This helps explain why one book about Apple has "Little Kingdom" in its title.

After resigning unceremoniously in 1985 when the Apple board felt that his skills were unsuited to leading the company, Jobs returned 12 years later to take the reins. He turned around Apple in one of the most remarkable feats in management lore. Some attribute this turnaround to the challenges Jobs experienced in leading his new firm, NeXT, while he was gone.[28] As Michael Moritz observed, "It is not too much of a stretch to say that Steve founded Apple not once but twice—and the second time he was alone."[29]

Jobs himself has never fully articulated Apple's culture and strategy for innovation. But it is ironic that an organization so often portrayed as being founded by eccentrics for eccentrics has followed a reasonably conventional path of internally consistent shared assumptions and values (if not always behaviors) necessary to produce its remarkable stream of innovations. This has occurred under Jobs' personal guidance, with his inspiration, and to his exacting standards for design—assets of priceless value. His most recent departure for a medical leave will, if it is for an extended duration, pose the kind of test during which the organization didn't distinguish itself on one other occasion.

Summary

Innovation is commonly described as invention plus commercialization. Without the latter, there is no innovation. It's like the proverbial tree falling in the forest that no one sees or hears.

Innovation is part of an entrepreneurial process that results from opportunities created by changes in the social, economic, technological, or legal environment—something that students of entrepreneurship call a change in "context."

Professional investors and venture capitalists bet on people with a track record of past entrepreneurial success and a competitively sound business model for achieving an "edge" in commercializing the opportunity.

Most innovations are what can be described as tactical—changes in features of existing products, services, or processes. They are often the direct result of efforts to create a culture of "continuous improvement." In contrast, strategic innovations can influence the entire direction of the innovating organization. Once in a great while, an organization may come up with a transformational or context-changing innovation that rewrites the competitive "rules of the game" for entire industries. Rarely can such organizations repeat the feat.

Organizations that have been especially successful in fostering significant innovation share beliefs in the importance of such things as individual and group initiative, the latitude to explore new avenues and generally determine how things are done, informed failure as a way to learn, and the willingness to trust inquisitive people from diverse backgrounds with the time and money needed to pursue their ideas. Conditions and behaviors that support innovative activities form "clusters" that include the following:

- Trust, engagement, and "ownership" through careful hiring, training, and expectations that are met
- Collaboration, inclusion, diversity, collocation, and transparency
- Latitude, individual initiative, and informed risk-taking
- Useful failure, boundarylessness, and learning
- Leadership, policies, and practices that support entrepreneurship

Successful formulae for innovation have changed little over the years. For example, practices at the most successful of today's highly publicized innovators such as Apple and Google can be traced back to 3M's policies and practices in the first half of the twentieth century. Few achieve the results of these organizations, however, without leadership from the top that both embraces values that support innovation and understands how creative people are best organized, recognized, and motivated.

9

Culture and Adversity

Do organizations with effective cultures deal more successfully with adversity? Does it matter what kind of adversity we're talking about—a single event affecting one competitor or a difficult environment affecting all? Do they perform better than competitors during times of stress? Do they come out of such times in a stronger competitive position? As with all complex phenomena, anecdotal evidence suggests that "it all depends." The question is: On what does it depend? Unfortunately, we have had an opportunity to explore these questions too many times in recent years.

Consider three organizations with cultures that have served them well over the years: Intuit, the maker of personal financial software; Southwest Airlines; and investment banker Goldman Sachs. One experienced a serious product flaw that threatened to tarnish the company's image with its highly loyal customers and employees. The other two experienced an industry meltdown that challenged their values and posed threats to their image. Compare these three with BP and the way in which its culture did or didn't influence and help its response to the explosion, fire, and oil spill associated with its rig in the Gulf of Mexico in April of 2010. To what extent were responses to the crises these organizations faced influenced by their cultures? And what difference did it make?

Adversity and Response at Intuit

Faced with the need to convince customers to buy their new check-writing and bill-paying software, Quicken, Scott Cook and Tom Proulx sought to establish a high level of trust with their customers shortly after founding their new company, Intuit, in 1983. They did so by means of an audacious guarantee: "If you don't like the product, just tell us. We'll refund your money whether or not you send it back." Fortunately, few took them up on their guarantee. But the lore it produced in the organization became the basis for a customer-oriented culture. This culture helped Intuit produce several important personal financial software products and services in an organization fostering transparency and populated with people who could work across functional lines in teams. These teams delivered software that could be understood by laymen, used with a minimum of delay or confusion, and serviced by unusually capable service representatives. As a result, Intuit's sales grew largely as a result of favorable word of mouth.

By 1994, Intuit had ridden this formula to more than $200 million in annual revenues. Then disaster struck.

On February 28, 1995, the head of Intuit's tax business was called by a reporter who had received a complaint from a user of one of Intuit's tax-preparation software products. The user had discovered that when he imported data from his Quicken files to his tax software, every thirtieth item on long lists was omitted. After unsuccessful attempts to reach the company's managers, he called a reporter instead.[1]

This direct challenge to Intuit's implied contract of trust with its customers (and employees) was discovered just 45 days before the deadline for filing tax returns for 1994—and in a way that did not reflect well on the company. Due in large part to how the company had been led up to that time, there was little question about what needed to be done or how.

In a sense, improving less-than-perfect products already on the market is in the DNA of many software companies. The basic assumption is that "perfect is the enemy of good." The best way to improve a product is to put it on the market and let the user participate in the improvement process. To facilitate the process, Intuit operates customer support (not call) centers staffed with highly trained people. These centers are designed to deliver outstanding service while collecting ideas for the next version of an improved piece of software. Of course, a product defect as serious as the one in Intuit's TurboTax and MacInTax products, given the timing, required extraordinary action.

In addition to setting about to create a fix for the software, a team led by then-President Bill Campbell crafted a message that was delivered within 24 hours by means of newspaper articles and radio and television interviews broadcast nationally:

> We have identified some calculation errors (in our tax preparation software) ... and are prepared to make it as easy as possible for any affected user to quickly correct any problem ... I want to assure all customers that our tax software is guaranteed accurate. In fact our guarantee states that we will pay absolutely any IRS (Internal Revenue Service) penalty because of a calculation error in TurboTax or MacInTax.[2]

But the Intuit team didn't stop there. They decided to make replacement programs available on Internet bulletin boards accessible to the public, in effect giving Intuit's software, which retailed for $35 to $40, to anyone who wanted it.

The Intuit team engineered a rapid recovery process without the aid of public relations consultants, lawyers, or Scott Cook, who was out of the office. The consultants argue for full and immediate disclosure, and the lawyers urge restraint in ways that are sometimes interpreted as cover-ups. There was no time for such debates. Instead, Campbell and his team produced a message that reflected the company's shared values and the way in which Intuit was led. As a result, the company experienced no noticeable reductions in sales during "tax season." The overall costs of the recall and guarantee were about $1.5 million, a small fraction of the company's revenue for the year. Six months after the incident, payouts on the guarantee to pay IRS penalties were only $15,000. *The New York Times*, in reporting the story, lauded the company for its efforts. *Investor's Business Daily* reported the matter under the headline "Intuit Moves Quickly to Avoid Publicity Nightmare."

The matter has been forgotten. It's as if it never happened, a nonevent. We tend to remember notorious crises that are handled badly, of which Toyota is a poster child, as we saw in Chapter 6.

Intuit, in contrast to Toyota's management response to adversity, has a culture of "just doing it" if one believes in what is being done. It's a product in part of the beliefs of a founder who continues to serve as chairman of the Executive Committee. Bill Campbell didn't have to consult anyone or anything other than his conscience before acting.

And he did it by putting into practice the values by which Scott Cook had led the company since its beginnings. In this case, Intuit's culture was a source of strength.

You could argue that Toyota's size made a rapid response difficult. But by the same token, the founding family and the CEO's names and reputations were at stake. Had the culture permitted it, Akio Toyoda could have acted as the Intuit team did. The culture didn't permit it.

Fortunately for Toyota, its time in the spotlight was eclipsed by the BP explosion and oil spill, a case in which the organization's culture provided it with too little direction and support.

Adversity and Response at BP

The BP story begins with a company called British Petroleum. Under that name, the company compiled a history of refinery explosions, worker accidents, and an extensive leak in its Canadian pipeline. Its reputation in the public eye became so bad that new leadership, headed by Lord John Browne, decided that a complete remake of the company was necessary.

The name was changed to BP. Its new "green" mission gave the initials BP a new meaning, "beyond petroleum." New emphasis would be placed on safety for employees and a customer orientation. Consultants were hired to help BP in its new mission. However, part of the way into this effort, an explosion and fire in 2005 at a Texas City, Texas refinery killed 15 people, casting doubt on whether management was "walking the talk" on values and goals. Two years later, Browne was forced by a personal scandal to turn over leadership reins to Tony Hayward, who once again pledged to put new emphasis on safety while at the same time initiating efforts to cut costs.

As the company's profits increased, workers reportedly continued to experience instances where cost control was placed ahead of safety on important decisions. Evidence of the promised green initiatives was limited. There was a large gap between espoused values and actual management behaviors leading up to the April 20, 2010 explosion, fire, deaths, and massive oil leak on BP's Gulf of Mexico oil rig. According to one report:

The spill also opened the door for an unflattering re-evaluation of the safety improvements Hayward often bragged about over the last year. The picture that emerged was of a company whose cost-cutting agenda drowned out its safety message, and BP was found to be in continuing conflict with both U.S. health and safety regulators and state officials in places like Alaska.[3]

Again, leadership's actions were apparently out of step with efforts to emphasize the values of the "new BP" and foster an improved culture. As suggested by the data in the study in Chapter 7, typically this is accompanied by a loss of trust in leadership and a further deterioration of a culture's strength and effectiveness.

In short, BP's culture provided no resource for coping with a disaster. Under these circumstances, it is perhaps surprising that management's response to the crisis was as good as it was. Within several days, management agreed with the U.S. government to establish a $20 billion trust fund to handle claims resulting from the disaster. But this did not offset a simple move by a member of the U.S. House of Representatives to force BP to provide a continual stream of images from the site of the oil leak—a constant reminder to the public of BP's mismanagement. It also reminded the public of the inaccuracy of the company's early announcements that underplayed the extent of the spill, perhaps on the advice of legal counsel. BP's actual delays in fixing the well and perceived delays in dealing with the cleanup effort only added to the negative image.

The well was capped, and the cleanup effort did go forward. But again, perceived progress in dealing with the spill was upstaged by several events, including the following:

- An effort by management to shift the blame for the explosion to BP's contractors, perhaps another result of legal advice
- Unscripted comments by Hayward that suggested an insensitivity to the seriousness of the situation

This prompted an advertising campaign featuring BP managers from the Gulf area who were assigned responsibilities for dealing with the crisis; it was received quite favorably. But by then the damage had been done in the public's mind. At the same time, it seemed as if the plight of the families of the 11 workers killed in the explosion had been forgotten. It was not surprising, therefore, when Hayward (from the United Kingdom) was replaced by Robert Dudley, a longtime BP manager from Mississippi with a good grasp of the situation and possible responses to it.

BP's response can be seen as massive, but too late and delivered with an insensitivity to the company's public and the needs of its own workers. It had to be crafted with little support from a set of assumptions, values, and beliefs whose sincerity already had been questioned both inside and outside the organization. What did BP get as a result of the most expensive disaster response in history (far more expensive than the response to the Bhopal chemical plant explosion in India many years earlier)? First, BP could receive a bill, and a charge to profits, for up to $20 billion for the cost of claims associated with the cleanup. To prepare its balance sheet for that possibility, BP sold assets worth billions of dollars. And as a result of the explosion and BP's handling of the disaster, its stock declined more than 50% in the two months following the event.

Organizations that embrace values that support timely and appropriate responses to short-term crises are better able to deal with them. It's quite obvious that this wasn't done at BP. You could argue that no organization could prepare adequately for the apocalyptic events that befell BP. Nevertheless, any company operating deepwater oil rigs prone to occasional failure would have to know about the constant possibility of disaster and the need to prepare for it. This point was impressed on me as I witnessed, during a visit to Southwest Airlines headquarters, a rehearsal for a mythical plane crash in New Orleans that killed everyone onboard. I found myself in a large group of people who actually boarded an aircraft in Dallas for the simulated trip to New Orleans. Everyone reviewed their responsibility for taking care of the needs of the relatives of a specific passenger onboard the crashed plane. Of course, such a crash has never occurred. In fact, no passenger has ever been killed as the result of a Southwest accident.[4] If such an event does occur, the exercise I experienced suggests that Southwest employees are ready to handle the disaster in ways that will address grief effectively and reflect well on the company and its employees.

Now consider two other examples in which the damages were industry-wide and potentially longer-lasting. In the situation facing Southwest Airlines after the 9/11 terrorist attacks in the United States, events leading to adversity were outside the company's control. Nevertheless, Southwest had to be guided by its shared assumptions and values.

9/11 and the Southwest Airlines Response

As we all know, the weapon of choice in the 9/11 terrorist attacks was the commercial airplane. This dealt a particularly heavy blow to the airline industry. People were less inclined to follow through with travel plans. And some pleasure travelers avoided air travel, at least for several months. During this time, U.S. commercial air travel fell by 23%, dealing a severe economic blow to an industry typically beset by high fixed costs. To deal with this problem, U.S. airlines cut nearly 69,000 jobs—13% of the workforce.[5]

New security procedures resulting from 9/11 hit one airline, Southwest, particularly hard. It had relied on fast turnaround of its aircraft to increase its productivity. It had made its reputation by providing point-to-point, low-cost, reliable, on-time service to business travelers over relatively short route segments. As a result, Southwest boarded more passengers per mile flown than any other major airline. But new restrictions slowed its efficient boarding procedure. In one instance, a frustrated Southwest pilot grabbed a scanner and waved passengers onto his plane so that he could take off on time.

In the face of this adversity, Southwest could have cut back on staff and service. That's what other airlines did. But Southwest's management saw this as an opportunity both to grab market share from its competitors and to energize employees who may have become complacent and self-satisfied, given their remarkable performance and the reams of favorable publicity it had generated over the years. It was viewed as an opportunity by Southwest's CEO Jim Parker, who was continually looking for ways to put to work a product of his imagination that had become a company value, a "Warrior Spirit." This encompassed the behaviors of "work hard, desire to be the best, be courageous, display a sense of urgency, persevere, and innovate."[6]

Many organizations would have regarded the new regulations as one more obstacle to profitable operations. At Southwest, this was seen as an opportunity to put its culture to work to deal with the new regulations—to reinforce an "underdog mentality" that was becoming harder to maintain.

True to its underlying assumption that loyalty to one's people in turn fosters their loyalty to the company, the management of Southwest Airlines did not lay off any Employees (always capitalized at Southwest) in the wake of 9/11. In fact, it didn't even cancel options for planes that it had on order. Instead, Southwest used this advantage to launch a job-sharing program in which all Employees voluntarily accepted fewer hours of work. This allowed the airline to preserve jobs as well as its base of talent for the upturn it believed would follow, thereby giving it a competitive advantage.

How well did Southwest do against its major competitors? Revenue data compiled for the period from September 2000 to December 2002, by which time the volume of air travel in the United States had recovered to pre-9/11 levels, provides one measure of industry health. Southwest's revenue declined much less than other airlines, partly because it gained share from those that had furloughed employees and taken planes out of service. As a result, Southwest was the only U.S. carrier to avoid losses in the third and fourth quarters of 2001. Per-share values of the common stocks of the largest U.S. airlines took a big hit as well. Figure 9-1 shows that the value of Southwest Airlines stock declined about 25%, and the value of five other major U.S. airlines dropped by an average of 40% in just the month of September 2001 alone. This heralded a period of time in which the value of Southwest exceeded that of the other five major carriers put together.

Adversity and Response at Goldman Sachs

The cultures at Goldman Sachs and Southwest Airlines share similarities. In both organizations, employees have repeatedly shown a willingness to put their organization before themselves. Both companies focus on their customers, assuming that this focus will produce profits for shareholders. Voluntary departures among employees are very low in comparison to competitors. This is particularly remarkable in the financial services industry, where explicit rewards are often regarded as more important than any other. But Goldman has enjoyed high rates of loyalty in both good times and bad. In every case, it has turned to its culture to provide stability during long-term periods of recovery from adversity. But in the immediate aftermath of setbacks to their industries, Southwest's culture helped it differentiate itself positively, while Goldman's, in my opinion, didn't. The question is why.

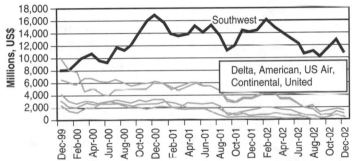

Figure 9-1 Market value of Southwest Airlines versus five other American airlines, December 1999 through December 2002

Having spent time working with investment bankers, my impressions confirm those of others with whom I have traded observations. While observing their plush décor and enjoying the fine food of their executive dining rooms, one gets the sense that in spite of the fact that their primary resource (and expense) is talent, they are by and large devoid of what might be called humaneness. As a longtime member of the faculty that has supplied Wall Street and The City (in London) with more talent than any other, I understand a graduate's rationale for going into the very demanding, exciting, seductive world of financial services: work long hours, sacrifice your personal life, and make a lot of money so that you can pursue your personal interests later (if later ever comes), regardless of what happens to the firm or your colleagues. A workplace populated with some of these largely self-centered Type A personalities can be energizing. One populated only with them can be pretty dreary.

Among these organizations, Goldman Sachs has always been regarded as different, a place where people work very hard to get ahead but look out for one another as well. At Goldman, an individual, instead of seeking "stardom," does her best for the good of the organization and its clients. Goldman's culture has been achieved through a rigorous recruiting, selection, and orientation process that inculcates a set of values, principles, and behaviors designed to promote a focus on clients, teamwork, prudent risk-taking, and long-term performance. It has produced an organization that, in the words of former co-chief executive Jon Corzine, "underpromises and overdelivers *to itself*."[7]

This has created the impression that Goldman largely has avoided the crises and scandals that have characterized its competitors. That impression is incorrect. The firm has had to survive, among other setbacks, a 1928 debacle involving trading money for others through its Goldman Sachs Trading Corporation, a 1970s Penn Central railroad bankruptcy that rendered nearly worthless bonds held by Goldman in its client's company, another commodity-trading disaster in one of its subsidiaries in 1983, and the arrest of one of its partners on charges of insider trading in 1986. The most recent, involving the fallout from government efforts to rescue financial institutions during the Great Recession of 2008, was different. Although the calamity visited the entire industry, Goldman Sachs and its leadership managed to distinguish themselves in the minds of the American public as the poster child for insensitive behavior in the dispute between Main Street and Wall Street. This was a significant distraction from the business of the day at best and a departure from the intent of the organization's values at worst. In the Great Recession, an underlying assumption of Goldman's culture—that it preserves the confidentiality of its clients' and its own business dealings, avoiding publicity if at all possible—may have worked both for and against it.

Goldman has been operated as a public corporation (versus a partnership) only since 1999. Its leadership has relied heavily on the loyalty (and resulting continuity in relationships) of its hundreds of managing directors or would-be managing directors to fulfill its first principle—primary focus on the client. Loyalty has been a product of the following:

- Careful selection of new recruits for "fit"
- Schooling in the organization's values (historically client service, integrity, and teamwork; more recently also strategic dynamism and commitment to change) and beliefs (shown in its "principles" statement in Chapter 4)
- Careful monitoring of both performance and behavior throughout one's career
- Rewards largely tied to the organization's, not the individual's, success

This does not mean that in times of stress, employment is guaranteed at Goldman. To the contrary, the firm has, when necessary, fired staff members below the rank of partner (during the time of the partnership) or, more recently, encouraged partners to leave (at the time of Goldman's incorporation and the opposition of some partners to it in 1999). This might be expected in a professional services firm in which talent makes up the lion's share of the costs and represents a significant cost-cutting opportunity. But it requires that the process be managed with primary concern for the health of the organization's culture. The resulting loyalty of those who remain helps ensure the continuity valued by Goldman's clients, the world's corporations, governments, and wealthy individuals who utilize the organization's services.

Goldman's strategic options are no different than others in its industry. It has not been particularly innovative. It left to Drexel Burnham the development of junk bonds and to AIG the development of credit default swaps, to cite just two examples. The company's strategy can be described as "rapid followership." In the past, those inside and outside the firm have been impressed with its resilience, lending support to the observation of one former senior Goldman executive that "Our firm's culture is the most sustainable competitive advantage that we have."[8] So how did the culture perform in the most recent crisis?

Goldman's receipt of government aid (as well as a major investment from Warren Buffett), whether or not it was accepted enthusiastically by management, called public attention to the seriousness of the Great Recession. This perhaps heightened interest in allegations that, in the months leading up to and following the recession, Goldman exacerbated the global downturn by doing the following:

- Creating and selling derivative instruments, called synthetic CDOs (collateralized debt obligations), designed to fail
- Trading against the positions of its clients, a natural result of market-making
- Providing advice and services that allegedly enabled weaker European nations to appear financially stronger than they really were

But a much more serious claim against an organization built on trust was that Goldman did not provide enough information to its clients to allow them to make informed decisions about the CDOs, particularly one requested by a client that was allegedly designed to fail so the client could benefit from others' losses. Specifically, in April 2010 the Securities and Exchange Commission accused Goldman of fraud. Maintaining that it had done nothing wrong[9]—essentially designing a product and making a market for it in which sophisticated investors could make their own decisions and trades—Goldman's management nevertheless settled the lawsuit for $500 million. As one observer put it, a possible perception resulting from the legal debate was that at Goldman Sachs "We make money for ourselves first, and our customers second,"[10] a clear contradiction of the principles. A perceived breach of trust for an organization built on trust is a serious matter.

The last of the major U.S. investment banks to sell stock to the public, Goldman for years was the most secretive in its industry. And perhaps this showed when the company had to face the spotlight cast on it by a mandatory government "bailout" loan and the attendant ire associated with it in the public's mind. Goldman admitted to nothing. But in defending itself against a variety of charges, it brought unwanted public attention to itself. It didn't help when Lloyd Blankfein, Goldman's CEO and perhaps poorly coached in the ways of offhand remarks, referred to investment bankers (probably with tongue in cheek) as doing "God's work" in an interview with a reporter from the *Sunday Times* of London. This provided a negative "sound bite" in an industry whose products and processes are puzzling to many.

This is evidence that Goldman's culture may have failed to serve it well. On the other hand, in the turmoil it was easy to forget Goldman's principle that the client's needs come first. The "public" may register an outcry, but it is not the client. And there is evidence that in continuing to serve its clients well, the company benefited from the same strong and effective culture that had served it so well for more than a century.

In 2008, Goldman faced the same economic pressures as its competitors. But it was uniquely successful in attracting private capital, maintaining relationships with its most valued clients, and retaining its senior talent. Much of this could be credited to the organization's reputation, a product of a culture emphasizing employee collaboration at the expense of "stardom" and focused on the needs of its clients. The result was that Goldman's return to a pattern of growth and profitability was more impressive than any other firm in the industry. Regardless of the continuing animosity of the public toward the financial industry in general and Goldman in particular, its culture continued to serve as the solid rock on which it relied for success.

So What?

Several factors influenced both the nature of the responses and the outcomes in these four organizations:

- The strength and health of the organizations' cultures
- The leadership present in each firm at the time of adversity
- The nature of the effect of adversity (death versus monetary loss) on customers and/or employees
- Whether the adversity was industry-wide (as at Southwest and Goldman Sachs) or "local" (producing a short- or long-term competitive disadvantage, as at Intuit and BP)

Upon reflection, one reaches the conclusion that at least three of the four organizations had better levels of performance than competitors prior to the crisis—performance attributed by informed observers in large measure to effective cultures.

In three of the four cases these organizations

- Suffered less than their competitors during the period immediately following the crisis.
- Gained market share following the quarter in which the crisis occurred.
- Saw their economic performance, whether in profits or market value, greatly exceed that of competitors.

But what about the fourth organization, BP? Here, we saw an organization not used to dealing with the "retail" public, either unwilling or unable to correct a relatively ineffective culture caused by a gap between values and behaviors at precisely the time it suffered a setback. In this case, BP's engineering-based culture worked against it at a time when it needed to present a more humane face to its workers and the public in general.

These four vignettes suggest that the degree to which culture is a factor in efforts to deal with adversity may depend on the fit between the following:

- The nature of the adversity (long-term or short-term, industry-wide or local?)
- The nature of the organization's culture (consensus-based, rewarding of individual initiative, proactive?)
- Leadership styles

The Fit Between Culture, Leadership Style, and the Nature of Adversity

When adversity strikes, many moving parts determine how organizations respond. The first, of course, is the *nature of the crisis*—its duration and whether it is industry-wide or local, as discussed earlier.

The nature of an organization's *culture* influences its responses to adversity. For example, an organization with a "communal" culture stressing consensus and internal sociability will respond quite differently from one characterized as mercenary and task-oriented. Ordinarily, a communal culture might inherently be the most attractive of these. But the most effective of these two cultures in a time of crisis may well be the mercenary culture, characterized by such things as speed, a relentless focus on the business, and intolerance of poor performance. However, if not tempered by behaviors fostered by a culture with some degree of sociability, the task-oriented culture can lead to longer-term negative fallout, as we saw at BP and Goldman Sachs.

Leadership styles may or may not meet the needs of particular crises. Organizations in which independent and proactive leadership behaviors are encouraged should foster more effective responses to short-term crises, as we saw at Intuit.

Leaders have special responsibilities to communicate with various constituencies during periods of adversity. Some are more comfortable with and effective at relating to their employees—creating just the right balance between confidence and reality, regardless of their personal feelings—than to those outside the organization.

The CEO of an organization may not provide the right "face" to the outside world for the organization. For example, Lloyd Blankfein, CEO of Goldman Sachs, has been criticized for the manner in which he represented his organization in his public comments. It is easy to forget that Blankfein was chosen for his job for capabilities more attuned to the needs of Goldman Sachs' internal organization. There the focus is on the organization's long-term performance, not a shorter-term economic downturn for which some think Blankfein's organization bore some responsibility.

In fact, leaders are rarely chosen for their skills in handling crises affecting individuals and communities outside the organization. Rather, the assumption is that they will steer the organization away from such crises. Whether prepared or not, it's the CEO who is expected to represent an organization in these kinds of situations. This was the case in the BP crisis. CEO Tony Hayward projected a somewhat smug and condescending attitude, further compounding the bad will that the company had already created for itself. The irony is that his direct report, Robert Dudley, head of U.S. operations, had earlier come across on television as serious, sincere, and informed. It was a clear case in which a CEO may have been better equipped for tasks other than representing the company's views to the world in a time of crisis. But it was impossible for the CEO to delegate the task of representing the company in so serious a situation.

How Cultures Help and Hurt in Times of Adversity

In this case and others I have observed, an organization's values can provide the guidelines needed to effect adjustments in bad times as well as good. Culture can be an effective competitive device as long as it does not lock an organization and its leadership into inaction. It can bring people together in the face of adversity. Crises can actually strengthen a healthy culture, forcing associates to question values and employ them in constructive ways. During these times, strong and healthy cultures also help do the following:

- Preserve an organization's capacity for recovery by retaining critical talent
- Foster latitude for action at all levels of the organization
- Provide the shorthand, common language reflective of shared assumptions that enable people to act when under attack

On the other hand, culture can have a negative impact on performance in times of adversity if it does the following:

- Leads to inaction in the name of values, such as favoring consensus as opposed to rapid response when the latter is needed
- Produces behaviors and actions that constrain otherwise logical strategies for recovery
- Leads to perceptions that necessary actions have too high a cost in terms of damage to the culture
- Delays the departure of those not contributing to the organization's success

Consider the challenges faced by Europe's medium-sized, largely family-owned enterprises during the Great Recession as characterized by Trumpf, a German manufacturer of high-value devices employing lasers to cut, weld, and imprint, among other things.

The demand for capital goods that accounted for Germany's remarkable ability to remain the second largest export economy in the world up to that time fell by 25% in 2009.[11] Most of these goods are produced by a group of medium-sized companies that are family-owned, known as the Mittlestand. Other major European economies have their own version of the Mittlestand. In Italy, it's a large community of businesses largely found in the states traversed by the Po River in the north. In France, the concentration is smaller, but the number is still large.

These family-owned businesses tend to have more paternalistic policies toward employees than their competitors. They are managed according to values, with a strong tendency to put employees before profits, and this is borne out by their actions. Trumpf's annual revenues, until the economic downturn, were approximately 2 billion euros. Revenues dropped sharply in the winter of 2008–2009. But as of the summer of 2009, Trumpf had resisted laying off any of its 8,000 employees. It used deferred "rainy day" funds accumulated during good times as well as government recovery resources to do so. However, it appeared that these funds were drying up. Company leadership seemed to be delaying any consideration of layoffs. As managing director Nicola Leibinger-Kammüller put it, "The responsibility I have for our employees is what is dearest to my heart. It's not the family's wealth. It's not our standing with the public."[12]

Leibinger-Kammüller's philosophy is a microcosm of a more general philosophy in Europe that employees and their jobs should be protected. This is reflected in stringent employment laws across the continent that make it difficult and costly to make personnel changes. This perhaps explains why Europe's productivity recovered much more slowly than that of the United States during the 18 months following the crash in the fall of 2008. Organization culture influenced staffing decisions, which in turn created a drag on productivity. It is too early to tell whether their cultures may have proven fatal to some of these midsized, family-owned companies. In Trumpf's case, its culture apparently helped preserve its talent base, enabling it to participate fully in Germany's strong recovery.

Culture as a "Filter" Between Adversity and Performance

With the foregoing as background, think of culture as a "filter" between adversity and performance, as shown in Figure 9-2. It suggests that perceptions of adversity in the organization are "filtered" by a combination of culture and leadership behaviors. This in turn tempers impressions of the nature and seriousness of the adversity among members of the organization. A possible range of actions is triggered, influenced as well by strategy and methods of execution. If the culture is strong, healthy, and reflected in leadership behaviors, the organization's perception of the adversity may lead to a conclusion that "We're under attack; we have to stick together to ward it off; let's figure out a way to do so." Talented people remain with the organization, producing relatively good performance.

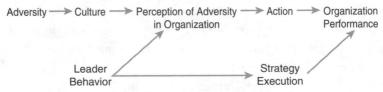

Figure 9-2 Culture as a "filter" between adversity and performance

On the other hand, perhaps the "filter" is perceived as overly leaky—that is, characterized by a weak or unhealthy culture and somewhat unclear or confusing leadership behaviors. In that case the perception of adversity may lead to a conclusion on the part of valued members of the organization that "It's time to abandon ship; everybody for himself; those in charge don't have a clue about how to react." The resulting actions may not be well coordinated or internally consistent. As a result, organization performance coming out of adversity can be expected to be relatively poor.

The challenge is especially great for leaders and their organizations in later stages of relatively successful growth and performance cycles. Too often, bureaucracy with its attendant layers of organization has replaced relatively flat organizations staffed with people rewarded for their individual initiatives. Often the big money has been made by individuals from the early growth in the organization's revenues and profitability, followed by a public offering of stock owned by those employed early in the life of the organization. Strategies reliant on new-product innovation and development may lose credibility in the face of few new successes. Compensation policies may be out of line with the competitive realities of the marketplace. For example, they may rely too heavily on stock options that no longer hold the attractiveness that they once did.

Leading on the way up is relatively easy compared to the challenges presented by a flattening of performance measures or a major setback. There is a need to encourage the most talented instead of the least talented people to stay with the ship and face the adversity. Under these circumstances, the role of the leader becomes one of putting the culture to work in marshaling the energy of the "believers" while weeding out "nonbelievers."

Summary

In times of adversity, a healthy culture aligned with strategy and methods of executing it can offer the following advantages:

- Bringing people together against a common threat
- Preserving the organization's capacity for recovery
- Fostering latitude—the authority to act on behalf of the organization at all levels
- Providing a shorthand and common language, based on shared assumptions, that facilitate action
- Providing guidance about how nonperformers are asked to leave and when (not just when jobs have to be cut back)

On the other hand, weak or nonadaptive cultures can do the following:

- Lead to inaction in the name of values and the need for consensus
- Produce behaviors and actions that constrain otherwise logical strategies

- Rule out necessary actions that are perceived as having a high cost in terms of damage to the culture
- Delay the departure of those not contributing to the organization's success

Factors that influence both the nature of responses to adversity and the outcomes include:

- The cultures themselves
- The leadership present in the organization at the time of adversity
- The nature of the effect of the adversity (death versus only monetary loss) on customers and/or employees
- Whether a crisis is industry-wide or "local" (producing a short- or long-term competitive disadvantage)

The degree to which culture plays a factor in efforts to deal with adversity depends on the following:

- The nature of the adversity (long-term or short-term, industry-wide or "local")
- The nature of the organization's culture (consensus-based, rewarding of individual initiative, proactive?)
- Leadership styles

Some leaders confronted with adversity may be better equipped to provide the organization's "face" to employees rather than to those in the "outside world." In particular, the CEO may not always be the best "face" to those outside the organization, even though he or she may need some visibility to avoid the impression that responsibility for dealing with adversity is being delegated.

Culture, along with leadership behaviors, can influence the organization's perception of adversity, serving as a kind of "filter" that may influence decisions on the part of employees about whether they intend to be part of the recovery.

In an economic downturn, it is important to reduce the right kinds of costs and make the right kinds of personnel changes in ways that are consonant with the organization's values. If done selectively and with good judgment—taking into account shared values, beliefs, and behaviors—those kinds of changes can actually strengthen a culture.

At times such as these, leaders and managers are especially challenged to use good judgment. Decisions have to be made with a demeanor suitable for the culture, regardless of how optimistic or pessimistic one might be about the future of the organization. If the culture is so weak that it provides no guidance, any decision will do.

10

Subcultures and Global Strategies

United Parcel Service's foray into Germany, its first outside North America, in 1976 was accompanied by high hopes at company headquarters in Greenwich, Connecticut. After all, the German market was growing, and UPS's biggest potential competitor, the Deutsche Bundespost, "didn't care much about service."[1] Germans were perceived as having much the same work ethic and basic values that had made UPS so successful in the United States. These qualities included punctuality; industry; the ability to work in a carefully engineered "time and motion" process consistent with the philosophy of "Taylorism," which was popular at the time the company was founded in the early twentieth century; and strong loyalty to the organization and the job. The company was so confident that it could apply these same concepts and values in Germany that it did not seek a German partner. It proceeded to organize its German subsidiary around much the same values, policies, procedures, and standards that were employed in the United States, including promotion from within and the opportunity for a long career with the company. Organized labor was not a concern for the largest employer of Teamsters in the United States.

Some adaptation was required. The company's ubiquitous brown shirts in the United States had to be redesigned with pinstripes to avoid association with the Nazi regime's uniform. As one account put it, "As it turned out, UPS might have spent less time considering shirt color and more on a crop of other cultural issues that undermined it those first few days."[2] These included tension over the amount of work required, routes with too few deliveries requiring too much driving, severe competition for labor, a generally unfavorable image of "truck drivers" in Germany, and even a reluctance of workers to be called by their first names.

As loads became larger, other cracks in the system began to appear. For example, the UPS fleet of "cars," the company's name for its highly engineered package vans, was dispatched each morning precisely on time. And just as precisely, the cars all returned at the end of the delivery shift, whether or not all packages had been delivered. This was unheard of in an organization that prided itself on doing whatever it took to get the job done—that is, get all packages delivered as fast as possible, regardless of the time required. In the United States, the day ended when all packages had been delivered. German drivers, regardless of the terms of their agreement, simply would not work beyond the customary quitting time to get their remaining packages delivered that day. As volume continued to increase, losses did as well, along with declining service. The "special sauce" of UPS's U.S. culture of hard work and ownership in the company's success had not had a chance to take root.

This story, involving one of the most highly respected U.S. companies, may be hard to believe. But UPS's leadership at the time had limited experience in international expansion. It had not made the effort to explore all the nuances of the German work culture, instead assuming that differences from those in the United States could be ironed out quickly. Both cultures valued punctuality, but German employees also had a penchant for working to the letter versus the spirit of an agreement. Having learned an important and costly lesson, UPS management performed a complete review. It recommended that salaries be increased, Germans be trained to take over the operation, and drivers be retrained to deliver UPS's quality service. These strategies led to profits several years later, long after the date in UPS's initial business plan.

This story illustrates both the importance of subcultures and the tendency of executives from one culture to project their assumptions about dealing with people from another culture. Although subcultures exist to some degree in all but the smallest organizations, one group of scholars and consultants calling themselves "culturalists" specialize in exploring subcultures in multinational organizations.

Enter the Culturalists

Cultural differences among people nurtured in various parts of the world are well documented. They are often the subject of jokes that compare stereotypes of one nationality with those of another, jokes that probably reveal more about the teller than the cultures being stereotyped. They are the subject of study by culturalists who could probably have been of great help to UPS as it entered Germany.

Culturalists, by and large, remind us that one should be cautious about generalizing about cultures. Then they proceed to generalize about cultures. They also remind us that because much of early management theory was developed in the United States, a country with a very different subculture than that in many other parts of the world, it reflects views based on assumptions about that culture. For example, Americans, to use one set of measures,[3] have very low uncertainty avoidance, high individualism, low "power distance" (human inequality), and high "masculinity" scores (clear delineation in the roles played by women and men) when compared with people from most other nations. So efforts elsewhere to motivate employees (based on work by McClelland[4] and other Americans), implement management by objectives (MBO) programs (using ideas generated by Drucker[5] and other Americans), or "reengineer" an organization (following the precepts of Michael Hammer,[6] an American), often are met with unexpected levels of resistance or apathy. When it comes to globalization, the relatively strong American fascination with human needs (characterized by Maslow's Hierarchy of Human Needs,[7] culminating in "self-actualization"), with management theory (such as Senge's ideas concerning learning organizations[8]), or with planning and control theories based on the work of Simons[9] and others) may not serve its leaders and managers well according to this culturalist theory.[10] (This book may be regarded as suspect under the same reasoning.)

The challenge, of course, is not limited to U.S. executives. Assumptions are a product of upbringing and national cultural biases. For example, managers at Toyota follow The Toyota Way, based on the 14 principles listed in Chapter 6. One of them is continual organizational learning, or Kaizen. Among other things, Kaizen in turn relies on Hansei, encompassing "responsibility and self-reflection" as well as organizational learning. To accomplish Hansei, according to Mike Masaki, erstwhile president of the Toyota Technical Center, "In Japan we would not point out the good things, but would focus on the negative... At Toyota, even if you do a good job successfully, there is a hansei-kai (reflection meeting)."[11] Japanese children who misbehave are told by their parents to do a Hansei.

American managers, brought up with a set of behavioral assumptions that emphasizes positive rather than negative aspects of performance, at first complained when efforts were made to implement Hansei in Toyota's facilities in the United States. Failure to understand Hansei made it extremely difficult, if not impossible, to bridge organization cultures between U.S. and Japanese members of the organization who were implementing a Toyota-General Motors joint venture in the United States. It required that Toyota's Japanese managers delay implementing Hansei until Americans understood its purpose, benefits, and importance to The Toyota Way.[12]

Regardless of the challenges facing them in their research, the work of culturalists can be directionally helpful. For example, Richard Lewis divides the world into three types of cultures with a sampling of contrasting characteristics:[13]

1. **Linear-active** (Scandinavians, Swiss, Dutch, WASP Americans, Germans, British, among others): Plans ahead methodically, does one thing at a time, works fixed hours, punctual, dominated by timetables and schedules, sticks to plans, unemotional, confronts with logic, uses limited body language.

2. **Multi-active** (Latin Americans, Arabs, Africans, Indians, Southern Italian, among others): Plans a grand outline only, does several things at once, works any hours, not punctual, timetable unpredictable, lets one project influence another, changes plans, juggles facts, emotional, pulls strings, uses unrestricted body language.

3. **Reactive** (Japan, China, Taiwan, Singapore, Turkey, Finland): Looks at general principles, reacts, likes flexible hours, punctual, reacts to a partner's timetable, sees the whole picture,

makes slight changes in plans, statements are promises, uses both firsthand and research information, uses subtle body language.

Lewis then goes on to point out that in 2005, statistics suggested to him that only slightly over 10% of the world's population fell into the linear-active category. The implications are that American management concepts may have less applicability than their proponents believe, and large challenges face any organization with linear-active roots when pursuing a global strategy.[14]

Although you might disagree with the framework or details of this kind of assessment, there is little doubt that cultural differences among various peoples do exist. Sensitivity to these differences becomes relevant when an organization seeks to pursue a global strategy involving people from another culture. As Lewis puts it: "When people from a linear-active culture work together with people from a multi-active culture, irritation results on both sides. Unless one party adapts to the other and they rarely do—constant crises will occur."[15]

Global Management Challenges from Cultural Differences

Cultural differences force an organization to decide certain things:

- Whether a single set of values, beliefs, and behaviors will serve for foreign subsidiaries
- How to integrate acquired organizations originating in a part of the world with a distinctly different business culture or social orientation than the one in the acquiring company
- The form of organization required to support a strategy centered around "one company" as opposed to one employing a highly decentralized set of policies and practices

The nature of an organization's activities, the demands of its clients, and competitive strategies chosen for meeting those demands influence responses to these questions.

The following sections consider the questions in the context of cultures fostered and strategies employed by three global companies. They look at Danish-based facility services company ISS, Mexican-based cement producer CEMEX, and U.S.-based marketing services organization Omnicom Group. These companies illustrate three strategies for meeting the challenges of cultural differences in the global organization: customization at the local level; one company, one culture; and a mix of both.

ISS: "Multilocal" Culture

ISS was founded in 1901 as a Danish security company. From its base in Copenhagen, the company recently employed 485,000 people in 53 countries on five continents. It provides facility service solutions centered around five basic service "pillars": cleaning, catering, security, office support, and property services. The company's goal is to serve the needs of large, globally operated customers, but in fact much of its business is regional or local. As a result, the custodians of the company's culture are heading up its operating units, often in competition with "mom and pop" providers in these localities.

Integrating newly acquired organizations is the task of a country manager. Other than establishing common accounting systems, the process is relatively simple and the central controls quite basic. This helps explain why the company has been able to absorb more than 600 acquisitions of relatively small companies in a recent nine-year period. It also helps explain why, among other things, ISS maintains what it calls a "multilocal" approach to doing business—one tenet of The ISS Way.

The nature of the organization's work—much of it performed out of sight and at odd hours by people whose work generally is recognized only when it is done poorly—has required it to focus on human resources issues. Several decades ago, management concluded that the "company's core business is not cleaning, but organizing and managing people."[16] For example, attention was given to the development of somewhat autonomous teams rewarded for such things as customer contract renewals and maintaining good results while using fewer materials and reducing costs.

ISS's culture and strategy are inseparable, as expressed in The ISS Way, largely a statement of strategy with its four "cornerstones" of customer focus, people management, integrated facility services, and the previously mentioned "multilocal" approach to business. Embedded in The ISS Way is a pledge to "(conduct) business in a responsible and sustainable manner." Shared values are largely reflected in its statement of corporate responsibility that addresses people ("... to realize our employees' full potential"), planet ("... to tread lightly as a responsible business"), profit ("... profitability and growth ... [without] corruption and bribery"), and partners ("customers and suppliers").

Reflecting the multilocal approach to business, it wasn't until 2003 that a Code of Conduct was developed for ISS Worldwide. Instead, the headquarters organization, ISS Global, has concentrated on providing common administrative systems and financial controls. It also provides mechanisms for the exchange of knowledge among managers, including ISS University (for senior managers), ISS academies (for the study of such things as work processes), excellence centers organized around the "pillars" of the business as well as regional business opportunities, and international forums.

With a 6% operating margin, the company has limited resources for the travel and face-to-face management cooperation necessary to sustain a "one company" culture. Nor is such a culture critical to the success of the business.

CEMEX: One Company, One Culture

CEMEX, one of the world's three largest cement and concrete manufacturers based in Monterrey, Mexico, fosters, in contrast to ISS, a "one company" culture. A single culture prevails even though CEMEX operates in more than 30 countries on five continents in a business that, because of the high cost of transportation for its products, comprises relatively small manufacturing facilities serving local markets. Why this is the case is worth some investigation.

CEMEX is the product of a common cultural experience. Since its founding in 1906, a large number of the company's senior management have graduated from the same school, Tecnológico de Monterrey. They were trained as engineers. And they are led by an engineer (by training), Lorenzo Zambrano, who has a penchant for information technology and its application to a multinational business. He told me a story about returning to Monterrey after completing graduate school and asking his father, the CEO at that time, to buy Zambrano a computer. His father asked what he could possibly want with it, and his request was denied. At that moment Zambrano vowed that if he ever became CEO, he would transform the company's IT infrastructure.[17] And he has.

Information technology has become the centerpiece of a strategy, called The CEMEX Way, to standardize all accounting, human resources, operations, and strategic planning systems within the company. Standardization is so comprehensive that it extends even to a common color scheme for painting pipes containing various materials in all its plants. The goal is to enable a CEMEX manager who is transferred to a company office or plant anywhere in the world to become fully operational in 15 minutes. This is important in a company that has realized substantial growth through acquisition. And it is important for managers who are moved from country to country repeatedly as part of a plan for their personal and creative development. It has made a "one company" mentality particularly attractive.

As we saw in Chapter 8, innovation also is given a high priority at CEMEX. This is surprising to those who regard the company as operating in a somewhat mundane industry. Innovation is critical to the success of a strategy that emphasizes providing solutions to customers—in the form of runways, buildings, sanitary conditions, or extra strength, as opposed to just cement or concrete—and growth by acquisition.

The "one company" mentality is centered around three values—collaboration, integrity, and leadership—as well as a set of beliefs described in the following sidebar. As the number of CEMEX acquisitions grew, management recognized that the values allowed room for a wide range of behaviors. For example, bribery was considered acceptable in certain countries in which CEMEX had acquired companies. As a result, the company adopted a common code of ethics in 1997. It carefully defines the limits of acceptable behavior. All employees are required to read, understand, and sign it. At times, its enforcement has led to difficult decisions and central edicts. But it is strictly (some new to the organization say too strictly) enforced world-wide. This is true even though such enforcement can lead to delays in obtaining licenses or the need to disengage from suppliers that may have been paid kickbacks by acquired companies.[18]

Excerpts from CEMEX's Code of Ethics

1. MISSION, VALUES, AND BELIEFS THAT DEFINE US

1.1 Our mission

CEMEX's mission is to serve the global building needs of its customers and build value for its stakeholders by becoming the world's most efficient and profitable building solutions company.

To achieve our mission, we work with our customers to build a better world, supplying them with the highest quality products and services and growing and positioning ourselves as the best option for our stakeholders within the global building materials industry.

1.2 Our values

We strive for excellence in our performance, creating long-lasting relationships based on trust and our essential values of collaboration, integrity, and leadership.

CEMEX values defined...

Collaboration: Work with others in a collective pursuit of excellence.

Integrity: Act honestly, responsibly, and respectfully toward others at all times.

Leadership: Envision the future and focus our efforts on service, excellence, and competitiveness.

1.3 Beliefs that define our character

We are convinced that our business success stems from being the best option for our stakeholders, and therefore...

We endeavor to develop and implement strategies that ensure our **leadership**, generating value for our customers, investors, employees, suppliers, and communities. We know that our continuous focus on effective service and competitiveness is fundamental to achieving our mission.

continued

We believe that, by acting with **integrity**, our employees give us a competitive advantage. By doing business honestly, responsibly, and respectfully, we will build lasting ties of trust and mutual benefit in all our interactions. We encourage clear and direct communication because we recognize that diverse backgrounds and opinions are enriching.

We are convinced that our **collaboration** speeds up our decision-making and helps us to achieve better results. We affirm our professionalism by keeping ourselves up-to-date, communicating effectively, and working in teams to share our efforts and knowledge. We proactively seek ways to satisfy the needs and expectations of our stakeholders by being innovative, striving for continuous self-improvement, adjusting to change, and doing our best.

These principles are the driving force of CEMEX people.

Source: CEMEX company document

Perhaps the greatest challenges to a "one company" culture come with behaviors. According to one account:

> In describing CEMEX's culture, employees used a variety of terms: young, agile, high performance, centered around high standards, execution-focused, fast-paced, intense, dedicated, persevering, collaborative, decisive, and, occasionally, impatient.[19]

This is not the normal widely held image of a Mexican-based culture. It has often led to challenges in resolving "gaps" in behaviors observed by PMI (post-merger integration) teams sent into companies acquired by CEMEX. For example, employees in newly acquired organizations often object to the long hours and intense focus on the business that is part of The CEMEX Way. This is usually mitigated to some extent by the willingness of veteran CEMEX managers—who typically descend in droves on acquired organizations and assume key jobs such as controller, treasurer, and head of procurement—to work alongside their new colleagues, sometimes putting in grueling hours at work. Objections are also offset by speed and decisiveness in decision-making that are perhaps characteristic of the engineering mentality that pervades the company. CEMEXers are reportedly willing to listen, learn, and adopt good ideas from acquired organizations. This is both the essence and objective of collaboration, one of CEMEX's core values. For example, at the time of a major European acquisition, the company decided to revise its code of ethics regarding whistle-blowing to reflect the fact that several European countries had made the practice illegal.[20]

Omnicom Group: A Mixed Model

The Omnicom Group is a holding company (thus Group in the name), the product of a 1986 merger of three large U.S.-based advertising agencies. It has increasingly grown organically, with 25% of its growth in the past ten years coming from acquisitions. Today, it is the corporate umbrella for nearly 200 "agency brands" comprising the second largest (but most profitable) provider of marketing services around the world. These include relatively well-known "brands" such as advertising agencies BBDO, DDB, and TBWA; public relations firms such as Ketchum, Fleishman Hillard, and Porter Novelli; and other organizations providing marketing services to various industries. Larger agency networks such as these are multinational. Others are national in operating scope.

Omnicom Group leadership has maintained an intense dedication to decentralized management, making no attempt to impose a common set of values or culture on its subsidiaries. Each of its acquired companies came to the Group with its own, often founder-inspired, culture with no pressure from the Group level to change it. According to former vice chairman Thomas Watson:

> We think a decentralized structure makes for better decision-making by the operating companies closer to the client, less "command and control" and more "convince and cajole." It is also key to our culture. Entrepreneurial values appeal to acquired company managements and prospective acquisitions. These values also are important in the recruitment and retention of talent.[21]

There are practical reasons for this, given that an advertising agency, for example, may not be permitted by its clients to serve a competitor in a given industry. Thus, Omnicom Group subsidiaries often compete against each other for the same client at the same time that they are encouraged to team with each other to provide more comprehensive service offerings to clients instead of soliciting each other's clients.

Services are made available to the Group's agency networks with a goal of minimizing "chargebacks" for them. These include such things as help in obtaining new business or making acquisitions as well as real estate, legal, financial, and procurement services. The Group offers management development programs through Omnicom University, which, according to one executive, has become the "cultural glue for the Omnicom Group." But agency networks may offer their own "universities" with much the same purposes.

What is true for the management of culture at the holding company level is not true for many of the subsidiaries, particularly those operating multinationally in the service of global clients. Many of the agency networks are operated on a "one company" basis to provide consistent quality and value to clients seeking consistency on a global basis. They become an engine to provide "one company" global marketing strategies for some clients that are unable to achieve such strategies on their own.

Strong, clearly stated values and behaviors are vital at the subsidiary (agency network) level, given their importance in recruiting talent, much of which is self-selected into these agencies. Even at this level, cultures of individual offices in networks with multinational reach take on the values associated with national traits and customs. This requires that management take steps to "bridge" differences among highly refined geographic cultures across a global network with common operating concepts. TBWA, for example, offers clients throughout its global agency network "disruption" as an operating philosophy—a process for developing creative ideas and marketing campaigns that are a distinct departure from the past or the norm. TBWA seeks individuals who believe in it and who can manage its internal business functions by such tenets as well. On the other hand, BBDO promises its advertising clients that it will focus on "the work" (creative ideas that deliver results), and it seeks talent that both wins creative awards and delivers results. The diversity of cultures and reputations among the Group's subsidiaries is thought to make them more attractive to clients with similar diversity and a need for successful "chemistry" in a relationship.

At the subsidiary level, the agency brand is important, because external reputation is what is used to attract new talent. And the agency brand encompasses values, beliefs, and behaviors that extend across national and regional boundaries. When new offices are opened or acquired in parts of the world formerly not served, an effort is made to inculcate commonly held values and beliefs. This can be a challenging task in cases where the office's predominant business is local or national. And it is further complicated in offices in which substantial portions of the business consist of local assignments for global clients and campaigns that are actually sold and created elsewhere in the world. This is one reason why global account directors often are assigned to ensure coordinated efforts across all offices handling global accounts.

The natural result of this strategy is that no effort has been made to impose a common culture from the holding company level. Instead, the Omnicom Group has focused on tight financial and loose operating controls, with operating plans made by the subsidiaries. It is the responsibility of the subsidiary agency networks to decide whether they want to develop shared services with sister subsidiaries under a corporate policy of encouraging both cooperation and competition among them. An effort is made to administer central financial controls, which involves setting goals and measuring against them. Shared costs are allocated among subsidiaries in ways that are designed to avoid setting subsidiaries against each other and discouraging cooperation. This is becoming increasingly relevant in a world in which large corporate clients seek comprehensive global marketing solutions provided by firms with diverse service offerings under one holding company brand.

What Do These Vignettes Suggest?

These examples suggest several things. The first is indisputable: In many cases, *a "one company" culture is very difficult, and may be uneconomic, to achieve.* This is particularly true if it requires that all subsidiaries be led and managed with the same set of basic assumptions. Important differences in behavior resulting from different basic assumptions from one culture to another may be quite subtle.

A common set of values may be the most that a global organization can hope for. But the same value may be interpreted in different ways depending on local assumptions. "Integrity" appears among the values espoused by many global organizations. But what does it mean to managers on an everyday basis in similar jobs around the world? How do they interpret it in practice? And where are lines drawn regarding its practice? For example, in some parts of the world, lavish entertaining that includes gift-giving is considered essential to doing business. Elsewhere, it may be viewed as crossing the line on bribery and even breaking laws. I recall remarking on the beauty of an oriental rug in the office of a senior manager at GM's New York headquarters. He told me it was the subject of some soul-searching in the organization. It had been proffered by an important local customer to a GM country manager in the Middle East, who had to decide on the spot whether to violate company policy by accepting the rug or risk insulting the customer. He decided to accept the rug, send it to New York, and have it registered as company property.

This leaves us with the conclusion that, in efforts to implement a "one company" culture globally, *it is most practical in the short term to give less emphasis to common assumptions and values. Instead, we should concentrate on behaviors, establishing and maintaining a common set of behaviors that can be made explicit, understood, measured, and controlled globally.* That's what CEMEX did in defining policies concerning bribery. Because learning about shared assumptions and values is such a complex and time-consuming task, the best way to access a "foreign" culture may be through its accepted behaviors while learning why those behaviors are important.[22] One team of researchers came to the following conclusion:

> Effectively shared practices are the reason that multinational corporations can function at all. Employing personnel from a variety of nationalities, they cannot assume common values. They coordinate and control their operations through worldwide practices inspired by their national origin...but that can be learned by employees from a variety of other national origins.[23]

Some behaviors are more universally effective than others, as pointed out by former GE CEO Jack Welch:

> Many outsiders often asked me, "How can the GE culture possibly work in various cultures across the world?" The answer to that question was always the same: Treat people with dignity and give them voice. That's a message that translates around the globe.[24]

Third, *culture both influences and reflects an organization's global strategy*. A common "one company" culture may be more important in some businesses than in others. The importance of global customers to a business may influence the path chosen regarding an organization's culture. Global customers often benefit from one point of contact with one set of rules for engagement. This suggests a bias toward a "one company" approach to values, beliefs, and even behaviors, especially if they are following such a strategy themselves.

ISS, CEMEX, and the Omnicom Group have all realized a substantial portion of their growth through acquisition. The culture of a potential acquisition target is an important factor in the decision. It can be a strong determinant of an acquirer's ability to retain talent. This is of special importance to the Omnicom Group, in which client relationships are often established and maintained at the level of the professionals, not necessarily the firm. CEMEX's culture of long hours and substantial travel and its custom of expending whatever effort it takes to get a job done is not for everyone. It is anathema to some, requiring CEMEX's management to take into account an acquiree's culture as well as such strategic matters as market opportunity.

In some respects, culture follows the brand as well. At the Omnicom Group, for example, a global brand is important at the agency network level (advertising agency BBDO or public relations firm Fleishman Hillard), where strong cultures do exist. Hence, up to now there has been little logic in imposing a "one company" culture across all its agencies in a business where personal relationships have much cultural significance. It will be interesting to see whether this policy has to be modified to accommodate a growing number of clients who now appear to be seeking comprehensive "holding company" solutions to their problems.

Fourth, the operating and economic *trade-offs of creating a "one company" culture vary*. Most global organizations have found common financial management and information technology to be effective, especially in the new world of the Internet. However, laws vary so greatly that a similar approach to legal services is less common. Efforts to maintain a "one company" culture can involve unusually high costs for travel, particularly in a culture emphasizing the importance of face-to-face contact, such as CEMEX's. It's not for everyone, because it can require stamina and take a toll on personal lives.

On the other hand, a "one company" culture can provide opportunities for the development of managerial talent that don't exist in a decentralized organization. At General Electric, a group headed by the CEO conducts a periodic "Session C" review of the top several hundred managers, regardless of business or location in the world. This leads to decisions about future individual assignments and development needs. This review takes advantage of the company's broad business reach to expand the opportunities available to each executive for further development.

Fifth, *organizations based on some national cultures may be more successful in integrating acquired organizations into a "one company" culture than others*. For example, it isn't an accident that a Mexican-based company employing large numbers of engineers has been singularly successful in merging organizations it has acquired into a "one company" global stance. These engineers have "linear-active" tendencies and come from a country that has a "multi-active" culture (to use terminology cited earlier). Chances are these engineers display less arrogance, more humility, a greater willingness to listen, and a tendency to adopt best-practice ideas from acquired organizations than managers from one of the world's "Big Five" economies.

Sixth, *effective cultures can provide a sense of purpose and direction that enables acquirers to bridge what I think of as a "culture credibility gap."* This gap is illustrated by an experience I had with a major pharmaceutical company. It brought together the country managers of its European subsidiaries to compare notes on the correlation between employee and customer satisfaction and the successful introduction of new products at the country level. As it turns out, the correlation on these dimensions was remarkably positive and high. The "problem" was that among the European countries represented at the meeting, Greece ranked much higher on all dimensions than Germany and France. Corporate executives were worried that unless the importance of the data was underscored by an impartial expert, country managers from those larger countries would discount the comparisons, just as they generally discounted most of the things done in the smaller Greek subsidiary. In any global organization, perhaps the most valuable function of headquarters is to encourage a best-practice mentality among subcultures in which good ideas are transferred from one part of the world to another. This requires bridging the culture credibility gap.

CEMEX's experiences, for example, in its newly acquired large U.S. subsidiary, a former competitor, suggest that one way to overcome an initial "culture credibility gap" is with a set of clearly stated and adhered-to values. This must be coupled with behaviors that work and make work life more satisfying.

Seventh, *all these organizations have "universities" or extensive management development programs.* As someone who has taught at leadership seminars in four of the companies described in this chapter, I have observed that formal education is probably the least important objective of such programs. Instead, they allow participants to get to know and learn best practice from each other, thus capitalizing on one of the real benefits of a global organization. At the same time, they share views about a common set of values and form business relationships that can endure over many time zones.

General Electric has made particularly good use of management development to encourage adherence to values such as speed, simplicity, and, most important, boundarylessness (willingness to share talent, other resources, and ideas across organizational boundaries). Its educational venture, centered at a campus in Crotonville, New York, is an extension of the critical "Session C" process of executive appraisal and development noted earlier.

One such program, the Executive Development Course, annually gathers groups of particularly promising senior executives. They study together and work in teams on a problem of particular concern to senior management at that point in time. As part of their assignment, teams are dispatched around the world in search of best practice both within and outside General Electric on such topics as continuous improvement, Six Sigma Quality, and administrative systems. At the climax of their work, the teams present their findings to top management. Whether or not their recommendations are accepted, they have shared an experience designed to both cement their dedication to a common set of values and foster boundaryless behavior.

Eighth, *the "cultural significance" of a company's business may affect the feasibility of a "one company" culture globally.* Although CEMEX executives might disagree with this assertion, there is less cultural significance in the act of manufacturing and distributing cement than in delivering marketing services in various parts of the world. Relationships with clients are less frequent, personal, and complex. CEMEX executives are less frequently confronted with the subtleties of language that the Omnicom Group's people face constantly. Freed of the complications of subtly different demands on each of its businesses, this makes a "one company" culture more feasible. Even at ISS, cleaning and other services may have a moderate amount of cultural significance. For example, what is "clean" in various parts of the world? How is it measured? And what does it take to deliver it by means of a process that is largely unseen and hard to supervise? Questions such as these raise a legitimate debate among the company's leaders about whether it should pursue a "one company" or more diversified culture.

There are few cases in which "cultural significance" mattered more than in Dutch-based Unilever's acquisition of Ben & Jerry's. Unilever purchased the premium ice cream maker based in Vermont as an addition to its North American Ice Cream Group in April of 2000. The Ben & Jerry's brand is centered around high-quality, innovative, fun ice cream products. (They are called "euphoric concoctions" in the mission statement shown in the following sidebar). Ben & Jerry's retains its strong, evocative mission and values regarding the environment and social issues. Unilever's acquisition raised questions about just what this large, diversified, global consumer goods manufacturer would make of its new purchase. The company was quick to resolve the uncertainty by making an unusual announcement: "Under terms of the agreement, Ben & Jerry's will operate separately from Unilever's current U.S. ice cream business (Breyer's), with an independent Board of Directors to *provide leadership for Ben & Jerry's social mission and brand integrity.*"[25]

Whatever the intent, Unilever tapped a 24-year company veteran, Yves Couette, to head up the subsidiary. For a period of several years, there was less talk of Ben & Jerry's social mission, until 2004, when Couette was succeeded as CEO (Chief Euphoric Officer) by Walt Freese, a B&J insider with experience in other large organizations. At the time of Freese's departure in 2010 to "pursue other values-led business and investment opportunities," he was lauded in a somewhat pointed statement for being "instrumental in *returning* Ben & Jerry's to its heritage of leadership in progressive social and environmental values ..."[26] So much for a "one company" culture at Unilever in the face of such differences.

These examples illustrate other issues of particular importance in several decisions critical to the success of a global strategy in an organization with a strong and effective culture: the selection of leaders, the way in which relationships between headquarters and subsidiaries are managed, and the ways in which effort is organized and controlled.

Ben & Jerry's Mission and Values

Mission

Ben & Jerry's is founded on and dedicated to a sustainable corporate concept of linked prosperity. Our mission consists of 3 interrelated parts...

Social mission: To operate the Company in a way that actively recognizes the central role that business plays in society by initiating innovative ways to improve the quality of life locally, nationally and internationally.

Product mission: To make, distribute and sell the finest quality all natural ice cream and euphoric concoctions with a continued commitment to incorporating wholesome, natural ingredients and promoting business practices that respect the Earth and the Environment.

continued

Economic mission: To operate the Company on a sustainable financial basis of profitable growth, increasing value for our stake-holders and expanding opportunities for development and career growth for our employees.

Values: We have a progressive, nonpartisan social mission that seeks to meet human needs and eliminate injustices in our local, national and international communities by integrating these concerns into our day-to-day business activities. Our focus is on children and families, the environment and sustainable agriculture on family farms.

Capitalism and the wealth it produces do not create opportunity for everyone equally. We recognize that the gap between the rich and the poor is wider than at any time since the 1920's. We strive to create economic opportunities for those who have been denied them and to advance new models of economic justice that are sustainable and replicable.

By definition, the manufacturing of products creates waste. We strive to minimize our negative impact on the environment.

The growing of food is overly reliant on the use of toxic chemicals and other methods that are unsustainable. We support sustainable and safe methods of food production that reduce environmental degradation, maintain the productivity of the land over time, and support the economic viability of family farms and rural communities.

We seek and support nonviolent ways to achieve peace and justice. We believe government resources are more productively used in meeting human needs than in building and maintaining weapons systems.

We strive to show a deep respect for human beings inside and outside our company and for the communities in which they live.

Source: Adapted from the company's web site, ben&jerrys.com

The Selection of Leaders

Few would dispute the notion that successful leadership in a global setting requires special sensitivity to the needs and mores of those being led. Such leaders often have cross-cultural backgrounds and experiences as well as the willingness and ability to learn languages and customs. This is in addition to such general qualifications as a sense of direction and a determination to achieve it, an open mind, an ability to listen, humility and perspective, and a good balance between pride in the organization and a constant effort to discourage arrogance. But beyond sensitivity, a leader may face cultural challenges as well. One story provides an interesting example of this:

> Managers in experienced multinationals like IBM, Unilever, and ABB are skilled at choosing the right person for each environment. Unilever recently needed a manager to supervise their marketing operations in South America. A Brazilian or an Argentinean might have been resented in some of the smaller countries and certainly in each other's. They chose an Indian executive and provided him with quality language and cross-cultural training. Not only did his nationality place him above interregional rivalry, but his keen perception and his Indian characteristics of people orientation, subtle negotiating skills and warmth made him someone Latin Americans could easily relate to.[27]

In addition to the usual travails of leadership, expatriate leaders in a multinational organization are exposed to the risks of culture shock, disorientation, and charges of cultural insensitivity or ignorance on the one hand and "going native" on the other. This is a particular affliction of nationalities comprising the world's largest economies, beginning with the United States, China, and Japan, according to one study.[28] Other studies point out that perhaps one-third of expatriates who are sent to manage in foreign environments return home prematurely, while many others remain abroad while suffering the continuing pain of disorientation.[29] Efforts to alleviate this problem through careful selection and preparation have been aided by the development of technologies enabling expatriates to communicate regularly on a face-to-face basis with colleagues at headquarters. If overused, however, such technologies can delay the expatriate executive's orientation to a local culture.

The practical costs of poor selection and training and, as a result, disorientation most often emerge during negotiation and the administration of contracts. Here it is important for each party to understand the basic assumptions and values that influence the behaviors and even the body language being observed at the negotiating table and beyond. Compound this with the necessity and advisability of employing interpreters for executives negotiating in a language other than their first, and it is easy to understand the challenges facing an expatriate leader.

Based on his groupings of cultural characteristics cited earlier in this chapter, Richard Lewis describes the kinds of behaviors they may produce during a negotiation:

> Germans will ask you all the difficult questions from the start.... The Japanese...must like you and trust you.... Like the Germans, they will ask many questions about price, delivery, and quality, but the Japanese will ask them all ten times.... Finns and Swedes expect modernity, efficiency, and new ideas.[30]

Contract negotiations also vary in important ways that, if not understood, can lead to costly disputes and litigation. Again, in Lewis' words:

> Americans, British, Germans, Swiss, and Finns are among those who regard a written agreement as something that, if not holy, is certainly final.... For the Japanese, on the other hand, the contract they were uncomfortable in signing anyway is merely a statement of intent. They will adhere to it as best they can but will not feel bound by it if market conditions suddenly change, if anything in it contradicts common sense, or if they feel cheated or legally trapped by it.... An Italian or Argentinean sees the contract as...an ideal scheme.... But the way they see it, we do not live in the best of worlds, and the outcome we can realistically expect will fall somewhat short of the actual terms agreed.[31]

If these generalities applied to all persons of any of these nationalities, managers could know what to expect in their negotiating activities. But of course they don't. Nevertheless, these generalizations underline the importance of preparation as well as opportunities afforded by everyday efforts to bring people of different backgrounds, assumptions, and values into continuing working relationships with one another.

Managing the Relationship Between Headquarters and Subsidiaries

From the perspective of managers at headquarters, who knows what bizarre things are going on in an organization's operating subsidiaries—things that require constant oversight and control? At the same time, those in the subsidiary believe that people at headquarters make poor decisions about resource allocation, have little understanding of how sales and profits are actually realized, and charge for services that could be purchased at much lower cost locally. This is true in any organization, but in the multinational it is exaggerated. Other challenges exist as well, including staffing, communication, and coordination.

Staffing

Unless international experience is valued as a condition of promotion, it will be difficult to entice talent to spend time in a foreign subsidiary, possibly as part of an effort to reinforce a "one company" culture. The assumption that you are "out of sight, out of mind" during time spent abroad may limit such assignments to senior members of the organization who have already been recognized and promoted for their work. I found this to be a particular challenge in staffing a European executive program offered by the Harvard Business School in the 1970s and 1980s. It was nearly impossible to convince a junior, nontenured faculty member to take the risk of moving overseas for two or three years and therefore out of the purview of colleagues who

would be making a joint decision on her promotion. Another partnership with a similar promotion review process, Goldman Sachs,
encountered this age-old problem as well when it sought to build a
strong position in European investment banking by establishing a substantial base in London in the early 1980s. According to one observer,
"For many years London was the Siberia of investment banking, a
place to banish those the firm hoped to forget."[32] In that case, international experience was established as an important consideration in
promotion to the rank of partner. This created a strong incentive for
those seeking a highly lucrative partner position to consider a potential transfer to London.

Communication

Too often, communication between headquarters and the field
takes its cues from the configuration of the organization chart—that
is, either top-down or bottom-up, with a stronger emphasis on the
former. To combat this phenomenon when she was CEO of the Girl
Scouts of the USA, Frances Hesselbein went so far as to encourage
a different mind-set. She created a circular organization chart that
emphasized the importance of communication around the perime-
ter as well as between the hub and spokes.[33] The problem of insuf-
ficient input "from the field" confronts all organizations, but it can
have disastrous results in a global organization in which challenges
of communication can take on added dimensions for subsidiaries
operating in different cultures. It can lead to everything from resent-
ment among employees to misfires in product introductions. Perhaps
the most frequently cited example of the latter was the introduction
of the Chevrolet Nova in Latin America. As the story goes, "No va"
translates into "Doesn't go" in Spanish, which hurt sales of the auto.
This story has always served as an example of poor communication
between GM marketing in Detroit and the field. Although the breakdown was probably exaggerated, because "nova" is not a Spanish
word, it's quite possible that some Latin American Nova owners who
became disgruntled with the car created a play on words. This occur-
rence might have been anticipated if more feedback from the field
had been obtained in advance of the launch.

There is a natural tendency for headquarters personnel—even those in finance, human resources, and other central functions charged with serving international subsidiaries—to perform for those nearest to them. They particularly want to impress those to whom they report and who control their fortunes in the organization. The natural reaction from the field is to recreate such staff support functions either regionally or nationally. Whether at global or regional headquarters, incentives can be developed to encourage central staffers to look outward rather than upward for performance rewards. This often requires substantial travel budgets, as we saw at CEMEX, even in an age of Internet conferencing.

Global organizations have turned to the adoption of a common language, often English, to facilitate communication. In my experience, this has had mixed results. First, it incorrectly assumes a common facility with the language, a shortcoming that continues to create communication problems. Second, members of such organizations often revert to their native language when given the opportunity, encouraging the formation of "cultural cliques" that exclude others.

Organizing, Coordinating, and Controlling Effort

The way in which efforts are organized can help in dealing with several of the challenges of the global organization just described. The most successful methods are based on several assumptions:

- In spite of remarkable new technologies to facilitate videoconferencing, there is no substitute for periodic face-to-face contact between personnel from headquarters and various regional or national subsidiaries.
- The most useful communication and cooperation take place around the organization's most important work.
- Projects with important missions, clear objectives, and explicit performance measurements and follow-up involving teams staffed from across an organization provide the most useful ways of facilitating a "one company" mentality. They also discourage biases toward strict hierarchies that exist in many cultures.

These assumptions underlie, for example, the global projects organized and carried out by multinational teams in GE's Executive Development Course for its highest-potential managers, described earlier.

The use of teams for project work deserves special attention. One observer has concluded, for example, that diverse teams:

> Generate more alternatives, respond better to cultural preferences in local markets, (do) better local forecasting (and)... critical analysis. They provide "broader perspectives" and achieve better product design.... Leaders emerge.... A language of communication evolves, as do problem-solving routines.... Everyone learns from everyone else.[34]

When the teams are international, interesting things occur. Geert Hofstede has cautioned that the success of teams in global organizations may depend on the nature of the task (favoring tasks that are clearly defined and urgent) or the team's composition.[35] The greater the diversity of team members, the less the likelihood that those from any one culture will dominate the work.

Senior managers without international experience often overlook the fact that methods of controlling effort have particularly strong cultural implications in a global organization. Although this is a vast subject, one example may make the point. U.S. organizations have often been stymied in their efforts to export management by objectives (MBO) initiatives to other countries. Hofstede, who notes that "planning and control systems for management largely were made in the United States," points out the following:

> MBO reflects an American value position in that it presupposes the following: (1) that the subordinate is sufficiently independent to negotiate meaningfully with his boss.... (2) that both superior and subordinate are prepared to take some risks.... (3) that performance is seen as an important criterion by both. Because these don't exist in many cultures, MBO too often fails as an export.[36]

This again underlines the importance of two-way, cross-organization communication in the planning, not just the implementation, of policies and processes for organizing and controlling effort in a global organization.

Implications for Subcultures in General

The basic question confronting the leadership of any organization, whether global or not, is whether to accept or change local subcultures.

Subcultures exist in all organizations of any size. For example, suppose you walk into the marketing and information technology units at ING Direct, the financial services organization that prides itself on its "Orange Code" culture discussed in Chapter 2. You will see distinct differences in everything from office décor to preferred dress to certain behaviors among people housed in the same building. Salespeople may operate from a different base of assumptions than the "techies" in IT, even if they are of the same national origin.

The most frequent approach to this issue is to create yet another subculture, this one for the entire organization. When it comes down to it, that's basically what this book is about.

Summary

Although it is dangerous to generalize, the work of "culturalists" in identifying differences in national or regional cultures can help you understand the things that distinguish global subcultures from one another. If they aren't understood, these differences can lead to blunders from strategy to staffing, sabotage negotiations, and discourage organization-wide efforts.

Culturalists divide the world into culture types. One such scheme sees people as being either linear-active (such as Americans and Swiss, who, among many other things, plan ahead methodically and are unemotional), multi-active (such as Latin Americans and Indians, who plan in terms of only grand outlines and are emotional), or reactive (such as Japanese and Chinese, who think in terms of general principles rather than specific plans and show little emotion).

The point is that some types of cultures don't mix well under certain conditions. Leaders' sensitivity to these possibilities is critical in assigning the right personnel to, and creating the right organization for, the task at hand. In general, leaders from the world's largest economies—the United States, China, Japan, Germany, and the U.K.—are thought to be more culturally "challenged" in fostering cross-cultural coordination than those from other economies.

Subcultures are common to all organizations. But global operations, unlike those conducted in relatively homogeneous cultures, produce subcultures in which assumptions and values are much more deeply ingrained than in the functional cultures—marketing, finance, or operations—found in a typical "domestic" organization. This poses a basic question for leadership of whether to try to achieve a "one company" culture—a formidable task—or whether to attempt to coordinate management efforts among subsidiaries with different cultures often influenced by national origins.

True "one company" cultures are built upon common shared assumptions and values. Their practical value results from the transactional efficiencies based on trust and even such things as a common operating language and "organizational shorthand" (resulting in messages that are received in the manner in which they were intended). Those who have sought to create "one company" cultures in multinational organizations have found that it may be most feasible to first achieve behavior change, with leadership setting the example, and then use that as a springboard to understand ways of changing values and even share assumptions. In most cases, the most that may be hoped for is the creation of a "center subculture" that is different and apart from the subcultures of global subsidiaries.

Practitioners of the "one company" philosophy may strive for a common set of values and behaviors in their organizations. But even those seeking a common set of values may be confronted with the problem of interpretation. For example, what does the commonly cited value of "integrity" mean among people who harbor different basic assumptions? This leaves us with a more realistic goal of achieving common behaviors fostered by "see and do" leadership across global subcultures.

Forms of organization that foster team efforts and continual cooperation between members of different subcultures are critical to a "one company" culture. In some organizations this is achieved through management teams made up of overlapping membership representing important businesses and offices located in financial markets around the world.

Educational programs combined with cross-cultural team assignments can be a particularly effective way to bridge cultural gaps.

Managing relationships between headquarters and subsidiary personnel is a situation ripe for mutual misunderstanding, condescension, and distrust. When put in a global context, decisions concerning staffing, communications, coordination, and control are especially critical in dealing with such natural tendencies.

It should go without saying that leadership in a global organization can benefit from international experience. This can be more easily spoken about than achieved, especially if there is little effort to counter the "out of sight, out of mind" mentality that encourages the best talent to stay close to headquarters and in the sight of senior managers who will be acting on their promotions. This often requires establishing international experience as a condition for ascending to senior management.

Candidates for senior positions should be sensitive to the fact that many administrative tools—management by objective (MBO), reengineering, kaizan, and others—are centric to a particular national culture (in these examples, the United States or Japan) and therefore are of questionable use in many cultures operating from a different base of assumptions.

Beyond this, when *staffing* to achieve a global strategy, it is important to emphasize always-important characteristics such as open-mindedness, the ability to listen, and boundaryless attitudes and behaviors.

Effective *communication* requires much more than establishing an official "global language," as many organizations with global aspirations have done. For example, organization becomes a critical factor in encouraging communication, particularly in the exchange of best practices. It can emphasize the use of teams and committees made up of members from diverse backgrounds focused on the organization's important work. It should encourage and reward "face-to-face" communication, by means of both the Internet and extensive travel. Budgets have to reflect the need for these activities.

Communication in successful global organizations involves heavy reliance on "field in" comments, suggestions, and inputs into important decisions involving such things as the design and introduction of new products intended for a global market or the implementation of new administrative practices. These take precedence over the temptation to create a "headquarters out" mentality.

Staffing and communication are reinforced by *coordination and control* in the global setting. For example, the most useful role for headquarters personnel may well be the identification and dissemination of best practices among global operating units. If so, performance measures and incentives for those at the center should reflect the importance of this activity. Firmwide incentives may be established along with those tied to a subsidiary's performance in rewarding managers employed in various parts of the world to encourage a "one company" mentality among everyone.

Several global company vignettes presented in this chapter suggest the following:

- A "one company" culture is difficult to achieve in a global setting.
- In implementing a "one company" culture, it is advisable to de-emphasize establishing common assumptions and values and instead concentrate on instituting common behaviors.
- Culture both influences and reflects an organization's global strategy.
- There are substantial trade-offs in creating a "one company" culture.
- Organizations based on some national cultures may be more successful in integrating acquired organizations into a "one company" culture than others.
- Effective cultures can provide the sense of purpose and direction that enables acquirers to bridge the "culture credibility" gap.
- Extensive management development programs can help provide the "glue" so important to a "one company" global strategy.
- The "cultural significance" of a company's business may affect the feasibility of a "one company" culture globally.

The bottom line is that culture has to play an exaggerated role in the strategic decision to expand globally. The culture of a potential acquirer of a foreign subsidiary or developer of a global opportunity can expand or constrain choices. Which will it be?

11

Mission-Driven Organizations: Special Challenges

Some organizations are intensely mission-driven. They "know why" they exist. It is usually to fulfill a mission of discovery (adventure and learning), altruism (putting customers or employees first), or heroism (changing entire industries or how we live), to use three of the categories developed by Nikos Mourkogiannis.[1] Those associating themselves with such organizations often have strong, clearly articulated reasons for doing so. They feel intensely about their association. Wendy Kopp, founder and CEO of Teach for America, in response to a question about how her organization creates a sense of mission, replied, "Maybe this is easier in our endeavor than some, in the sense that we're looking for people who are magnetized by this notion, this vision, that one day all children in our nation should have the opportunity to attain an excellent education."[2]

Particularly strong cultures form around such missions. Although many not-for-profit organizations fit this description, these phenomena may occur in for-profits as well, as we saw earlier with Service-Master, ING Direct, and Ben & Jerry's. Mission-driven organizations have an extra sense of urgency to succeed. They also present special challenges for leadership.

Supergrowth

Because of its nature, a mission-driven organization often has demand in excess of supply for a social service (feeding the hungry, as at CARE) or product (special medicine to cure the sick). The organization also has a built-in desire to grow as fast as possible. Rapid growth and the maintenance of a healthy culture are not always compatible. This was the challenge faced by the leadership of Willow Creek Community Church several years ago in carrying out its mission to "save souls."[3]

Willow Creek is a leader in the "megachurch" movement. It was a pioneer in attracting the "unchurched" to its church in suburban Chicago through "seeker services" largely devoid of religious icons and featuring music and drama along with entertaining sermons. Seekers are encouraged to become "believers," for whom separate services are conducted. Believers also join "ministries" ranging from book discussion to auto repair groups that provide outlets for their talents and interests while making the megachurch seem smaller.

Not only does founder Pastor Bill Hybels provide inspiration from the pulpit, but he also applies his skills and interests to the task of making Willow Creek a well-managed organization. For example, every sermon is rated for its quality through the organization's quality control process. Ministries are created only when a member steps forward to volunteer to lead one. The church campus, called "Main Street" and with the feel of a mall, is maintained up to Disney World–standards as part of an effort to maintain the church's image. So far, so good.

Several years after its founding, Willow Creek reached a point where its Sunday services were attracting as many as 20,000 people, most of them "seekers." Planned interactions between "seekers" and "believers" at these services were not occurring for many in attendance. The "traffic ministry" had to be out in force to direct thousands of cars to the church's parking lots. The church had reached a point at which fewer seekers were becoming believers. Without believers, the church's stewardship would falter. Clearly, growth threatened Willow Creek's future.

Hybels and his leadership team decided that the organization's mission and culture were being diluted. In an organization with a strong bias toward growth, the church took a courageous step, especially for a religious organization. It decided to stop making an effort to encourage new seekers to attend services until it could formulate a plan for the future that would enable it to grow while maintaining its basic mission.

The planning effort led to a dramatic strategic decision. To accommodate growth and maintain the local "feel" of its religious experience, Willow Creek's leadership decided to neither expand its mother church nor establish another. It chose instead to create the Willow Creek Association, a kind of franchising organization responsible for assisting local churches with similar evangelical beliefs around the world to improve the quality of their services. The Association, for a modest fee, each year provides organizing plans, text for sermons, quality control methods, religious study materials, and leadership training events in more than 250 cities in 50 countries. Currently, the Willow Creek Association has enlisted more than 10,000 member churches in 35 countries.[4]

Loss of Focus: "Mission Creep"

Focus: HOPE was founded in the wake of the 1967 racial rioting in Detroit. The riots left entire neighborhoods with burned-out wreckage that quickly deteriorated into what one resident described as "property that would be improved by a strong tornado." Its founders were a priest, Father William Cunningham, teaching in a suburban seminary school, and the mother of several of his students, Eleanor Josaitis. Cunningham and Josaitis didn't just vow to do something to provide "intelligent and practical solutions to racism."[5] They moved into the neighborhood (at great emotional cost to Josaitis, who incurred the wrath of her family and in-laws for taking her five children into the inner city). They took up their task in a nearby parish. First they opened a food bank as part of a longer-range effort to meet their goal of helping people better themselves and their families through improved health and good jobs. Cunningham, a charismatic figure, and Josaitis, a determined, organized manager, made a good team whose abilities complemented one another. They saw an opportunity to partner with Detroit's dominant economic institutions—its automakers.

They set out to convince the auto companies to help fund and equip a training facility to prepare people to work in local auto manufacturing plants and to hire Focus: HOPE's graduates. They achieved some success and learned from some setbacks. The biggest lesson was that many people were not prepared to learn. In response, Focus: HOPE created more basic educational programs. The students' children needed nurturing while they were in training and afterward. This led to the creation of one of the most impressive nursery schools I've ever visited, designed to take in children from the age of six weeks. Rather than prepare people for low-paying, menial tasks, Focus: HOPE acquired computer-aided machinery for instruction in state-of-the-art skills and higher-paying jobs. In 1997, after Cunningham's death, Josaitis not only continued the mission but rebuilt the organization facilities after a tornado actually did hit the community. Her success was due in part to a clear mission coupled with a set of values that have produced behaviors that can be characterized with terms such as "no-nonsense" and "tough love."

Ironically, Focus: HOPE became almost too good at what it does, ministering to the residents of inner-city Detroit. At the peak of its success, it was asked by the city's mayor to take the lead in rebuilding the area around its facilities, at the time a wasteland of deteriorating homes and vacant lots. The offer was attractive. After all, this would contribute directly to the redevelopment of the organization's neighborhood and benefit the lives of some Focus: HOPE students and graduates. Even more important, it would help create jobs for the organization's students, although not the jobs for which they were currently training.

Focus: HOPE's challenge is common to successful organizations in the social sector. They face the possibility of "mission creep." When asked about fear of failure and how it influences decisions, Wendy Kopp said that one of the things she had learned from the near-failure of her organization, Teach for America, was "the importance of focus, and saying no. There was so much momentum and we were launching new, good ideas. But they took away resources and energy from the fundamental core of what we do, which we came back to believing was the most important thing."[6]

Back in Detroit, Josaitis ultimately decided to reject the mayor's proposal because it represented a poor fit with Focus: HOPE's strategy and would distract the organization from its partnership with the auto industry. Just as important, there was concern that the initiative would dilute the organization's culture by introducing trainees with a different set of interests than those already being served by Focus: HOPE.

Making a Large Organization Seem Small

The rapid growth associated with many organizations operating in the social sector (or in commercial organizations with altruistic or heroic missions) can be an enemy of maintaining an effective culture.

Cultures are intensified in smaller organizational units. That's why Willow Creek Community Church created ministries centered around the interests of its members as the church grew. At Walmart, the basic organizational unit around which a culture forms is the store. At Nucor, the steelmaker, it's the minimill employing no more than a couple of hundred employees, of which Nucor currently operates 21. It explains why ING Direct limits the size of its service centers that field calls and requests from its banking customers to 250 employees, requiring the creation of seven centers in four cities by 2010. These small centers do the work that one large center could do, but with greater devotion to maintaining a strong and supportive culture and level of customer service. It helps explain why ING Direct earns the highest customer service ratings among all financial services companies in the United States.

Small, team-based units have the additional benefit, as discussed in Chapter 6, of creating a work environment in which team members exert peer pressure on each other. This enables management to delegate responsibilities to teams with some assurance that they will be met.

Deploying Human Resources: The Challenge of Volunteer Labor

Mission-driven organizations often do not devote the effort to recruitment that it deserves. People, attracted by the mission, select themselves into mission-driven organizations. Self-selection has both benefits and consequences, particularly in organizations utilizing volunteer labor. People know why they are volunteering to work in a mission-driven organization, or at least they think they do. But there can be a tendency to glamorize the opportunity. People want to be put to work on important tasks. And too often, the selection process is too casual. Not enough attention is given to describing the reality of the job, the bad times as well as the good times.

Another problem is that volunteers often want to work on meaningful tasks on their terms, perhaps a few hours here and there that fit their schedules and other commitments. For some time, this was a challenge confronting the leaders of Habitat for Humanity. This organization is dedicated to "eliminating substandard housing and homelessness worldwide and to making adequate, affordable shelter a matter of conscience and action."[7] Habitat for Humanity, founded in 1976 by Millard and Linda Fuller, has constructed hundreds of thousands of homes around the world for those in need. The organization uses a great deal of contributed materials and the labor of volunteers, including those who occupy the housing when it is finished.[8]

The challenge of keeping volunteers usefully occupied on projects employing up to 6,000 volunteers building 100 homes in a week is daunting. People volunteer their hearts and minds, but not necessarily their skills, to Habitat for Humanity. People can get hurt building a house if they lack knowledge of or skills in certain jobs. Training is often necessary, even for those volunteering for a few hours. Methods have to be worked out for scheduling volunteers, making sure they are trained for the jobs to which they might be assigned. They are encouraged to volunteer for as many hours or days as possible or, better yet, the completion of a piece of work or a specific assignment. All of this has to be designed for a group of people who feel very strongly about the organization's mission, values, and beliefs.

Volunteers are selected for attitude. Are they joining up for the right reasons? What beliefs do they bring to their work? In particular, do they expect to be given extra recognition because of the value of the time they are volunteering? If so, they may not make good candidates. Some may have to be turned down. Because they often don't devote enough effort to recruitment, many mission-driven not-for-profits take on volunteers who later prove difficult to organize and manage.

Organizations utilizing volunteers can learn from other mission-driven enterprises, some in for-profit businesses. For example, Viacom's television venture MTV has made extensive use of 18-to-24-year-old volunteers who subscribe to MTV's mission to be "a vehicle for rebellion." The volunteers are the ages of MTV's target audience. They enjoy the working atmosphere of constant buzz, music, and entertainment with others just like them. They credit their affiliation with the company as being a great source of "cool dates." But the company is careful to structure jobs in which volunteers can actually contribute to the work being performed while helping keep management "young" and in tune with MTV's viewers.

There are few rules at MTV. But one concerns the ubiquitous TV sets placed strategically throughout the company's U.S. headquarters that were mentioned in Chapter 1. They may be turned down for important business, but they may not be turned off. As a result, MTV's volunteers constantly hear and react to the content being broadcast. And they influence those programming the channel's content. It is a way of keeping MTV eternally fresh for a rapidly changing target market.

In a sense, people "volunteer" in large numbers to work in organizations such as Google, Apple, and Facebook. As a result, an extra burden is placed on those employed in the selection process for those organizations. It requires that an organization decide exactly what it is looking for, perhaps based on the qualities of people who are already succeeding in the enterprise.

Measuring and Rewarding Effectiveness Among an Organization's Subcultures

Traditionally, board members in for-profit organizations have assumed that their primary responsibility is to the shareholder. The main question raised in meetings is: "Is this strategy or decision in the shareholders' best interests?" If only things were that simple in the typical not-for-profit. Here the proverbial "multiple bottom line" results from the need to deliver results to those served by the organization (often hungry, ill, or indigent) as well as those providing the sources of funding for the enterprise. In addition, staff and board members have to feel that their efforts are being rewarded, at least in intrinsic ways. This becomes even more complicated when a not-for-profit also seeks to pursue unconventional "for-profit" avenues as well as to become self-supporting. This was the situation that Seattle-based Pioneer Human Services (PHS) faced several years ago.[9]

Pioneer was founded by a former alcoholic to rescue alcoholics jailed for crimes. It was established to provide them with rehabilitation, housing, training, and job placement. Initially the organization survived on contributions from wealthy individuals, many of them recovering alcoholics. But under the leadership of Gary Mulhair, PHS became a national leader in the emerging "entrepreneurial not-for-profit" movement, with much of the organization's revenue based on earned income. Successful "graduates" of Pioneer's programs began shouldering more and more of the financial burden, enabling the organization to acquire real estate for housing and other purposes. Among other businesses, Pioneer even acquired an old hotel in a convenient location in downtown Seattle, which it converted into two blocks of rooms—one for recovering alcoholics and one for tourists. The hotel employs those being rehabilitated.

All of this would not have been possible without a dramatic reorganization that was necessitated by confusion about the mission, values, and measures by which the organization was to be run. Pioneer's early successes and increasing reliance on revenues earned by the organization produced a natural tension between those responsible for not-for-profit services and those responsible for revenue-producing businesses such as real estate and other operations. For example, Gary Mulhair commented on the disparity in wages between those managing businesses and human services this way:

> The human services managers complain that they are not being paid on a par with business managers. That often evokes a response such as "If you don't like it, maybe you should be a machinist rather than a therapist."[10]

Questions arose about what the organization's goals really were and how performance should be measured and recognized. The multiple bottom line threatened to destroy a budding entrepreneurial not-for-profit.

At that time Mulhair took a step that few not-for-profits have been willing to take. With the support of his board, he reorganized PHS into separate divisions responsible for real estate, other business streams of revenue, and not-for-profit services. Each had its own targets, measures of performance, and sources of recognition. The move restored order to the multiple bottom line and eliminated many of the questions about first- and second-class "citizenship" among staff members.

Even these moves didn't eliminate all the tensions. Not only did measures need to be maintained for each part of the enterprise, but policies needed to be devised to handle situations in which the organization's social and financial goals came into conflict. As Michael Burns, Mulhair's successor, put it: "Because the need is always greater than the available cash flow, we constantly confront a struggle between the parts of the organization providing human services and those creating jobs and running our businesses."[11]

In spite of the tensions, Pioneer has expanded its enterprises, each of which employs Pioneer clients. Today they include such things as precision sheet metal manufacturing, both internal and for-hire construction, wholesale food distribution to nonprofit organizations, catering and café operations, institutional food services to hospitals and others, and contract packaging for several major corporations. In 2009, even in a difficult economic environment, Pioneer took in nearly $61 million in revenue that was used to serve nearly 12,800 clients.[12] Its reports reflect measures of effectiveness used by the organization. They contain graphs of such things as changes in net assets and return on average equity.

Coordinating Efforts with Other Mission-Driven Organizations

Mission-driven organizations rarely "play together" well. A census of organizations providing community social services in any large metropolitan area will reveal that tens and sometimes even hundreds of organizations provide essentially the same service or seek the same results. Discussions among leaders of such organizations that I have facilitated have suggested that they find it very difficult to coordinate their efforts, no matter how desirable this may be. Several things get in the way:

- Differing underlying assumptions resulting from such things as religious faiths
- Differing philosophies about how to achieve the same objective
- Preservation of the jobs, especially that of the CEO, in the cooperating organizations
- Opposition from boards of directors with members committed to a certain set of assumptions and values as well as a mission

Rarely do such organizations merge. Instead, they reach agreements about how they will cooperate, such as creating boundaries in serving children of different ages or in serving the same children with different needs. Such agreements include processes for referring clients across organizational boundaries rather than "hoarding" them. These agreements have enabled cooperating organizations to produce better results with fewer resources.

Some of the most successful partnerships have occurred between for-profit and not-for-profit organizations. City Year, for example, recruits urban youth (more than 14,000 to date) to work in teams that are "adopted" and funded by various commercial organizations. The workplaces then enlist their employees to help a City Year team with its community improvement work. Much of this work has been with at-risk children. It has "engaged more than (a million)...citizens in service" in 18 U.S. cities as well as London, U.K., and Johannesburg, South Africa.[13]

Such partnerships between for-profit and not-for-profit organizations have been used effectively by the for-profit partner to build "engagement" among talented employees seeking to become involved in community activities as part of a good "day job."

Managing Board and Leadership Conflicts Concerning Basic Assumptions

Board members in many commercial organizations typically recognize the fine line between governance and management, adhering to an "advise and consent" mode concerning proposals made by management. They know that management, not they, will have to implement proposals. Although board members are aware of, and sometimes make reference to, issues regarding an organization's culture, it is not a frequent topic of conversation at board meetings. Compare this to the mission-driven organization, in which the mission, values, and beliefs are often the primary reasons why people agree to serve as board members. They care. And they often express stronger views on issues affecting the mission or values than on the organization's strategy and how it is executed. This was the primary issue confronting many of the CEOs of not-for-profit organizations with whom I worked for several years in an educational venture called The Denali Project.

The Project had a primary goal of encouraging social entrepreneurship. Twenty participants per year, after studying experiences of other organizations such as Pioneer Human Services, were encouraged to prepare business plans making use of some underutilized asset to form a business providing nontraditional sources of support for the organization's primary social mission. The plans were varied and imaginative. Some offered real promise for significant "profit," a word that we used deliberately in the program instead of the more typical not-for-profit equivalent of "surplus." Some plans were implemented. Some were not. The biggest obstacle to implementation proved to be boards that questioned the appropriateness of such activities for their organizations, often with the comment, "I didn't join this board to get into for-profit businesses." In short, a distinct difference in basic assumptions as well as values arose between Denali participants and their boards. Rifts developed in these organizations' cultures. In at least one case, the rifts resulted in directors firing their CEO and shutting down the entrepreneurial initiative.

The moving force behind the Denali Project, Bill Strickland, founder and CEO of the Manchester Bidwell Corporation in inner-city Pittsburgh, faced a reverse governance challenge.[14] Strickland's primary interest is in creating a place where at-risk high school students can be encouraged to remain in school through special instruction in the arts at his Manchester Craftsmen's Guild. Having achieved some success at this, he was asked to inherit Bidwell Training Center, a nearby nearly defunct jobs training center for the unemployed.

He saw both efforts as an opportunity for community revival, with the jobs training center producing revenue from public grants and place-ment fees that could support the art programs. But each organization had developed its own board of directors. Those associated with the Guild were interested in saving at-risk high-schoolers through the arts, using private gifts and government grants. Those on Bidwell's board were accustomed to meeting budgets through job-creating, revenue-producing enterprises such as computer repair and the weatherization of buildings. Transfers of funds from one organization to another, as well as any kind of coordinated planning, were achieved only with what Strickland termed "mutual trust and belief in the overall mission."

It was clear that this informal process would become much more challenging. Plans were made for a 70,000 square foot office build-ing to house both Manchester and Bidwell staff and provide rental income. A 40,000 square foot greenhouse would be built, in which orchids could be grown commercially and people trained for horticul-tural jobs. A music concert series and commercial recording venture would be undertaken. And the Manchester Bidwell concept would be replicated in other cities. Strickland and his boards agreed that it was time to bring in management consultants to provide counsel on the best governance structure going forward. The result was the creation of a super board responsible for both organizing a campaign to build the endowment and reviewing and screening all proposed projects.

The transition was not easy. According to one description:

> An MCG board member called Strickland to announce that she would "resign before playing a subordinate role in the board structure...." An attorney who had just joined the MCG board...indicated that it would be very difficult for him to vote for any venture that might generate significant income that could be tapped by a Super Board.... (Strickland himself believed that he was) "giving up power. But that's what you have to do when you're in the big leagues."[15]

The super board has, over the years, worked to Manchester Bidwell's advantage, but only through the loss of some board mem-bers and the careful selection of their replacements. It has developed both a growing endowment and support for the ventures proposed at the time of its creation, all of which have been accomplished. But most important, it has allowed very different subcultures to flourish in what is now known as the Manchester Bidwell Corporation.

Controlling Zealous Behavior

We talked earlier about the fine line between the development of pride and arrogance in organization cultures. In mission-driven organizations, the issue more often becomes one of managing the line between well-meaning behaviors and what I would call zealotry. For zealots, the ends justify the means. Just as problematic, the ends may color interpretations of the meaning of the organization's core values. Zealotry helps explain sometimes-puzzling actions without diminishing the importance of their effects.

For example, Google has been accused of violating everything from privacy to copyright laws in the name of "organizing and making accessible the world's information." For many observers, it often appears that the zealots are led by Google's founders, Sergey Brin and Larry Page, who are sometimes seen as failing to adhere to the company's core value of "do no evil." History has shown many times, however, that zealotry colors a person's view of good and evil. In Google's case, it may have produced an insensitivity to unintended harm that Google has done to customers, partners, and competition in general.

Walmart, the world's largest private employer, has been excoriated for its personnel policies. Critics say that Walmart has produced hundreds of thousands of underpaid, uninsured, part-time employees who can subsist only by relying on such things as government-provided food stamps and free medical care provided by munificent hospitals. It's interesting that most of the criticism has come from outside the organization, particularly labor organizations (who just might be seeking to organize Walmart employees) and state governments. Walmart employees, given their numbers, have been relatively silent on such issues, with only a few exceptions.[16] Among the possible reasons are that Walmart senior executives themselves are probably underpaid, especially by standards of compensation experts for organizations of its size. They spend relatively large amounts of time in the field working alongside employees in the stores. And they carry on the "we're all in this together" tradition established under the leadership of Sam Walton. As Richard Tedlow has graphically described it:

> Wal-Mart, in other words, was not for everyone. If you wanted to march with the righteous few to lead the customer out of the high-priced house of bondage to the low-priced promised land, Wal-Mart was the company for you. If you were less fervent, there were plenty of other nice companies which were happy to spend on their executives rather than save for their customers where you were welcome to find employment.[17]

But the question remains: How can an organization like Walmart justify such low wages and benefits? One answer is in its mission as "the agent for the customer." That mission gives Walmart a great deal of leverage in dealing with suppliers of everything from products to labor. Any supplier will tell you that Walmart buyers are tough when they're negotiating for their customers. The same is true for human resources. What employees do not receive in pay they are assumed to gain as customers in the form of the everyday low prices. That explains why a visitor to Walmart's Bentonville, Arkansas headquarters doesn't witness guilt on the part of senior executives. Puzzlement at times over complaints against the company? Yes. Guilt? No.

Nevertheless, in recent months Walmart's leadership has announced, as part of a "commitment to cultivate talent within the company," a program to provide online degree programs from an organization that will offer tuition discounts to Walmart's U.S. employees. In addition, Walmart is contributing $50 million over three years to help pay for books and tuition.[18]

Summary

Mission-driven organizations are made up of many people who have selected themselves into the organization with a passionate belief in the organization's shared assumptions and values. This is true whether or not the organization seeks to make a profit. Self-selection can produce savings in recruitment costs. But it poses special challenges to leaders responsible for harnessing the energy of those who believe fervently in the organization's mission.

Mission-driven organizations often face the following challenges:

- Supergrowth resulting from demand that outpaces supply
- Loss of focus
- Preserving the "smallness" of the organization
- Leading volunteers
- Measuring the effort's effectiveness
- Coordinating efforts between organizations
- Managing conflicts between leaders and their boards
- Avoiding zealotry in the pursuit of a mission

Demand often outpaces supply for many mission-driven organizations, particularly those that provide free services, often in the social services sector. When efforts to control growth, often over the objections of organization members, fail, it may be necessary to declare a "time out" to appraise ways of dealing with the situation.

Successful not-for-profits are besieged by expectations that they can do anything successfully. This can subject them to "mission creep," which threatens to produce "culture creep." This requires a mechanism for defining limits and the willingness to say no, often contrary to the wishes of contributors or board members.

Growth inflates organizations, creating the challenge to make them seem small to members expecting an "intimate" relationship as part of their membership. This may require organizing into small groups, such as the "ministries" at Willow Creek Community Church, comprising people with specific interests and skills who can organize themselves in service to the church and its mission. Such efforts help foster "scalability," particularly for organizations facing strong pressures (or a calling) to grow.

Mission-driven organizations often rely heavily on volunteers. Volunteers can be demanding, expecting challenging, interesting work on their own terms, when such expectations are unrealistic. This necessitates special care in the selection process, one in which volunteers are given a frank grounding in what to expect.

Organizations that engage in both for-profit and not-for-profit activities have to establish policies and practices appropriate for each. This requires different measures of performance and compensation practices, among other things, designed to help bridge the gap in subcultures that inevitably develop in such organizations.

Mission-driven organizations generally do not "play together" well. Nor are they good candidates for mergers, particularly in the not-for-profit sector. Rather, they often need to seek agreements to exchange clients and provide complementary services. By way of contrast, mission-driven for-profits and not-for-profits have been successful at working together. In particular, not-for-profits have provided a vehicle by which for-profit partner organizations can signal their concern for social responsibility and offer inspiring, exciting ways to bring employees together away from the job.

Board members agree to serve with a mission-driven organization because of a strong identification with the organization's shared assumptions and values. Their service often involves a special passion. It creates a situation ripe for potential conflict between leadership and the board, especially if the leadership seeks nontraditional sources of income (even for-profit activities) to support the core mission. In such situations, it may be necessary to create separate governance structures for the core and "fringe" activities of the organization, with a "super board" to coordinate plans and activities of the subsidiaries as a whole.

Passion in pursuit of a mission can produce zealous behaviors that lead to decisions that seem puzzling to the world outside the organization—decisions that can have adverse effects for suppliers, partners, and even employees. Where this occurs, it may be necessary to establish processes to ensure that the effects of a pending decision are reviewed by nonzealots with a degree of objectivity.

An organization's culture faces many challenges associated with its mission. Many of these result from a rapidly changing social, economic, competitive, and legal environment. We turn to these issues next.

12

Dealing with Forces That Challenge Organization Cultures Today

Organization cultures develop and take shape from within beginning with a founder or leader. But they are influenced over time by forces at work in the environment. Conventional wisdom is that cultures at their core—the assumptions as well as the values and beliefs on which they are based—change slowly, if at all. In fact, the greater the need for flexibility in responding to a changing environment, the greater the utility of a strong foundation provided by a culture with widely accepted assumptions, values, and beliefs that enable individuals to respond quickly and appropriately to a changing need.

On that dimension, the Catholic Church ranks high. Why has it survived for more than 500 years? Obviously, it is built on a firm set of shared assumptions and values anchored in religious beliefs that give it tremendous strength. But there must be something about those assumptions and values that have allowed it to adjust to many regional cultures and centuries of conflict, misfortune, attack, and even criminal behavior within its ranks. I was reminded of this once when visiting a cathedral in a remote part of Guatemala. The priest, a circuit-rider with responsibilities in several churches, had departed for the day, but my family was invited to assemble with others behind the cathedral for an extracurricular sacrifice of a chicken, a practice certainly not condoned by the Church, but one with which the Church coexisted.

Today, of course, the Church faces challenges directly related to its core beliefs about such things as celibacy and contraception in a world (including many Catholics) highly and justly critical of the behavior of some of its priests. It is characterized by changing beliefs and behaviors, even among its own members. As it has always done, it will rely on core values to guide it even while examining the relevance of current policies and practices that it advocates in an effort to maintain its relevance and adaptability.

Any organization that spans regional cultures and seeks to be truly global has to operate from a strong set of core beliefs. At the same time, it must be able to tolerate regional differences. This can be characterized by something as lasting as shared assumptions and values or as flexible as policies and practices. For example, earlier we were introduced to ServiceMaster's core value of "to honor God in all we do." Some might consider that a constricting value, one that could limit an organization to those holding only Christian beliefs. But Bill Pollard, former CEO of the company, has told of company management meetings in Japan that began with a Shinto prayer. Different God, same value.

But surely the confluence of forces that we face today can have a profound effect on an organization's culture. These forces include the development of new information and communication technologies, the entry into the workforce of new generations with different mindsets and working habits, the increasing emphasis on teams as an organizational device, changing employment and deployment strategies, the rise of free agency with its multiple jobs, and the psychological shrinking of the world. The questions this poses are: How will these trends, if they continue, affect the strength and health of cultures?—and—What kinds of cultural adaptations represent adequate responses?

Information and Communications Technology

Word of an indiscretion by a Tiger Woods can spread instantaneously throughout the world despite efforts on his part to contain the information. Anyone seeking just identity, not necessarily notoriety, through such media as Facebook and YouTube, has to accept the possibility that little about his or her life may remain confidential. Similarly, organizations today are either blessed or beset by new information and communications technologies that have changed the operating face of business, government, and society. An example is the vast extension of 24-hour global news coverage of cable television to more than 900 million broadband subscribers and 5.2 billion cell phone subscribers[1] (as of 2010), many capable of receiving and broadcasting pictures and text. This turns nearly everyone into a potential reporter and broadcaster. The impact on government organizations has been profound, making it impossible even to restrict access to classified documents and messages.

An academic and public servant of great insight, Harlan Cleveland, forecast the impact of such technologies years ago when he wrote:

> The information resource, in short, is different in kind from other resources. So it has to be a mistake to carry over uncritically to the management of information those concepts that have proven so useful during the centuries when things were the dominant resources and the prime objects of commerce, politics, and prestige.[2]

As Cleveland predicted, information, unlike most manufactured products, is expandable (as it is used), compressible, substitutable (for capital, labor, or physical materials), highly transportable, hard to hoard or keep secret, and shared, not exchanged.[3]

The development and rapid spread of these technologies have changed behaviors and artifacts of all organizations. But how deeply have they affected thinking at the core of a culture—thinking that influences basic assumptions and hence values and beliefs? It's clear that a society centered around communication technology that provides ubiquitous information and makes it possible for workers to telecommute will behave differently than one centered around large groups of workers assembling daily in a factory. As a society, we're in the process of finding out just what those differences are. This is having profound effects on the basic assumptions on which the cultures of organizations are based today. Furthermore, the generation gap in the use of technology between the growing ranks of the youngest generations in the global workforce and their older colleagues is having similarly jarring effects on organization cultures.

Technology that enables us to organize and communicate information at the speed of light that did not exist 15 years ago is taken for granted today. It has fostered dramatic increases in the productivity, for example, of customer-facing personnel. At the same time, it has fostered one kind of communication, Internet-based, while replacing the face-to-face communication necessary to satisfy certain human needs in an organization. The fear of "using technology as a crutch" has prompted Ray Gottschalk at the Alcone Marketing Group to begin tracking the incidence of "face-to-face" meetings as opposed to electronic conferencing, especially for activities such as presenting creative concepts to clients. Although this involves added travel, it complements and improves electronic communication.[4] For example, many organizations are finding that face-to-face meetings enhance the effectiveness of teleconferencing by enabling managers to associate live faces with voices and better interpret the body language that can be seen on high-definition television monitors.

Handheld communication devices have similarly tested the etiquette representing long-held values. Taking calls and texting during meetings, for example, are increasingly being ruled out as acceptable behaviors. "E-mail-free" hours are being set aside to enable workers to concentrate on ideas associated with their work. Other organizations are relaxing expectations about answering (as opposed to receiving) e-mails after certain hours. All of this suggests that organizations with strongly held values and clearly communicated expectations regarding accepted behaviors are in a better position to come to terms with the demands of new technologies.

Of greatest import, however, is the fact that information and communications technologies facilitate other phenomena such as telecommuting and outsourcing that can result in "fragmented" cultures characterized earlier as having both low sociability and low solidarity.[5] In addition, such technologies have contributed to pressures for greater transparency.

Increasing Emphasis on Transparency

Transparency, access to information, is a byword in many organizations. But those proclaiming its importance have found that it cuts many ways. Two questions confronting managers today are: "Just how transparent should we be?" and "Do we any longer have a choice?" Vineet Nayar, founder and CEO of HCL Technologies, an information technology services company based in India that contracts outsourced work from companies around the world, believes he knows the answers.

Nayar is a firm believer in the importance of transparency in achieving a high level of trust in an organization. In his words:

> All HCL's financial information is on our internal Web. We are completely open. We put all the dirty linen on the table, and we answer everyone's questions. We inverted the pyramid of the organization and made reverse accountability a reality.
>
> So my 360-degree feedback is open to 50,000 employees—the results are published on the internal Web for everybody to see. And 3,800 managers participate in an open 360-degree (involving feedback from subordinates, peers, and superiors) and the results—they're anonymous so that people are candid—are available on the internal Web for those who gave feedback to see. So, that's reverse accountability....
>
> We started having people make their presentations and record them for our internal Web site. We open that for review to a 360-degree workshop, which means your subordinates will review it. Your managers will read it. Your peers will read it, and everybody will comment on it.
>
> What happened?... You cannot lie.... You are going to put your best work into it...(and) you didn't learn it from me.[6]

In another interview, Nayar commented that "We are trying, as much as possible, to get the manager to suck up to the employee." This can be difficult for the top twenty or so managers whose ratings are posted. As one put it, "It was very unsettling the first time."[7]

Transparency can pose other challenges. It can be costly. Reporting systems have to be changed. Without accompanying changes in other values and behaviors, transparency can have painful effects. It is has led to such things as the departure of key managers. Others may require retraining and preparation. And yet, as a vehicle for establishing trust, it has no peer if management is consistently constructive in its use.

The benefits of transparency may, at least for certain kinds of information, outweigh the costs. At Zappos, the online shoe retailer, suppliers receive much of the same data that is available to Zappos' buyers. According to CEO Tony Hsieh, "It's like having an extra 1,500 pairs of eyes to help us manage the business.... Even if some data end up with rivals, the benefits outweigh any costs."[8]

Today, in an information age in which knowledge rules, communication is instant, and transparency grows through Internet-based e-mailing, blogging, and "friending," there are few secrets. The Catholic Church, like many other organizations, is finding this out to its regret. Sex abuse scandals and the speed with which information about them travels have raised questions about leadership in its culture. It remains to be seen how deeply these questions will penetrate to the very shared assumptions and values of the Church's culture in an age in which responses to revelations are as important as the revelations themselves.

New Generations of Employees

An industry has arisen to study, analyze, and make pronouncements about "Gen Y-ers" or Millennials, those who began entering the workforce shortly after the turn of the twenty-first century. No generational impact since perhaps the end of World War II with its returning veterans has been greater. In the United States, for example, this group is made up of more than 70 million people and constitutes the largest living generation.

This generation was raised in relative affluence and stability by doting parents born in the wake of World War II. More important, Millennials take for granted and know how to exploit the power of information and communication technology. Relatively speaking, they have been denied little. Their achievements, no matter how insignificant, have been praised frequently by fawning parents from the United States to China. In fact, the effect has been magnified in China under a regime seeking to limit families to one child. It has produced a generation with somewhat different expectations regarding wealth and personal development as well as a heightened social idealism. Furthermore, in the words of one manager, "they have expectations, but they have the highest expectations first and foremost for themselves."[9]

A recent Pew Research Center poll found that Millennials in the United States are very tolerant and expressive and connect with others (often through the newest social networking technologies).[10] They are not controlled by technology. Instead, they often use it in ways that its designers did not anticipate. They have been told by their parents that they are special, and they believe it. This may account for the fact that, however much recent global economic difficulties may have restricted job opportunities, Millennials are confident they will earn enough money in their lifetimes.

Anyone who has worked with Millennials on a daily basis, as I have, will also point out that their social skills are better honed, they team up (often through technology rather than face-to-face collaboration) more effectively, and their working habits are less regular and predictable than their predecessors. They prefer what appears to others as nearly chaotic working conditions. Remarkably, they often can produce what they promise on time. And their work can be of excellent quality.

The influx of Millennials into the workforce has profoundly changed the results of surveys intended to identify "what workers want" in their jobs. For example, among the values listed in Chapter 1, Millennials strongly value the "fairness" of their boss. But they place greater weight than preceding generations on such things as personal development and growth, a clear path to the future in their job assignments (not necessarily in the same organization), and frequent recognition and feedback. They place less weight on long-term employment or compensation other than as a form of recognition. This may require a reconsideration of the behaviors featured in many statements of mission, values, and behaviors.

Recruiting Millennials: The "Haves"

Google is one of the foremost employers of Millennials. It has been held up as an organization that epitomizes the "future of management."[11] It was founded and is led by Larry Page and Sergey Brin on the basic assumption that Google will "do no evil." However, in pursuit of its lofty mission to make the world's information readily accessible through its vast library and search routines, it has been accused of such things as compromising privacy in China, violating copyright laws and royalty agreements, and hastening the decline of various traditional media. A basic shared assumption at Google reflects its engineering roots. It is a belief in science and fact as opposed to instinct or opinion. It may be reflected, in the words of one observer, as "not just a disdain for public relations, but also a whiff of arrogance."[12] Its values include transparency (including the display of progress reports of ongoing research on its Web site, googlelabs.com), personal development (allowing engineers 20% of their time for work on projects of personal interest), and a belief in the ultimate importance of teamwork.

These are characteristics of an organization seeking to be an egalitarian meritocracy. Google has also been described as an extension of the university culture that the founders experienced at Stanford University.[13] These values provide a good fit with a Google strategy and organization described as follows:

- "Dramatically flat, radically decentralized"
- Comprising "small, self-managing teams"
- Providing "the freedom to follow your nose"
- Encouraging "rapid, low-cost experimentation"
- Fostering a "continuous companywide conversation"
- Providing "differential rewards" for the development of superior ideas[14]

In short, Google's values and behaviors, reflected in its organization, are made to order for the Millennials who are strongly attracted to it in large numbers. This creates a special need for Google to be very selective in those it elects to hire.

At Google, people have to sell themselves into the organization by demonstrating a superior intellect. After they are hired, they must find their place in the organization (a "bozo-free zone" that embraces others like themselves). They also must sell their ideas to others in a purposely ill-defined organization emphasizing the generation of ideas and innovation. They have to either join a team or recruit one on the strength of their ideas. There is no place for a person seeking structure or the solitude of work away from the seeming chaos and confusion of the group. For those able to select themselves into the organization, Google appears to be an ideal place to work, regularly appearing at or near the top of Fortune's "100 best companies to work for."[15] But like all organizations with a strong culture, it is not for everyone.

Cisco Systems is another organization with success in not only recruiting but keeping Millennials, 98% of whom are still with the organization after two years. A program called Cisco Choice is credited with helping the company achieve its successes. After a week of general orientation, new recruits are exposed to a week of presentations from Cisco's managers. After selecting five business units in which they would like to work, candidates interview executives in those units and then make their final choices—even who they'll be working for. Most get their first choices.[16]

What relevance do the Google and Cisco experiences have for other organizations? Does, for example, Google rely too heavily on one path breaking idea—a superior algorithm for retrieving information linked to an advertising model that enables the company to monetize its technology—to provide a useful example? Has the phenomenal success of one idea provided the often elusive financial security needed to foster a culture of employee services and individual time to reflect and think at Google? Can it duplicate the feat? Will Google's and Cisco's success and growth eventually dilute cultures, as has happened in other organizations? Time will tell, but it is likely that Google's and Cisco's cultures provide models for organizations that will rely on large numbers of Millennials for their future success.

Recruiting Millennials: The "Have Nots"

Many industries are not recruiting their share of Millennials. There may be many reasons:

- Lack of desire to cope with the challenges Millennials bring with them
- Unwillingness to adjust behaviors, organization, and even strategies to accommodate them

- Cultures emanating from stringent regulatory environments that have constrained organization choice to forms providing strong controls
- Simple inertia

Whatever the reason, Michael Costonis and Rob Salkowitz point out that a number of industries—including insurance, transportation, utilities, and manufacturing—are confronted with aging ranks, traditional organizational hierarchies, and a heavy blanket of bureaucracy. They are repulsive to the very Millennials who could achieve the very technology-based operating solutions that their customers want. Such factors are preventing these industries from keeping pace with the demands of the marketplace. In discussing implications for the insurance industry, for example, Costonis and Salkowitz point out that "Insurance and other traditional industries may be a less-than-ideal fit for American-born Millennials, but globally, there are nearly 3.5 billion people under 30.... The future of insurance resides in this young world of new talent."[17]

Team-Based Work

It is probably no coincidence that the influx of Millennials into the workforce has been accompanied by a renewed interest in team-based work. This augurs well for the creation and sustenance of effective cultures. The organization form reminds team members of the importance of culture. It generates the peer group pressure needed to ensure adherence to values and behaviors. It fosters the transparency described earlier. And it facilitates the delegation of responsibility for performance by assuring senior management that such responsibility will be borne by several people interacting with one another rather than with just one manager.

I pointed out in Chapter 6 that teams may not be appropriate for all kinds of work, particularly if members are not hired and trained with team-based work in mind. It requires team-based performance measurement and compensation, as well as a clear definition of leadership and responsibilities. But when applied effectively, team-based work can be a powerful anchor for an organization's culture.

Employment and Deployment Strategies

Staffing strategies that have the greatest impact on cultures are those centered around the use of part-time employees, remotely based work, telecommuting, and outsourcing. All require careful consideration of ways to impart a sense of engagement and "ownership" to such employees. Efforts to get them to put their organizations' interests above their own become particularly challenging.

Part-Time Employees

The siren song of part-time employment has always been a flexible work schedule for those with other commitments. Employers like it because it means relatively inexpensive labor and usually few or no nonwage benefits. The song becomes dissonant as workers string together two or more part-time jobs as part of a full-time employment strategy and become less reliable and engaged on any one job. The culture-based challenge that part-timers represent is that they can easily feel like second-class citizens on the job. Perhaps because retailers are the largest employers of part-time workers, it is no surprise that some of the best cultures for part-timers exist in organizations such as Starbucks, Walmart, and Whole Foods Market.

At Whole Foods Market, for example, part-timers confront a strong culture characterized by a Declaration of Interdependence for "a community working together to create value for other people." The company's motto is "Whole Foods. Whole People. Whole Planet."[18] Employees are interviewed and hired by teams within each store who are responsible for the performance of a store's department. Teams control staffing as well as some of their sourcing and pricing decisions. They are rewarded in part on the profitability of their departments as well as, in many cases, the overall performance of the company through stock options widely distributed to employees. Because performance data is shared at the store level, there is peer pressure to do well. Success begins with determining how much labor is needed and hiring people with the right attitudes and capacity for work. At Whole Foods, teams are highly motivated to make sure that any part-time people they hire are properly oriented and trained and acquire the cultural traits that have made the company so successful. Again, this culture is not for everyone. But for part-timers who are attracted to it, many want to graduate to a full-time position with the company.

In terms of impact on an organization's culture, the employment of part-timers is a balancing act. Too many in relation to full-timers can dilute the culture, with ramifications for everything from internal communication to customer relations. Circuit City, a well-known U.S. retailer of electronics and office equipment that shifted its employment base from full-time to part-time, found this out too late to avoid bankruptcy and death several years ago.

Remotely Based Work

It is ironic that the very advances in information and communications technologies that have enabled organizations to perform work remotely have also increased the challenge of communicating effectively with members of a far-flung, largely home-based workforce. Because much of their work is done on the Internet, ways have to be found to accomplish inclusion largely through that medium.

Much reservation work is performed remotely. For example, Jet-Blue employs an army of homemakers in Utah to handle phoned-in reservation requests. Ramada Inns has successfully deployed teams of inmates to take reservations in prison-based facilities.

The question for us is whether any kind of dedication to a mission or set of shared values can be created among such employees. The answer is a qualified yes. But it requires that remotely based workers periodically interact with other members of the organization, typically through regional meetings or even in-home visits by the person responsible for their work.

Remotely based work, as opposed to that performed by telecommuters, often is repetitive and routine. But variety can be introduced into the work by providing employees with some latitude to solve customers' problems, for example. This has to be preceded with an investment of time and effort to make remote workers familiar with the mission and values of the enterprise, something that some organizations are unwilling to do.

Communication is critical. The natural medium is the very Internet on which remote workers perform their work. Rapidly declining costs have made Internet conferencing much more affordable. Even simple computer cameras can enable supervisors to maintain contact with employees in the far corners of their remote organizations. The goal is to maintain morale, remind workers of the importance of the mission they are pursuing, and point out how their work fits with that performed elsewhere in the organization and why it is important.

Failing frequent communication, remote workers are more likely to become bored, more likely to become closely affiliated with customers than with the organization, and more likely to forget the reason for their work. The consequences soon become quite obvious to customers and others. But the effects, according to one study, depend on individual traits. For example, well-organized extroverts fare the best in a remote setting. Stuart Duff, who conducted the study, concluded that "Mobile workers...are far more organized, personally, than their office-bound counterparts."[19]

Telecommuting and Flex Time

Telecommuting, a form of remotely performed work, offers a number of benefits to workers and managers alike. But nevertheless it presents questions for an organization attempting to preserve its culture. It can be attractive to a group of talented people responsible for complex, creative work who otherwise might quit to fulfill family responsibilities or find a job with a shorter commute. But their absence from the office or the team with which they work can be critical to a culture and must be managed by mutual agreement. This is best done by requiring a presence in the office and alongside those with whom they work on certain days and hours of the week to permit the kinds of face-to-face meetings on which strong cultures are often constructed. Again, the success of this practice depends on the people involved and the tasks they perform, suggesting special care in recruitment and selection.

Flex time, offering a flexible work schedule to accommodate other commitments, has become popular in jobs such as scientific work in laboratories in which collaboration may be unimportant. It often is left to the individual to determine when to arrive at and leave the job. But it's important to schedule a minimum of overlap of everyone's schedule for both collaboration and organization-building activities. On the other hand, flex-time policies imply trust, can demonstrate an important value of the culture, and may in some cases even have a beneficial effect on productivity.

Outsourcing

It may appear at first that outsourcing a set of tasks to another organization perhaps located on foreign soil has little effect on efforts to build an effective culture. There are several reasons why this is not the case.

First, outsourcing is associated with more than just a loss of jobs at an organization's center. It implies an underlying assumption that an organization can no longer afford to perform a set of tasks itself and will do whatever is necessary to remain competitive. This assumption is often made by those at the top of the organization with little input from those most directly affected by the outsourcing decision, potentially damaging trust. Of course, if the culture is relatively ineffective to begin with, it may have little impact on an organization.

Second, if contact with customers is being outsourced, an organization may be ceding control over an important element of its customer relationships. No matter how carefully organizations attempt to exert control over the quality of interactions, there is a real contrast for American customers between service representatives whose first language is English and those whose first language is not. This may in turn reflect on other aspects of customer relationships, the firm's image, and even the firm's mission and values.

This raises the question of how outsourced service organizations can be brought under the umbrella of the same set of values and behaviors, with extra care given to maintaining a standard of quality, as that of the enterprise outsourcing its work. At the least, it requires the same kind of orientation and personal development provided to full-time, in-house employees.

The Rise of Free Agency

The Great Recession accelerated a trend that has been building globally—that of individuals leaving large organizations to create their own. It has extended even to less-developed economies where micro-lending, for example, has made it possible for increasing numbers of people to finance their own small businesses.

This raises the question of whether and how free agents—representing themselves and their own best interests—may be induced to subscribe to a given set of values and behaviors. Several large organizations, for example, have experimented with the issuance of stock to the free agents with whom they deal as a means of aligning the interests of both organizations. Others utilize customer surveys as a means of tracking the quality of work performed on their behalf by free agents.

The Psychological Shrinking of the World

Thomas Friedman pronounced that "the world is flat" in a book of the same title. His message was both simple and complex.[20] The simple side of it was that new technologies and ease of travel have brought us together in ways that allow us to understand one another better.

His message was brought home to me when I participated in an experiment to test high-definition television technology being developed in the 1990s by Mitsubishi. The company created a virtual classroom in which I facilitated a case discussion between Japanese students located in classrooms in Boston and Tokyo. The experiment involved graduates of Harvard Business School programs who were familiar with the case teaching method. It required westbound and eastbound satellite networks as well as a third network to connect 3,000 observers in Japan with classrooms that were equipped with large screens showing outgoing and incoming high-definition video signals. A member of the faculty of the Tokyo Institute of Technology explained the pros and cons of the case method relative to the lecturing with which observers were more familiar. Naturally, I was somewhat apprehensive about whether this somewhat unique and very expensive (costing at least six figures) test could succeed in a "fishbowl" created in space.

I shouldn't have worried. Within five minutes of the start of the experiment, participants became comfortable with the complex technology. Given their common experience with the case method, classroom participants began confronting each other in ways unfamiliar to the Japanese observers. High definition allowed us all to read each others' name tags and address each other by name. Some of us knew each other through our previously shared experiences. For the next hour, our world was "flat" as we discussed a case about Scott Cook and his company, Intuit.

Of course, technology was important to the success of the experiment. But it paled in significance to the fact that it was preceded by both conditioning (in this case, familiarity with the case method), personal familiarity, and even friendships among participants. These were the things that enabled a bridging of a broad cultural gap. The experience provides a metaphor for what is going on in organizations around the world today that are faced with the challenge of creating a "one company" culture while recognizing and even preserving the cultural differences among members of the organization.

Summary

Organization cultures, after they are established, are constantly tested by trends in both the external environment and management practices.

Developments in information and communication technology coincide with the entrance into the workforce of Millennials. They have a somewhat different outlook on work than their predecessors, as well as the ability to employ technologies more effectively. They bring with them a bias for greater transparency in management methods, an inclination to work in teams, and a comfort with working across cultural barriers. They appear to put more emphasis on working relationships, personal development, recognition for the quality of their work, and the quality of their colleagues than on monetary rewards (other than as recognition). These factors on balance augur well for organizations that can adapt their cultures to meet the needs of this generation.

Organizations with the greatest success in attracting Millennials are those with inspiring missions that are willing to provide the job qualities just cited, as well as a certain amount of self-determination in the nature of their work and how it is performed.

At the same time, employment and deployment strategies largely facilitated by information and communication technologies pose real challenges to the maintenance of effective cultures. These include a greater reliance on part-time employees, remotely based work, telecommuting, outsourcing, and free agents. All threaten to dilute an organization's culture if they are not accompanied by efforts to bring people together physically from time to time. Such meetings can facilitate more "virtual" relationships and are needed to reinforce the importance of shared values and behaviors as well as foster trust, engagement, and ownership to the extent possible. In some respects, culture matters even more to individuals detached in time and place from their employer. The Internet affords a natural link with which an organization can communicate that it is noticing and that it cares.

A "flatter" world may bring us together through the widespread use of new technology. But unless it is accompanied by travel and face-to-face exposure, the foundations for an effective multinational organization culture may not be accomplished.

In sum, change is the constant in an environment that demands increasingly flexible responses faster. If anything, this increases the need for a shared set of clearly understood assumptions, values, and beliefs. They are essential in fostering a possible range of actions that individuals can take with the assurance that they are representing their organization and its values well. How is this accomplished? Primarily through leadership, to which we turn next.

13 ――――――――――――――――――

Leading Culture Change

Those who can see the need for "useful change" and achieve it through others can claim to be leaders.[1] When this is done with an intense sense of purpose and a large dose of humility, you can claim to be a "Level Five" leader of the highest order.[2] When the change involves culture, it is truly the personal responsibility of a leader. A. G. Lafley, then CEO of Procter & Gamble, in commenting on what only CEOs can do, quoted Peter Drucker to the effect that "CEOs set the values, the standards, the ethics of an organization. They either lead or they mislead."[3]

Leading successfully requires an organization that is willing to follow. Remember the first of the reasons cited in Chapter 1 for why people like their jobs? It was "My boss is fair." This covers many aspects of behavior, beginning with judicious decisions about people. It is also demonstrated by important elements of the culture cycle, such as meeting expectations as part of the "deal" (to use a term from Chapter 6) and the trust that results from this. It includes such things as sensitivity (concern for the problems of others in the organization), humility (among other things, a willingness to do what is necessary to get a job done), and the ability to project an even-tempered, reassuring personality, especially in times of adversity.

Why do we admire displays of this kind of leadership so much? Is it because we see it too infrequently? Consider the stark example of Capt. Chesley B. "Sully" Sullenberger III of US Airways flight 1549. After making one of the few successful crash landings of a commercial aircraft on water, he personally ensured that every one of the 155 people onboard was off the plane before leaving the plane himself and later dealing modestly with fawning reporters. After that experience, one suspects those passengers would have followed Sullenberger in almost any endeavor.

The ultimate test of leadership ability may be leading a change in a dysfunctional culture. This takes a great deal of time and effort. It requires not only a return to an organization's shared assumptions and values but also its people, how they were selected, and their reasons for joining the organization. It's like producing a new strain of plant by not only grafting on new branches but also switching out all the roots. As the ad for a high-performance car says, "Professional driver. Don't try this with your automobile." This calls for an example from the auto industry.

A tough task faced chairman Edward Whitacre, Jr. and CEO Fritz Henderson as they successfully brought General Motors out of bankruptcy in 2009 and began to lead a "new GM." You could argue that the "old GM" was a victim of its success as well as leadership by an insular group of men with similar backgrounds ("car guys" with upbringing in Michigan and education at GM Technical Institute) who exhibited some admirable qualities, such as a willingness to put their loyalty to the company before their own ambitions.

As a consultant to GM working on projects involving service and parts supply in the late 1970s, I worked with managers who had some very attractive qualities. They were plainspoken people who were true to their word, something a consultant values in a client. However, I observed behaviors that were not representative of a healthy culture. For example, I discovered one day when I arrived at the GM Technical Center in a Ford Pinto (the last rental car on the lot at the airport) that one didn't drive competitors' products at GM (even though this could have produced valuable information).[4] My hosts never let me live that one down. Then there was the head of a GM operating company who swore that GM dealer service was outstanding, even though he was loaned a new GM auto every six months and never had to have it serviced himself. He stood his ground until his daughter called him during one of our meetings to complain about the treatment she was getting at a GM dealer's service department.

You might ask why I cite experiences that occurred more than 30 years ago. Comments from others who have worked with GM in the interim have suggested that little changed, in terms of culture, until recently.

At GM, long-term success bred an unintended amount of arrogance along with a great deal of pride. The saying at GM was, "At Ford, you have a job. At GM, you have a career." With the arrogance came creeping parochialism, not just toward those outside the GM "family" but also toward GM dealers and others. GM's leadership either ignored the parochialism or didn't realize that it existed. They were products of the organization that fostered the mentality.

Of course, its culture was only one of the challenges confronting the management of GM. Its wage structure and health insurance obligations were especially daunting. They were a legacy of better days before GM's decline began in earnest, days of market dominance that appeared at that time to an overly confident (some might say arrogant) management team to be endless.

Culture change starts with leadership. When he announced the "new GM" in the summer of 2009, CEO Henderson, a GM veteran, cited a change in culture as one of three pillars of the company (along with "cars" and "customers") as it emerged from bankruptcy. In his mind, culture encompassed three elements. He described the first as "You make culture change virally. It's how you spend your time, how you behave." The second involved getting out of the office. He reminded himself that "I need to go back to hitting the road.... (It's about) getting out of the office...seeing your people." The third element was "accountability for results, being transparent." In the words of one of his colleagues, he sought to make GM "the most public private company on earth."[5]

Henderson, in initial moves that suggest just how bureaucratic the organization had become, cut four-hour meetings to two hours, reduced the number of attendees, and eliminated "pre-meetings" in which agendas and other preparations for real meetings were organized.[6] We'll return to GM later, but it's clear that Henderson faced a formidable task of changing an entrenched culture.

How Do You Know Change Is Needed?

An organization that waits for a significant downturn in growth and profit to signal the need for change is doomed to fail. These often are the results of internal rot associated with a nonperforming culture that has existed for some time. Other triggers for change need to be found. For example, new assumptions, beliefs, and behaviors may be called for when an organization takes on a new mission, is merged with another, or simply faces its possible demise. However, there are more subtle indicators of the need for change.

The telltale signs that a dysfunctional culture is developing are many. They may include a poor sense of mission, often resulting from the hiring of people with the wrong motives. These often involve too great an emphasis on extrinsic rewards that run counter to the intended mission. Other signs include constant planning and replanning, with a chronic inability to meet plans. This suggests the inability to identify a coherent, realistic strategy with sufficient long-run potential to enable an organization to meet its goals. It is often accompanied by frequent reorganization and turnover in leadership positions, an increase in the politicization of the organization with an attendant rise in bureaucracy, levels of management, the frequency of "studies" as a means of deferring decisions, time spent in committees, managers supervising other managers, and the inability to make timely decisions.

The most important indicators of the need for reviewing an organization's culture are the Four Rs—referrals, retention, returns to labor, and relationships with customers. Gaps between desired and actual results of the Four Rs will appear long before financial setbacks. But contributors to these gaps appear much earlier in the culture cycle. It requires that leaders monitor how employees are doing in performing their roles at each link in the culture cycle, as shown in Figure 13-1. Data from the profile of RTL, Inc. from Chapter 7 illustrates this point.

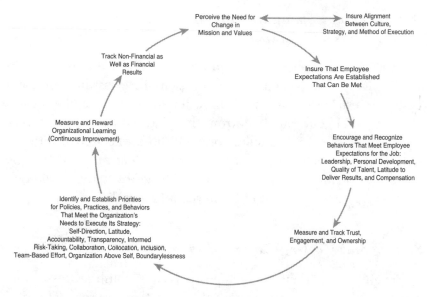

Figure 13-1 The role of leadership in the culture cycle

Monitoring Links in the Culture Cycle: RTL, Inc. Revisited

A review of selected data from the RTL, Inc. example in Chapter 7 (shown in full in Appendix C), when reorganized in terms of the culture cycle, illustrates the importance of the monitoring process for activities such as the following:

- Defining and communicating mission and shared assumptions, values, and behaviors
- Setting and meeting expectations
- Encouraging and recognizing desired behaviors
- Building trust, engagement, and ownership
- Shaping policies, practices, and behaviors that support important initiatives
- Ensuring a learning organization
- Tracking and achieving desired results
- Perceiving the need for culture change

Defining and Communicating Mission, Shared Assumptions, and Values

A leader's first responsibility in the cycle of activities resulting in an effective culture is to ensure that mission, shared assumptions, and values are established and communicated to everyone in the organization. At RTL, only one item from the RTL 2010 employee survey is helpful here, but it is a telling one. Of those who agreed with the statement, "The actions of our office are consistent with our strategic objectives and mission statement," only 58% agreed with it in the Baltimore office compared with 81% in the Minneapolis office.

Setting and Meeting Expectations

The next important leadership task is to establish processes that shape employee expectations and the ways they are met. The processes begin with recruitment of an individual employee and continue through her tenure with the organization. The best way to measure the effectiveness of the processes is to ask those who are affected by them. When this was done at RTL, the following responses provided a mixed picture of how well leadership was doing in the Baltimore and Minneapolis offices.

	Baltimore[*]	Minneapolis[*]
In my office, senior leadership's actions are consistent with what they say.	54	67
I know what is expected of me at work.	76	94
My supervisor clearly communicates his/her expectations of me.	66	58

[*] The percentages show the share of employees surveyed agreeing or agreeing strongly with each statement (4 and 5 on a 5-point scale).

Encouraging and Recognizing Desired Leadership Behaviors

It's a leader's role to encourage and recognize desired management behaviors that help ensure that expectations are met. We've talked a lot about what employees say they want in their jobs. Given the data just shown, we would expect Minneapolis to fare better than Baltimore on this criterion. But we might not have expected such large differences.

	Baltimore	Minneapolis
My supervisor routinely provides feedback that helps me improve my performance.	56%	61%
Here you are required, not just encouraged, to learn and develop new skills.	33	72
I have the opportunity for personal development and growth here.	41	86
In my office, senior leadership shows by their actions that employee training is important.	36	63
My total compensation is fair for the work I do.	23	28
Those who contribute the most to the overall success of the office are the most highly rewarded.	11	34

Here we see the first real evidence of a potential problem in Baltimore. There is a serious gap between the two offices in perceptions of personal development, growth, the effort devoted to employee training, and the "fairness" of compensation. In today's world, it is difficult to retain anyone not perceiving growth on the job, let alone the creative talent required for the kind of work performed by RTL. And although dissatisfaction with compensation may exist to some degree in every work environment, there appears to be room for a great deal of improvement regarding communication about the kinds of contributions that warrant reward, and generally how differentials in rewards are determined.

Note now how these differences play out in terms of trust, engagement, and ownership.

Trust, Engagement, and Ownership

Inadequacies on dimensions of learning and personal development, when combined with expectations that, once set, have not been met as well in Baltimore as in Minneapolis, are magnified when it comes to issues of trust, engagement, and ownership.

	Baltimore	Minneapolis
In my office, management is trusted (trust).	30%	69%
I am highly satisfied with my job.	32	61
I would recommend my company as a great place to work (engagement).	27	77
I am actively encouraged to volunteer new ideas and make suggestions for improving our business (ownership).	71	86

Given the culture cycle relationships shown in Figure 13-1, management at headquarters should need to go no further in determining that new leadership in the Baltimore office is needed. Without establishing trust with employees, there can be little hope of accomplishing the goals set for the Baltimore office. For example, although employees indicate that efforts are made to tap into the "ownership" tendencies of employees with requests for new ideas and suggestions, there is no evidence to suggest that employees are responding to the requests.

Policies, Practices, and Behaviors

Employees' perceptions of the policies, practices, and behaviors with which they are expected to perform their work show similar contrasts between RTL's Baltimore and Minneapolis offices.

	Baltimore	Minneapolis
I have the freedom to make the necessary decisions to do my work properly.	63%	83%
In my office, senior leadership communicates relevant information in a timely manner.	60	61
We emphasize teamwork. People who do not collaborate are not tolerated.	41	67
My colleagues are willing to go beyond what is expected for the success of my company.	87	92
We have no room for those who put their personal agenda ahead of the interests of our clients or the firm.	44	69
I have the resources and tools needed to do my job.	37	78
My team has a climate in which diverse perspectives are valued.	60	86

This data, combined with employees' views that Baltimore's management is not getting the best work out of its employees (discussed next), is, in a perverse way, encouraging. It suggests that with the proper leadership, this office could improve its performance substantially.

Organizational Learning

Although RTL management tracks individual learning among employees in its offices, this data contains few useful measures of organization learning. What there is suggests that, as we would expect, learning among employees is greater in the Minneapolis office. One reason why this may be the case is suggested by earlier data that indicates that so much time is being devoted to getting the work done in Baltimore that there is little time for reflection and learning.

Results

Given the indicators just presented, there is little need to look at the results. We already know what they should be. However, they suggest that the full impact of the data just shown has not yet been fully felt in the two offices. For example, the employee defection rate is higher in Baltimore, but it may grow, given larger differences in "intent to stay on the job" between the two offices.

Client defection rates are substantially higher in Baltimore. However, the numbers may be misleading because of an intent on the part of management to "weed out" less desirable clients across the network.

All this adds up to significant differences in operating profit on revenue.

	Baltimore	Minneapolis
Annual employee defection rate, 2009–2010	21.4%	19.2%
I intend to stay with my company for at least another 12 months.	46	72
My team constantly strives to find innovative solutions to clients' problems.	83	86
Annual client defection rate, 2009–2010	48.5	31.7
Annual average operating profit on revenue, 2009–2010	3.1	22.5

Most organizations track employee and customer perceptions on a regular basis. But too few organize the data in some useful conceptual way. By organizing it in terms of the culture cycle, management can begin to see cause-and-effect relationships that provide a look into the future, not just the past, of financial performance.

Other Signs of a Counterproductive Culture: "Culture Creep"

Behaviors associated with a counterproductive culture include an unwillingness to face the real issues while debating peripheral ones, a tendency to "shoot messengers bearing bad news" or squelch useful dissent (phenomena that appear to have characterized the cultures at both Enron and Worldcom), confusing rank with reason in discussions, and an inability or unwillingness to deal with members who violate values and behaviors in everyday management activities.

Maintaining an effective culture requires constant vigilance. Dysfunction doesn't arise overnight. Neglect leads to "culture creep" and a need to revive a culture. This task often involves an effort to lead change in behaviors, not necessarily basic assumptions or values. Note how culture creep was dealt with in the following three situations: the inability to face issues, paralysis in making complex decisions, and the loss of speed and agility in executing a strategy. Correcting this problem is a task that need not take years.

Avoiding Even Constructive Confrontation

Ursula Burns took on an element of "culture creep" as the incoming CEO of Xerox. Consider the following account of Burns' speech to her Xerox management team about what she calls "terminal niceness":

> "We are really, really, really, really nice." Maybe the "Xerox family," she says, should act a bit more like a *real* family. "When we're in the family, you don't have to be as nice as when you're outside of the family," she says. "I want us to stay civil and kind, but we have to be frank—and the reason we can be frank is because we are all in the same family."

Nods of recognition ripple across the audience.

"We know it. We know what we do," she continues, describing meetings where some people present and others just listen. "And then the meeting ends, and we leave and go, 'Man, that wasn't true.' I'm like, 'Why didn't you say that in the meeting?'"[7]

Burns is referring to one of the signals of an ailing culture. Richard Tedlow describes it as denial characterized by positive responses to the question "Do the real issues of the day only come up in the hallways after meetings are finished?"[8]

Returning to more academic terms used earlier, scholars would say that Burns is seeking more "communal" behaviors for her company. Such behaviors include high sociability and solidarity as well as a willingness to confront ideas and proposals in a timely way without destroying the organization's social fabric.[9]

Carrying Consensus Decision-Making to an Extreme

Values and behaviors can have a significant impact on how groups arrive at decisions: how fast they do so, the quality of the outcomes, the assignment of responsibility (credit or blame) for results, and how satisfied people are with the process. A frequent concern about "culture creep" in high-sociability organizations is that they begin to rely too heavily on a consensus mode of decision-making. This slows the process and creates a series of "veto screens" through which it is difficult to get anything approved. In this kind of organizational setting, many, perhaps too many, decisions are made by groups of interested parties. This may help explain why Toyota's management response to claims of defects in its products was regarded by many as far too tentative and slow.

This kind of behavior pattern, if perceived as dysfunctional, is difficult to break. It may require the introduction of a major initiative aimed at behavior change. For example, GE implemented a process called "Work Out" in the early 1990s when it was perceived that important, complex decisions were being delayed too often because of a lack of communication among parties to the problem or managers' unwillingness to address complex issues.[10] Work Out brought together interested parties for two or three days to solve the "knottiest" problems that had been avoided. The responsible manager was divorced from the discussion, but he or she had to return at the end of the process to rule on proposals from the group ("yes," "no," or "we'll consider it"). The manager was pressured to accept as many of the recommendations as possible. As you might guess, discussants were enthusiastic about the process, but managers were not. At first, managers were given the option to implement Work Out. When that didn't work, "coaches" were brought in to help with the process, and it was made mandatory. Over time, it changed basic decision-making behaviors for particularly challenging, complex decisions involving people from several interest groups inside and outside GE. It became part of a more cohesive, faster-moving culture.

Loss of Speed and/or Agility

During the early months of his tenure as CEO of GM, Ed Whitacre was said to walk up to the clay models of new GM car designs and ask why they couldn't be in dealers' showrooms within a year.[11] GM designers assumed that Whitacre's question reflected the naïveté of a newcomer to the auto industry. Any GM designer knows this process takes three years. Or does it? Whitacre's question, repeated often, suggested that possibly painful change might have begun, especially in GM's design division.

It doesn't take an outsider like Whitacre to recognize culture creep that leads to a loss of speed or agility or both, but in some ways this may be a more difficult task for an insider. GM's neighboring competitor, Ford, had reached this conclusion earlier when it brought in Allan Mullaly from outside the industry to head the company. One result was a company that had regained its agility. Ford achieved superiority in acting faster and with more agility than GM.

Whitacre realized that a longer and longer product development cycle increases the probability that an auto design may, when it is finally introduced, be out step with the market—something for which GM had become notorious. Worse yet, the loss of speed and agility discourages people from taking risks, because a poor decision can be very costly when coupled with a slow production development cycle.

For this reason, speed and agility lie at an important intersection between an organization's strategy and culture. Faster and more agile organizations enable people to make decisions faster, realizing that if they are wrong, their mistakes can be corrected before the market passes them by. This message had been overlooked by GM insiders.

"Culture creep" may or may not show up immediately in measures of employee trust, engagement, and ownership. But eventually it will produce gaps between expected and actual behaviors, as well as frustration with the pace at which decisions are made. This will discourage and drive away the most talented and engaged employees while negatively affecting the organization's ability to meet the needs of customers and its reputation as a place to work.

The warnings provide a basis for early action. Just what kind of action is the question.

Changing a Culture

We know a lot about how change is managed. One set of ideas put forth by Michael Beer posits that the probability of success in managing change depends on the degree of dissatisfaction with the status quo, the quality of the model for change, and the quality of the process for change, all in relation to the perceived cost of change (typically high) in an organization.[12] Beer's "model" also can be applied to the subtle, complex, and time-consuming task of shaping culture change. The application of these ideas is suggested by the inner circle of relationships shown in Figure 13-2.

Leading a change in culture is not something that should be undertaken lightly or as a project divorced from a review of strategy or how it is executed. As suggested in Figure 13-2, the effort has a logical sequence of steps, which may include the following:

1. Reviewing the need for change, using gaps between expected and actual results on the Four Rs, innovation, profit, and growth
2. Where it does not exist already, establishing dissatisfaction in the organization with the status quo

3. Selecting "change agents"

4. Proposing changes in mission, shared assumptions, values, and behaviors from the top

5. Conducting an organization-wide referendum on the proposed changes

6. Finalizing the revisions

7. Overcommunicating every step of the way

8. Personally demonstrating the new behaviors

9. Sorting out the "nonbelievers" in a timely way

10. Combining patience for long-term results with an impatience for early wins to validate the effort in the eyes of members of the organization

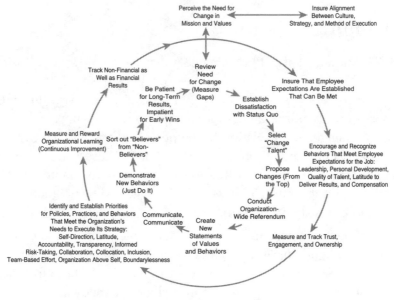

Figure 13-2 The role of leadership in culture change

Dissatisfaction with the Status Quo[13]

Dissatisfaction in the culture cycle should result from disappointing results in such things as the Four Rs rate of innovation, growth, and profit. Long before disappointing financial results begin to occur, the organization may have incurred several years of dissatisfaction among employees tempered by acceptable bottom-line results. Regardless of views at lower levels of management, if the level of dissatisfaction with the status quo at the top is not very high, change may be difficult to achieve. Where this is the case, dissatisfaction may have to be generated. Consider three cases involving different levels of dissatisfaction.

GM

At GM, it was not necessary to create dissatisfaction with the status quo. Plenty already existed. Here a once-proud organization was emerging from bankruptcy after outside intervention in which the U.S. government bought a sizeable share of GM's stock and loaned it money. GM employees knew that something had to change.

Baptist Health Care

Al Stubblefield, CEO of Baptist Health Care in Pensacola, Florida, understands very well the need to create dissatisfaction with the status quo. He was practicing it when he walked into a board meeting in October 1995 and committed his organization to raising patient satisfaction scores from the 18th percentile to the 75th percentile among Baptist's peer hospitals in just nine months. As he relates it, "When I walked out of the room after making that announcement, one of my senior officers took me aside and said, 'Do you realize what you just did in there? You set us up for failure!'"[14] As it turns out, Stubblefield had committed the organization to success, a new status quo.

Stubblefield had concluded that Baptist did not have the resources to outspend its rivals on technology, facilities, or programs. It had already pursued several strategic options by acquiring a community mental health center, establishing partnerships with two area rural hospitals, and creating a company for affiliated physicians. In the process, patient perceptions of quality had declined. Baptist's reputation as a place to work had not fared much better, even though there was no sense of an urgent need for change, other than among some board members. That's why Stubblefield took matters into his own hands, as did William Bratton at the New York Police Department (NYPD).

NYPD

Even before assuming his job as Commissioner of the New York Police Department, William Bratton realized the challenge he faced.[15] Here was an organization with a strong culture situated at the intersection of a proud tradition, policing, and a community, New York City, that naturally gave its work a high profile, including the fame of being featured on a highly rated television series, *NYPD Blue*.

It was not a promising atmosphere in which to change anything. Even worse, members of police organizations must have a strong loyalty to each other. After all, they trust each other with their lives every day. This naturally results in the "thin blue line" between the police and the public, which supports a culture of "us versus them," strict confidentiality, and the separation of administrators from street cops.

But the NYPD was an organization that, in Bratton's view, needed serious, sweeping change. For example, he was determined to change the department's mission from "fighting crime" (requiring effort) to "reducing crime" (requiring results). He needed a way to drive a wedge of doubt into the organization, a way to create dissatisfaction with the status quo and capitalize on the existing dissatisfaction. This explains why he ordered a "cultural diagnostic" in which an outside consulting psychologist interviewed individual police officers, encouraging them to disclose their real feelings about the department.

Police officers hated the diagnostic. But as a result of the interviews, the psychologist reported that officers identified their highest priorities on the job in terms of activities that had little to do with fighting, let alone reducing, crime (as opposed to "going through the motions," such as answering 911 calls and issuing summonses). The interviews uncovered nonproductive behaviors and illogical practices, such as officers on drug details working daytime shifts amenable to their lifestyles rather than working at times when most drug trafficking was being committed. The process also yielded information about a number of concerns among police officers about everything from a shortage of equipment to biases in scheduling shifts—concerns that, once identified, led to a general realization that they needed to be addressed. Police officers may have hated the interviews, but the process gave them an opportunity to express their frustrations concerning such things as the need for clearer lines of authority.

Quality of the Model for Changing a Culture: Assumptions, Values, and Beliefs

At GM, the model for change embraced cars, customers, and culture. It signified that both strategy (largely economic issues) and culture (symbolizing the need for organization change) would be addressed simultaneously. But it turned out they would have to be addressed without CEO Fritz Henderson's help. An insider with 25 years of GM experience, Henderson apparently named too many other insiders to his team to suit his board. They feared he would not move fast enough, so they replaced him with their fellow board member, Chairman (and outsider) Whitacre, who assumed Henderson's job as well. Whitacre soon asked several executives to leave or accept other assignments. Even Bob Lutz, widely known as the father of several successful GM auto designs, left. He commented that "In the past, GM was accused of not enough change. You have to find the balance between the pace of change and trauma to the organization."[16]

To GM's and Whitacre's credit, the change in culture was launched in tandem with basic changes in strategy that required a new culture. Entire brands have been sold, allowing the firm to focus on just four. Dealerships have been reduced to those that will be most critical to GM's new brand and pared-down cost structure. Manufacturing processes are being altered to help GM reduce the inventory of autos in its pipeline to dealers, a decision that will require more timely decision-making by managers. So "car guys" won't be sitting around talking about abstract changes in culture; they will be discussing concrete steps to change behaviors that are critical to the new strategy and methods of executing them. Apparently gone are the days of GM as a "career." North American President Mark Ruess has commented, for example, that "What we were doing didn't work. The time of providing for everybody, no matter what their performance, is gone."[17]

In terms suggested by Michael Beer, GM appears to be working on changes to both the economic model (actions producing economic change) and organization model (including culture). Beer has pointed out that this approach has more promise than one that addresses these matters sequentially.[18] The idea is that changes in strategy that have economic significance (such as divestitures or downsizing) can poison the atmosphere for subsequent changes in culture if the two are not implemented concurrently. On the other hand, changes in organization and culture executed substantially ahead of economic change risk damage to levels of trust, engagement, and ownership to the degree that subsequent changes in strategy involve significant downsizing and other changes. Simultaneous initiatives on both fronts may be challenging, but they help avoid many of the issues in addressing them sequentially.[19]

Baptist Health Care's model for change, by comparison, didn't follow this pattern. It began with strategic, economic moves involving the acquisition of other health care organizations and partners, at least until it became clear that this wouldn't be enough to secure the organization's competitive success. It then turned to organization and cultural change with the establishment of Five Pillars of Operational Excellence (people + service + quality + financial = growth) through a process designed to engage large numbers of people. Responsibility for change was essentially turned over to employees, who were organized into teams to accomplish the task along with training designed to support their efforts. Efforts began immediately to alter employee selection. Candidates who did not have an attitude consistent with the Five Pillars or the ability to work in groups with responsibilities for improving each of them were weeded out.

At NYPD, Commissioner Bratton, a student of management, had already begun to conclude that significant changes in strategy and organization were necessary, based on his experiences in the same job in Boston. In addition to changing the mission from "crime fighting" to "crime reduction," he concluded that the organization would have to be changed as well. In response to calls for clearer lines of authority from officers, he decided that a cornerstone for change would have to be organizational. His 76 precinct commanders would assume primary responsibility for reducing crime, through greater involvement of police officers in the life of the community and a lower tolerance for petty crime. In talking with precinct commanders individually, however, Bratton discovered that only one in three believed that crime levels could be managed downward to the degree he had envisioned. Another one-third agreed but were unwilling to subscribe to the goals he had in mind. The final one-third rejected the idea completely. (By the way, this is consistent with experiences of other organizations.)

Concluding that you can't fight a battle as basic as culture change with a reluctant army, Bratton had to return to square one and begin moving two-thirds of his precinct commanders to other jobs, because union rules did not permit their dismissal. This slowed the process of change but was critical to its accomplishment. At the same time, items of importance to the police force, such as equipment upgrades and perceived bias in assignments, were addressed.

Quality of the Process for Changing a Culture: Behaviors, Measurement, and Actions

As soon as dissatisfaction with the status quo and a model for change have been established, John Kotter suggests a time-tested process for how change can be led:

- Establish a sense of urgency by getting the leadership team to face unpleasant facts.
- Create a powerful guiding coalition.
- Provide a clear and concise vision.
- Effectively communicate the vision.
- Remove obstacles such as organization structure, incentive systems, and those who refuse to change.
- Plan for and create short-term wins.
- Resist the temptation to declare victory too soon.
- "Anchor changes in the corporation's culture" by making it "the way we do things around here" and showing people "how the new approaches, behaviors, and attitudes have helped improve performance."[20]

The last step again underlines the importance of culture in the change process. It also suggests how a culture itself can be changed.

At this point, we know little about the process for changing the culture at GM, other than what we can surmise from the organization's early economic success, which is likely reflected in greater employee engagement. For example, when GM announced that it was repaying government loans ahead of schedule because of its economic success, its message was probably more important for GM's employees than for its lenders or shareholders. And it was executed through a national advertising campaign showing groups of proud employees as well as the company's products.

Al Stubblefield was determined early on that process would not undermine efforts to change Baptist Health Care's culture. He set out to create a process that would lighten the burden of perceived change. With employee participation, "key characteristics of a healthy culture" were identified: open communication, a sense of ownership, a no-secrets environment, and a no-excuses organization.[21] Then goals and policies for each were established. For example, recruitment and selection processes were altered to identify and engage people who could thrive in an organization with such characteristics. Behaviors involving everything from frequent recognition to ways of addressing fellow employees and patients were modeled, starting with CEO Stubblefield and those at the top. To support open communication, "BHC Daily" meetings are held at the beginning of each shift to go over the "lineup" as well as special circumstances each team might encounter. (This strategy was borrowed from the Ritz-Carlton organization after a BHC management benchmarking exercise was held at a Ritz-Carlton hotel to inspire change by observing the Ritz-Carlton's best practices.) Service teams are required to set standards for quality in activities for which they are responsible.

Realizing that behaviors have to be modeled as part of the change process, William Bratton utilized every opportunity to send messages as he recognized outstanding service or condemned certain behaviors among those in the NYPD. For example, early in his tenure, he publicly retired the badges of two officers convicted of corruption with a carefully crafted comment: "so that no one else will ever have to wear those disgraced badges." He also became an advocate for his officers, getting them more modern equipment, even in times of budget constraints, and instituting a reengineering process to reduce the time needed to process arrests and give testimony, tasks they generally regarded as distasteful.

Bratton's cultural diagnostic at the NYPD, described earlier, also disclosed that a high proportion of police officers had joined the organization because of the sense of power their jobs conveyed. For example, they enjoyed using police cruisers and other equipment and carrying weapons and being able to use them at least in target

practice. Given the NYPD's new objectives to reduce crime by antici-
pating it, officers instead needed to get interested in becoming part
of a community and its day-to-day activities. This was not what many
members of the department had signed on for. So hiring practices
had to be altered to communicate the nature of the new NYPD and
the kinds of people it was looking for. It began hiring recruits with
different motivations than in the past. This kind of change would take
years.

But the most important process change at NYPD is one that has
been so effective in reducing crime that it has been adopted by police
departments around the world. This process game-changer is called
Compstat (for computerized statistics). Compstat is much more than
a crime counting and reporting system. It brings together the NYPD's
76 precinct commanders for Monday morning meetings to discuss
ways of reducing crime. This is based not only on crime statistics but
also on information about "hot spots"—concentrations of drug dealers, gun owners, and people with criminal records, three determinants of major crime. Discussion is concentrated on precincts that
have particular challenges, and clear plans of action are formulated,
some involving "boundaryless" efforts in which precincts can help
each other. The process is not a favorite of all precinct commanders, but it has gained adherents as they see how it can improve their
crime-fighting capabilities.

Sustaining Culture Change

Culture change requires continuity and long-term follow-through.
The effort to change GM's culture may be continuing, but it is continuing under rapid changes in leadership, something that is usually
the death knell of such efforts.

GM

As we saw earlier, just months after GM's emergence from bankruptcy, Chairman Whitacre assumed CEO Fritz Henderson's job
in December of 2009 after announcing that Henderson would be

leaving the organization. Just three months later, Whitacre announced wholesale changes in the company's senior leadership, shuffling jobs and people to place more emphasis on marketing and sales in its four remaining divisions. GM's early successes following its bankruptcy gave Whitacre some credibility and bought him time to establish other initiatives.

Only time will tell whether a sustained effort to truly change the culture will be made. But there has been little mention of culture (as opposed to sales and market share) since the initial announcement. One veteran observer commented after Whitacre assumed the CEO's job that "The moves are a sign of Whitacre's impatience, but may not be wise because it generally takes 12 to 18 months for people to become effective in their jobs.... Whitacre...is all about convincing people to buy GM's products rather than improving them over the long term.... This is an illusion of take-charge as opposed to actually working on strategic visions...."[22]

To his credit, Whitacre began visiting GM's manufacturing facilities that hadn't hosted top management in years, signaling a new era by his own behavior. The goal of repaying the government rescue loan was achieved ahead of schedule. It was replaced with the goal of putting the company in position for a stock offering that would enable the U.S. government to sell its stake in the company, thereby fully returning GM to the private sector and enabling it to gain full control over the management of its affairs, a goal that was also successfully attained. Whitacre sent a companywide e-mail roughly nine months into the job stating that "I want to reassure you that the major leadership changes are behind us."[23] But several months later he turned his responsibilities over to fellow board member Daniel Akerson, who, like Whitacre, came from the communications industry.

Four CEOs in two years is not a good prescription for any kind of useful change in culture. According to one commentator:

> The board wants him to build a nimble, high-performance culture and groom the next CEO.... Above all, Akerson will have to complete Whitacre's reengineering of the corporate culture: trimming bureaucracy, cancelling meetings, and avoiding the strategic analysis paralysis that comes when managers share responsibilities....[24]

Given Akerson's reputation for confrontational, no-nonsense behavior, it will be interesting to watch his progress in leading GM from what was characterized earlier as a "networked" management culture (people-oriented, highly social) to one that is more "mercenary" (task-oriented, meritocratic, but potentially ruthless).

Baptist Health Care

Back at Baptist Health Care, teams were established to help sustain the early gains made in the quality of the workplace. They were given organization-wide responsibility for such things as culture, communications, employee loyalty, customer loyalty, and physician loyalty. This transformation occurred without an edict from top management. It influenced everything from selection and orientation of new employees to training in general. Nonbelievers or those unable to adapt to the new set of values and behaviors were asked to leave in a timely manner. For example, the executive who suggested that Al Stubblefield had "set us up for failure" in promising the board dramatic improvements in patient satisfaction scores was one of the first who had to go.

More important, responsibilities are still assigned and actions executed on a daily basis according to the Five Pillars of Excellence. Behaviors consistent with the values continue to be observed and, if necessary, corrected, further reinforcing the importance of the values.

The efforts described earlier appear to have worked. The organization has maintained a quality of service rating from its patients that has placed it in the 99th percentile when ranked against other U.S. health care organizations for many of the years since 1996. It has also been named one of the best places to work in the United States in some of those years and has sustained its economic performance as well. Just as significant, employees took matters into their own hands when, in one year, they saw a decline in patient satisfaction from the 99th to the 98th percentile among American hospitals. They renewed their efforts to counteract small signs of arrogance in behaviors of staff members and restored the 99th percentile ranking, a far cry from the 18th percentile that Al Stubblefield confronted in 1995.

NYPD

At the NYPD, granting precinct commanders and their charges responsibility and authority for managing crime in their precincts also raised the possibility of police brutality. This required creating a team to address such issues with a new set of policies regarding the handling of suspected criminals as well as new goals in the reduction of such incidents. It's an example of how the organization's new culture was sustained and strengthened.

Bill Bratton has not been associated with the NYPD for some years. But some of the initiatives he sponsored live on. Among these, Compstat continues to be used. In fact, it has been adopted around the world, providing police departments with the kind of information needed to reduce crime.[25] But it has done something much more profound. It has fostered the reorganization of police departments to establish focused authority to utilize the information produced by Compstat. This has led to further changes in policing practices designed to enable police to identify causes of crime and the people most likely to perpetrate it so that they can more effectively deal with crime-fighting challenges.

Sociologists and criminologists still debate whether crime levels can be managed in the face of changing economic and social conditions. One analysis attributes Bratton's success to a dramatic increase in the size of the police force prior to Bratton's arrival. It ignores the fact that there were no increases for several years following his short two-year tenure.[26] And the reality is that New York has continued to enjoy a declining crime rate in nearly every year, in good times and bad, with or without increases in the force, since Bratton's departure in 1994. Compared to their peak in 1992, major crime rates have fallen by more than 70%, changing one of the most dangerous cities in America into one of the safest. Bratton himself (until his recent return to the private sector) employed more or less the same formula to change an organization's culture as Commissioner of a troubled Los Angeles Police Department with similar results (and critics).

Conclusions

Several themes run through all these vignettes. Together, they form a kind of "scorecard" for predicting the effectiveness of efforts to lead culture change:

- The task of nurturing and changing culture is an important responsibility of the CEO; it has to be led from the top. If you don't believe it, don't do it. Let the culture shape itself. It will represent just one more "unknown" to deal with, albeit an important one.

- Broad involvement in shaping shared values and behaviors helps ensure the effective implementation of the change.

- The task is made easier by dissatisfaction with the status quo, often accompanied by poor performance. If dissatisfaction doesn't exist, it is the role of the CEO envisioning the need for change to create it.

- Necessary changes in behaviors have to be modeled from the top. They can, however, be reinforced through such things as performance evaluations placing as much emphasis on "managing by the values" as "making the numbers."

- Culture change that reflects or accommodates changes in strategy and methods of execution has the best chance of success.

- Longer-term, more sustainable changes in culture require a reexamination of an organization's shared values and even the assumptions on which they are based. They require time, often more time than the tenure of one leader, placing a premium on continuity in leadership.

The application of this "scorecard" to the three extended examples cited in this chapter suggests that culture change at GM may have the lowest probability of success. There questions remain about the breadth of organization involvement in the process of culture change, the modeling of behaviors necessary to the change, and the continuity of leadership.

The Role of the Leader in Reshaping Culture

Effective leadership often involves delegating responsibilities and authority. But one responsibility that can't be delegated completely is reshaping and maintaining an effective culture. Delegation is difficult because it requires that values be adhered to and behaviors be acted out from the top of the organization. When it comes to culture, people take their cues from the top as well as from those around them. When people tell us that one of the most important things they want in their job is a boss who's fair, what they are really saying is that they want someone who is honest, who meets expectations, who is forthcoming, and who can be trusted to make the right decisions, especially when it comes to people. These kinds of behaviors are modeled at the top, as the earlier vignettes illustrate. These stories also suggest the following:

- Leaders perceive the need, regardless of current performance, for changes in the organization's mission, as well as its shared assumptions, values, and behaviors. Bruce Philp calls this "leading from the front." "You see what is next before everybody else does, and you have to be ready."[27]

- Seeing what's next requires constant measurement of things that suggest the need for culture change, starting with the nonfinancial symptoms in the culture cycle, including levels of employee trust, engagement, and "ownership" resulting from the ability or inability to fulfill employees' expectations.

- Leaders determine the causes of dissatisfaction and lack of trust. These include hidden agendas and disappointments as well as a lack of transparency; unwillingness to hold people accountable for their actions; absence of latitude to solve problems; and an absence of teamwork, diversity, and willingness to put the organization's interests before one's own personal interests.

- Leaders monitor the organization's learning capability, indicated by the presence of, and responses to, benchmarking and best-practice initiatives as well as its speed and agility in decision-making.

- They track performance on such dimensions as the Four Rs; rates of innovation; and profit and growth. In this effort, financial measures reveal very little; by the time they start to decline, it's very late in the game to begin a process of culture change.

- If necessary, and based on continuing measures, leaders create dissatisfaction with the status quo and present the case for change.

- Leaders take personal responsibility for deciding on the goals of a culture change effort and articulating a new set of values and behaviors and, if necessary, shared assumptions and even mission, ensuring that they are in alignment with current and planned strategies.

- Leaders codify values and behaviors that "feel right" and make great places to work. Start at the top, submit them for validation to the organization, and make final revisions back at the top.

- They assign "believers" as change agents and replace "nonbelievers" early in the process.

- They form a "contract" with employees that specifies expectations of all parties.

- Leaders ensure that the organization and its individual managers meet all commitments, a basic condition for building trust, engagement, and ownership.

- Leaders personally act out the values and behaviors. They just do it. And they do it consistently.

- They emphasize the importance of managing by the numbers—the *nonfinancial numbers*.

- Leaders establish policies, practices, and behaviors that are made possible by trust, engagement, and ownership—including such things as self-determination and latitude, accountability, transparency, informed risk-taking, collaboration, clustering, inclusion, boundarylessness, and a willingness to put the organization's interests before one's own.

- They build in adaptability and agility through continuous employee-centered, customer- and supplier-driven, and innovation-focused improvement.

- They turn "not invented here" on its head.

- They preserve the culture through everyday behaviors, measurement, and timely corrective actions, beginning with managers exhibiting behaviors that run counter to the values.

- Leaders give the change process the time it requires but are impatient for early results.

A. G. Lafley, former chairman and CEO of Procter & Gamble with whose comments we began the chapter, maintains that there are four tasks that only a CEO can do. One of them is "shaping values and standards." According to Lafley, this requires a leader to "interpret the organization's values in light of change and competition and to define its standards. This was a top priority in my first year as P&G's chief executive, after setting goals but ahead of strategy." This required "focusing first on what would not change—the company's core purpose and values...trust, integrity, ownership, leadership, and a passion for winning—while reorienting them toward the outside and translating them for current and future relevance."[28] As one example, Lafley described reshaping "a passion for winning" this way: "A passion for winning was often a matter of intramural competition; we redefined it as keeping promises to consumers and winning with retail customers."[29] In short, Lafley and his team redefined behaviors, not values, as a way of reshaping P&G's culture.

The process may test the patience of more impulsive leaders. But if a change in culture and the complete brand are led from the top, they are sustained throughout the organization. The subtle transfer of responsibility for an effective culture from the top to all levels of an organization characterizes all successful efforts over the long term.

Summary

The real test of a leader comes in changing a culture before it is necessary to ensure the organization's success in executing its strategies. Much of the task can't be delegated. Only the most confident and farsighted even try, because a change in culture requires a level of trust and time that few leaders possess. A comprehensive change in a culture requires that behaviors, values, and even the mission and basic assumptions underlying the values be examined and altered where necessary. Typically, this process requires five to ten years and a great deal of patience. This helps explain why short-term "wins" confirming the value of culture change are so important. Culture change is beyond the tenure of most CEOs, placing success in the hands of two or more leaders. Therefore, continuity in leadership is critical. This may help explain why the odds of success are not more than one in four.

Here are some telltale signs that a dysfunctional culture is developing:

- A poor sense of mission, often resulting from hiring people who have the wrong motives
- An emphasis on extrinsic rewards that run counter to the intended mission
- Constant planning and replanning, with a chronic inability to meet plans
- Frequent reorganization and turnover in leadership positions
- An increase in the politicization of the organization with an attendant rise in bureaucracy and levels of management
- The frequency of "studies" as a means of deferring decisions
- Excessive time spent in committees
- Managers supervising other managers
- The inability to make timely decisions

Behaviors associated with a counterproductive culture include an unwillingness to face the real issues (and disrupt the organization's "social" character) while debating peripheral issues, a tendency to "shoot messengers bearing bad news" or squelch useful dissent, confusing rank with reason in discussions, and an inability or unwillingness to deal with members who violate values and behaviors in everyday management activities. Needed changes in behaviors can be modeled by leadership and generally can be achieved in a relatively short period of time. This is often mistaken for a basic change in culture, but it may represent the most practical kind of change that can be achieved in the tenure of one leader.

The effects of changes in behavior can be measured through employee perceptions, organized on the "stations" of the culture cycle:

- The degree to which employees' expectations, once set, are met
- The levels of employee trust, engagement, and ownership that this generates

- The extent to which trust leads to productive policies, practices, and behaviors associated with such things as latitude with accountability on the job, transparency and informed risk-taking, collaboration and teamwork, inclusion, boundarylessness, and the tendency to put the interests of the organization before one's own

- The organization learning that these conditions and behaviors foster, including external benchmarking and internal best-practice comparisons

- The results associated with the Four Rs—referrals, retention, returns to labor, and relationships with customers; innovation; and lastly, the financial performance that this produces

More basic changes in core values and even shared assumptions require organization-wide involvement in a reexamination of what people really believe is critical to the organization's long-term success.

Engaging an organization in discussing a change in strategy or execution is relatively easy compared to a change in culture. People like to talk about the "business of the business," the stuff of strategy and execution. Perhaps for this reason, some of the most successful changes in culture have occurred where a change is considered essential to the success of a strategy. Furthermore, changes in strategy can yield the short- and intermediate-term results needed to buy the time necessary for the culture change to be accomplished and take effect. This is consistent with the idea that the probability of success for a change in culture may be highest when it is begun in tandem with a change in strategy.

Vignettes of several efforts to effect changes in culture tell us about the role of the leader in the process. It involves the following, among other things:

- Perception of the need, regardless of current performance, for changes in mission, shared assumptions, values, and behaviors, based on the tracking of key measures of the strength and health of a culture (as well as conventional financial measures)

- Acceptance of personal responsibility for articulating a new set of behaviors and, if necessary, values and shared assumptions, ensuring that they are in alignment with current and planned strategies

- Taking the lead in submitting proposed changes to the organization and finalizing and communicating the results
- Consistently demonstrating new behaviors while promoting the new values in public ways
- Constantly reminding the organization of its new shared values and assumptions
- Ensuring that processes and mechanisms are in place to populate the organization with "believers," to rid it of "nonbelievers," and to take the organization's culture into consideration in all major decisions

This requires a choice between a "quick fix" through a modeling of new behaviors from the top and a longer-term effort to reevaluate the organization's shared values and basic assumptions. And it requires patience and time to involve the large numbers of people necessary to the successful implementation and sustenance of basic, long-term culture change as well as impatience for short-term "wins" that confirm that constructive change is being achieved.

Clearly, leading an organized effort to change a culture at its core can be a high-risk endeavor. However, if successful, it can have a remarkably long-term positive impact on an organization's performance. It may well be a leader's most important responsibility and legacy.

14

Answers and Questions

Cultures are not abstract notions. They enable strategies and ways of executing them. They are direct contributors to the bottom lines of both for-profit and not-for-profit organizations. But, perhaps most important, they influence how we work—together or alone, sharing or protecting ideas, with a sense of community or individual responsibility—and with what amount of joy, personal development, and satisfaction.

Cultures are a distinctly human product of ideals, notions, and actions. They influence both the decision-making process and decisions. In times of adversity, they are the glue that holds people together in the service of common goals.

Cultures directly influence economic performance through the people they attract and the ability of those people to serve customers and each other well, and, in a for-profit organization, profitably. There is nothing "soft" about them.

A central purpose of this book has been to explore the range of ways in which culture affects the results that an organization can achieve, both in economic and noneconomic (behavioral) terms. Along the way we've examined the impact of culture on innovation, recovery from adversity, global strategies, mission-driven organizations, and ways of coping with changing forces in today's society. But our primary interest has been the ways in which an organization's culture affects its people, customers, partners, strategies, methods of execution, and ultimately owners through its performance. The order is important; it starts with people.

Characteristics of Effective Cultures

The cultures of the more successful organizations we've examined share all or most of a number of characteristics:

- They result from a mission, basic assumptions, values, and behaviors that are the product of leadership from the top, often beginning with a founder. They define "the way we do things around here."
- They evolve over time into serving their organizations well and are employed to recruit new members who subscribe to their precepts.
- They both influence and reflect strategy and how is it executed, requiring alignment among culture, strategy, and execution.
- They can be shaped, at least to a point, through a process described by a "culture cycle" involving the following:
  - Identifying and communicating the mission as well as shared assumptions and values, creating the basis for expectations
  - Setting and meeting expectations among organization members
  - Thereby establishing trust, engagement, and ownership among employees
  - Enabling the policies, practices, and behaviors that characterize great places to work
  - Fostering the learning behaviors critical to long-term organization performance
  - Producing the economic and noneconomic results that confirm the rightness (or wrongness) of a culture, an associated strategy, and the way both are executed
  - Periodic reviews of the mission as well as shared assumptions, values, and accepted behaviors
- Largely through peer interest and pressure, they encourage those who join to place the organization's needs alongside (and often above) their own and encourage "nonbelievers" to leave the organization.
- They foster trust, engagement, and ownership, often through extraordinary efforts to share important information about processes and outcomes and generally meet expectations.

- They do not utilize the "star system," instead emphasizing contributions to a team-based effort.
- They encourage work through teams invested with a high degree of decision-making latitude and responsibilities for managing themselves.
- They are inclusive, recognizing the advantages of diversity in innovation and other activities.
- They seek ways to create organizations that seem small even though they may be very large.
- They focus on and reward results, not just effort.
- They benefit from continuity in leadership that is most often provided by promotion from within.

At the same time, to be effective over the long term, these cultures foster change and encourage constant attention to it. They do this by doing the following:

- Building trust among organization members that encourages openness and cooperation while providing assurance that those suggesting change will not be penalized. For example, as I write this, the issue of trust faces all branches of the U.S. military, including the Marine Corps with its particularly strong culture, as they implement policies that replace the "Don't ask; don't tell" policy associated with the enlistment of gays and lesbians in the U.S. armed forces.
- Encouraging the constant questioning of assumptions and recommendations during the process of deliberation, not afterward. As you saw in Chapter 13, this was Ursula Burns' challenge when she assumed the job of CEO at Xerox.
- Promoting boundaryless behaviors such as benchmarking, the sharing of ideas and resources across the organization, and internal best-practice comparisons, as at GE.
- Fostering ownership among both employees and customers by soliciting ideas for new products, services, processes, and policies, as well as referrals of new employees and customers. For example, about 85% of the Mayo Clinic's patients, according to one survey, have recommended to others that they seek treatment there. On average, each has generated five new patients for the Clinic.[1]

An organization's culture can have a profound impact on both its economic and noneconomic outcomes.

Economic Outcomes: Profit and Satisfied Stakeholders

In a theoretical example based on generalized experience, I showed how an effective culture can produce distinct competitive advantage. As described in Chapter 5, the "Four R" model is composed of the following:

- A higher rate of employee *referrals* of new candidates and reduced recruiting costs for the organization
- Higher employee *retention* that leads to lower costs of recruitment, selection, and training
- Higher productivity, or *returns to labor*, that produce a favorable compensation/revenue cost ratio
- Better *relationships with customers* that result in more customer loyalty and referrals of new customers

The sum of these effects, in the example shown in Chapter 5, was more than an 8 percentage point boost in margins that could spell the difference between profit and loss.

A field test of the Four R framework in several offices of a global marketing services firm, described in Chapter 7, confirmed that in an organization in which a large proportion of employees are customer-facing, *as much as half of the difference in operating profit performance between offices can be attributed to culture*.

Behavioral Outcomes: Great Places to Work

Organizations with effective cultures are often very demanding places to work. They may purposely be staffed to a level that assumes a high rate of employee capability and productivity. If this is the case, why are many of these same organizations, such as The Container Store or ING Direct, regarded as great places to work? Why aren't they places that instead experience high rates of employee fatigue and burnout, failed family relationships, and poor health?

There are several explanations for this. Foremost among them is leadership that understands the culture cycle and ensures that mutual expectations between the organization and its employees are established and met. This creates the trust that reduces anxiety and makes possible other conditions and behaviors that define great places to work. These are places in which individual and organizational learning occurs, producing excellent economic and noneconomic outcomes.

For example, these organizations go out of their way to grant employees control over their work, beginning in some cases with a choice of starting jobs. Employees determine how their work is done. The focus is on results rather than process. Often, members respond by working harder and sometimes longer than they would under stiff controls.

Great places to work foster recognition, celebration, surprise, and fun—behaviors that characterize an effective culture. Activities are organized either formally or informally. Required behaviors are taken seriously and are modeled by those at the top of the organization.

An effort is made to look after the physical well-being of employees. SAS, one of the world's most successful custom software developers, perennially is regarded as a great place to work. This is in part because of the amenities employees receive, ranging from outstanding child care to great food to first-class workout facilities to beautiful surroundings. The goal is to remove as many concerns as possible while providing incentives to individuals to improve their health and welfare. The result is perhaps the highest employee retention rate of all software developers. Employee retention provides the staffing continuity needed to develop complex, often customized software.

Most important, people select themselves into these organizations. They do so with assurance because of the clarity with which values and behaviors are stated. For example, anyone who can't demonstrate that they really want, not just *say* they want, to put patients (as opposed to physicians and staff) first will have little interest in the Mayo Clinic, particularly after they learn what that means in practice. Nor will the organization have much interest in them, regardless of their clinical skills. The resulting alignment creates an environment in which people of like mind work more easily together, spend less time arguing about priorities, and put aside bureaucracy and politics in the service of the client.

All this—in spite of the unusually high demands placed on members to produce—reduces tension, stress, and fatigue for employees faced with deadlines and demands for high-quality work. Jeffrey Pfeffer regards this phenomenon as determining the very "sustainability" of an organization and its people over the long term. It comprises things that make some organizations great places to work and other organizations, according to a large body of research data, sources of destructive stress, poor family relationships, economic inequality, and eventually poor employee health and even high morbidity.[2]

Some Final Thoughts

In the introduction to this book, I mentioned that I was puzzled by one aspect of visits to Walmart and Southwest Airlines that triggered the work on this book. Although one of the founders of Southwest was a graduate of the Harvard Business School, none of its senior executives hold MBAs from "big name" business schools. Walmart has only a small cadre of senior leaders with such degrees. Why is it that two of the most successful companies in the United States—one of them the world's largest private employer—employ only a few graduates of our leading business schools? Is it the relatively low starting pay and an unwillingness to trade extrinsic for intrinsic forms of income? Is it the time it takes to work up through the organization to a senior position? Is it the amount of time a manager is required to spend with frontline employees? An excerpt from the letter I previously mentioned receiving from Herb Kelleher, at the time chairman and CEO of Southwest Airlines, provides another answer:

> Rightly or wrongly, we believe that there is a vast untapped potential in many of our people to soar far beyond what their educational attainments would appear to indicate is their capacity and that their fundamental intelligence, judgment, wisdom, and creativity need only be liberated and stimulated in order for them to effect remarkable accomplishments. It has been my experience that in many cases their approaches

to solving problems are perhaps less trammeled and more pragmatically ingenious than those of their better educated colleagues....[3]

Kelleher's comment implies that Southwest Airlines is pursuing a strategy that preserves a successful culture and a great place to work, apparently quite successfully if one judges from the number of people applying for every job there. This is the product of a conscious choice. And the graduates of "leading" business schools are in the atypical position of not being permitted to make it.

But that leaves me with other questions: Why is it that some of the most engaged, satisfied managers and employees I have met were at Walmart and Southwest Airlines? Why were some of the least engaged, least satisfied people well-paid employees of a leading investment banking firm that I visited during the course of my work on this book? The latter were nearly all graduates of leading business schools. They told me that they had put their personal lives on hold and were working day and night to make enough money to enable them to do what they really wanted to. This gave me a great deal of pause for thought when writing this book.

I began by asking why job satisfaction has fallen to new lows in the United States, which may be a precursor to similar trends in the rest of the world. This book has attempted to supply some answers. And the biggest headline should be reserved for unmet expectations. Today's entrants into the workforce expect jobs where the boss is fair, the feedback is frequent, the opportunities for personal development are high, people are recognized for their accomplishments, the quality of the work team is beyond question, latitude is provided (within limits) to deliver results to others, and the compensation is reasonable. When these conditions are met or exceeded, both economic results and intrinsic rewards can be remarkable. But clearly they are being met all too infrequently. What's the answer?

If job satisfaction is to be revived in this world, new as well as current members of the work force have to adjust their expectations downward, employers have to seek ways of meeting expectations, or both. My hope is that the answer is not an effort to manage expectations downward with little attention to an organization's underlying culture. Rather, my hope is that an increasing number of organizations will realize the sizeable competitive opportunity represented by a culture that is in alignment with an organization's strategy and how it is executed. This culture should foster such things as trust, the right amount of self-direction, the opportunity to fail, and inclusiveness.

An examination of why and how culture matters is an inexact science. It's too complex to sort out completely. But an awareness of the ways in which it matters, as well as ways of ensuring that it matters for the better, will lead to the kinds of choices that produce a better world in which all of us can live and work.

A

Sample Questions for Measuring the Strength and Health of a Culture[*]

Circle the number that best represents your agreement with each of the following statements. 7 equals Agree Completely, 4 equals Neither Agree Nor Disagree, and 1 equals Disagree Completely. For statements about which you are unsure, circle 0.

Strength of a Culture

Mission, Shared Assumptions, and Values

I know what the organization's mission is.	7	6	5	4	3	2	1	0
I identify personally with the mission.	7	6	5	4	3	2	1	0
The organization's mission was an important reason I came to work here.	7	6	5	4	3	2	1	0
The values by which this company is managed are very clear.	7	6	5	4	3	2	1	0
"The way we do things around here" is well known among employees.	7	6	5	4	3	2	1	0
The values and beliefs in this organization:								
Make a difference in how I carry out my work.	7	6	5	4	3	2	1	0
Make me a more effective manager.	7	6	5	4	3	2	1	0
Help the organization achieve its goals.	7	6	5	4	3	2	1	0

[*]Keyed to the Culture Cycle in Chapter 6, Figure 6-2

Health of a Culture

Expectations Versus Experiences

What is expected of me is made very clear.	7	6	5	4	3	2	1	0
I have a chance to express what I expect from the organization in return.	7	6	5	4	3	2	1	0
My manager manages by the values.	7	6	5	4	3	2	1	0

My experiences to date on this job have met my expectations regarding the following:

The person to whom I report	7	6	5	4	3	2	1	0
The capabilities of the colleagues with whom I work most closely	7	6	5	4	3	2	1	0
My own learning and personal development	7	6	5	4	3	2	1	0
My opportunity for advancement	7	6	5	4	3	2	1	0
Decisions made about who gets hired, recognized, and let go	7	6	5	4	3	2	1	0
The feedback and counsel I get from my boss	7	6	5	4	3	2	1	0
The latitude I have to deliver results to clients	7	6	5	4	3	2	1	0
The recognition I get for what I do	7	6	5	4	3	2	1	0
Actions taken on the basis of my suggestions	7	6	5	4	3	2	1	0
The reasonableness of my compensation	7	6	5	4	3	2	1	0
My boss is fair (he/she hires, recognizes, and terminates the right people).	7	6	5	4	3	2	1	0

Trust, Engagement, and Ownership

I trust the person to whom I report.	7	6	5	4	3	2	1	0
I trust the organization.	7	6	5	4	3	2	1	0
I trust those with whom I work.	7	6	5	4	3	2	1	0
I have all the "security" (likelihood of continued employment) I need in this job.	7	6	5	4	3	2	1	0

I would recommend my organization to a friend as a good place to work.	7	6	5	4	3	2	1	0
I have recommended my organization to friends as a good place to work (circle 7 for yes or 1 for no).	7	6	5	4	3	2	1	0
I have made suggestions for new ways of doing our work (circle 7 for yes or 1 for no).	7	6	5	4	3	2	1	0
I have suggested potential new products or services to those responsible for them (circle 7 for yes or 1 for no).	7	6	5	4	3	2	1	0

Policies

I determine how I get my work done.	7	6	5	4	3	2	1	0
I have latitude to deliver results to customers or others who are expecting them.	7	6	5	4	3	2	1	0
I am held accountable for my work.	7	6	5	4	3	2	1	0
I hold myself accountable for my work.	7	6	5	4	3	2	1	0
I have all the information I need to do my job.	7	6	5	4	3	2	1	0
In my job I have the latitude to engage in informed risk-taking.	7	6	5	4	3	2	1	0
I am encouraged to collaborate with coworkers.	7	6	5	4	3	2	1	0
We accomplish much of our work in teams.	7	6	5	4	3	2	1	0
My work space is near others with whom I work frequently.	7	6	5	4	3	2	1	0
Our organization is made up of people with diverse skills and backgrounds.	7	6	5	4	3	2	1	0
In this organization, people often put the needs of the organization before their own.	7	6	5	4	3	2	1	0

Organization Learning

In this organization, we have the freedom and the budget support needed to acquire ideas from other organizations and sources.	7	6	5	4	3	2	1	0
There is a lot of opportunity to learn in this organization.	7	6	5	4	3	2	1	0
We engage in a great deal of benchmarking and best-practice exchanges with other organizations.	7	6	5	4	3	2	1	0
There is a strong tendency here to listen to ideas from employees.	7	6	5	4	3	2	1	0
There is a strong tendency here to listen to ideas from customers.	7	6	5	4	3	2	1	0
Once we decide to act, things happen fast around here.	7	6	5	4	3	2	1	0

Measurement of Results

A great deal of emphasis is placed on tracking employee satisfaction, loyalty, and engagement.	7	6	5	4	3	2	1	0
A great deal of emphasis is placed on tracking customer satisfaction, loyalty, and engagement.	7	6	5	4	3	2	1	0
A great deal of emphasis is placed on tracking innovation in this organization.	7	6	5	4	3	2	1	0
A great deal of emphasis is placed on "making the numbers" in this organization.	7	6	5	4	3	2	1	0
This organization places as much emphasis on employee loyalty and engagement as on making the numbers.	7	6	5	4	3	2	1	0
This organization places as much emphasis on customer loyalty and engagement as on making the numbers.	7	6	5	4	3	2	1	0

B

Four R Assumptions and Computations*

	Office		
	Chicago	**Baltimore**	**Minneapolis**
First R: Savings from Employee Referrals			
Number of new hires referred			
2009	1	0	0
2010	15	2	3
Average total compensation per employee			
2009	$102,350	$158,700	$100,960
2010	116,000	135,000	114,470
Cost of hiring referred persons (at 100% of average annual compensation)			
2009	$102,350	0	0
2010	1,740,000	270,000	343,410
25% discount on cost of hiring by referrals			
2009	$25,590	0	0
2010	435,000	67,500	85,850
Total revenue (in thousands)			
2009	$22,608	$16,617	$8,203
2010	22,443	16,379	9,644
Savings from referrals/total revenue (in percentage points)			
2009	.1	0	0
2010	1.9	.5	.9

continued

* Keyed to the data shown in Chapter 7, Table 7-2, for Three Offices of RTL, Inc., 2009 and 2010

	Office		
	Chicago	**Baltimore**	**Minneapolis**
Second R: Advantage from Employee Retention (Cost of Defections)			
Number of employees departing voluntarily			
2009	4	1	3
2010	39	10	7
Number of employees departing involuntarily			
2009	0	10	0
2010	8	0	4
Cost of voluntary departures (100% of average annual compensation)			
2009	$409,400	$158,700	$302,880
2010	4,524,000	1,350,000	801,290
Cost of involuntary departures (50% of average annual compensation)**			
2009	$0	$793,500	$0
2010	464,000	0	228,940
Portion of cost attributed to culture***			
2009	50%	50%	50%
2010	50%	50%	50%
Total cost of retention/defection attributed to culture as a percentage of revenue			
2009	.9	2.9	.9
2010	11.1	4.7	5.3
Third R: Returns to Labor			
Labor costs as a percentage of revenue			
2009	45.5%	51.8%	46.6%
2010	49.4	46.4	45.6
Improved returns to labor due to culture equal to 25% of differential in labor costs (in percentage points based on the office with the best performance each year)			
2009		1.6	.3
2010	.9	.2	
Fourth R: Relationships with Clients			
Number of clients lost			
2009	24	36	13
2010	15	24	9

	Office		
	Chicago	**Baltimore**	**Minneapolis**
Average annual revenue per client			
2009	$508,040	$335,700	$293,000
2010	701,000	429,000	386,000
Total revenue lost (assuming the average loss was for one-half year)			
2009	$6,096,000	$6,043,000	$1,905,000
2010	5,258,000	5,148,000	1,737,000
Portion of revenue lost due to culture (50%)			
2009	$3,048,000	$3,022,000	$953,000
2010	2,629,000	2,574,000	868,000
Lost revenue compared to total revenue			
2009	13.5%	18.2%	11.6%
2010	11.7	17.9	9.0
Effect on relationships with clients due to culture (in percentage point differentials based on the best performer for each year)			
2009	1.9	6.6	
2010	2.7	8.9	
Savings from client referrals****	—	—	—

** Assuming fewer sales and profit lost for each employee who leaves involuntarily.

*** This is at the higher range of estimates for all organizations, because culture represents a significant factor in determining retention in a professional service organization.

**** Information regarding client referrals was unavailable.

C

Complete Results of Employee Surveys, 2009 and 2010, for Three RTL, Inc. Offices*

	Chicago	Baltimore	Minneapolis
Response rate	70%	80%	75%
Employee engagement index**	3.93	3.53	4.17
	Average Agree Scores***		
Intent to Stay			
I intend to stay with company for another 12 months.	70	46	72
Male	86	44	
$25,000 to $50,000 in salary	73		
$100,000 to $125,000 in salary	58		
Female	64	46	78
$25,000 to $50,000 in salary	79		
$100,000 to $125,000 in salary	55		
Ages 20 to 29	66	50	
Ages 30 to 39	58	36	
Ages 40 to 49	83	45	
Ages 50 to 59	92		
1 to 3 years of tenure	71	30	
4 to 6 years of tenure	36	27	
7 to 9 years of tenure	77		

continued

* Source: Company records

	Chicago	Baltimore	Minneapolis
Communication *(% responding 4/5)*			
I am actively encouraged to volunteer new ideas and make suggestions for improving our business.	77	71	86
In my office, senior leadership communicates relevant information in a timely manner.	51	60	61
Customer/Client Focus *(% responding 4/5)*			
My team constantly strives to find innovative solutions to client problems.	81	83	86
My team does a good job of resolving client problems when they occur.	93	88	97
My team is extremely good at building long-term client relationships.	83	88	92
Client satisfaction is a top priority at our company.	89	88	94
My colleagues are passionate about providing exceptional client service.	84	88	78
My team keeps the client informed about issues affecting their business.	83	80	94
My team regularly discusses the results of client satisfaction feedback.	67	54	70
Employee Morale/Loyalty *(% responding 4/5)*			
I feel my supervisor takes interest in my skills and career development.	65	56	69
I am highly satisfied with my job.	53	32	61
I get a great sense of accomplishment from my work.	61	46	75
I am proud to work for my company.	67	39	77
I intend to stay with my company for at least another 12 months.	70	46	72
I would recommend my company as a great place to work.	58	27	77
The amount of work I have keeps me challenged, but not overwhelmed.	44	17	33

	Chicago	Baltimore	Minneapolis
Empowerment (% responding 4/5)			
My job makes good use of my skills and abilities.	66	60	75
My team does a good job of delegating work to the appropriate level.	63	46	72
I have the freedom to make the necessary decisions to do my work properly.	70	63	83
Leadership (% responding 4/5)			
In my office, senior leadership's actions are consistent with what they say.	46	54	67
In my office, senior leadership has a sincere interest in the well-being of employees.	54	54	86
My supervisor routinely provides feedback that helps me improve my performance.	62	56	61
My supervisor clearly communicates his/her expectations of me.	66	66	58
My supervisor inspires the people on my team.	58	59	74
In my office, management is trusted.	46	30	69
In my office, management gets the best work out of everyone.	34	23	65
Learning Orientation (% responding 4/5)			
Here you are required, not just encouraged, to learn and develop new skills.	57	33	72
In my office, senior leadership shows by their actions that employee training is important.	41	36	63
We have high-quality training opportunities to improve skills.	35	21	47
I have the opportunity to work on challenging assignments that contribute to my development.	60	54	75

continued

	Chicago	Baltimore	Minneapolis
Quality *(% responding 4/5)*			
The quality of supervision on client projects is uniformly high.	62	63	60
The quality of the professionals in our office is as high as can be expected.	55	54	69
My supervisor holds me accountable for the quality of my work.	88	93	89
My team produces outstanding-quality work.	87	88	94
In this office we set and enforce very high standards for performance.	71	73	89
Stake in the Outcome *(% responding 4/5)*			
My total compensation is fair for the work I do.	42	23	28
Those who contribute the most to the overall success of the office are the most highly rewarded.	31	11	34
I understand how my job contributes to the success of my company.	88	78	92
My colleagues are willing to go beyond what is expected for the success of my company.	67	87	92
Implementation *(% responding 4/5)*			
I have seen positive changes made based on the results of the last survey.	37	34	26
Long-Term Focus *(% responding 4/5)*			
We invest a significant amount of time in things that will pay off in the future.	55	19	56
Teamwork *(% responding 4/5)*			
We are focused as a team on specific goals.	63	45	69
We emphasize teamwork. People who do not collaborate are not tolerated.	47	41	67

	Chicago	Baltimore	Minneapolis
Strategic Planning/Focus (% responding 4/5)			
I know what is expected of me at work.	91	76	94
The actions of our office are consistent with our strategic objectives and mission statement.	62	58	81
I know exactly what my office is trying to achieve strategically.	65	53	75
We regularly discuss our progress toward our strategic objectives, not just the financial goals.	55	48	83
We have a real commitment to high-quality work, and we tolerate nothing less.	67	63	75
We have a real commitment to high levels of client service, and we tolerate nothing less.	75	68	78
My work goals fit with my company's business practices and direction.	77	68	86
Work Environment (% responding 4/5)			
We have no room for those who put their personal agenda ahead of the interests of our clients or the firm.	46	44	69
I have the opportunity for personal development and growth here.	59	41	86
I have the resources and tools needed to do my job.	67	37	78
My team has a climate that values diverse perspectives.	74	60	86
People within our office always treat others with respect.	68	53	75
I receive recognition or praise for doing good work on a regular basis.	68	59	72
My company has a strong culture.	44	39	81

** A composite of key attributes: (1) I would recommend my company as a great place to work, (2) I intend to stay with my company for at least another 12 months, (3) My colleagues are willing to go beyond what is expected for the success of my company, (4) I am proud to work for my company, (5) My colleagues are passionate about providing exceptional customer service, and (6) I understand how my job contributes to the success of my company. A perfect score on a 6-point scale of 0 to 5 with a midpoint of 2.5 is 5.00.

*** Average agree score equals the respondents agreeing or strongly agreeing with a statement, equivalent to 4 or 5 on a 5-point scale.

Endnotes

Introduction

1. See, for example, the results of a survey of seventy-five investment analysts in John P. Kotter and James L. Heskett, *Corporate Culture and Performance* (New York: The Free Press, 1992), p. 36.

2. See John H. Fleming and Jim Asplund, *Human Sigma: Managing the Employee-Customer Encounter* (New York: Gallup Press, 2007), p. 161. Fleming and Asplund define engagement in terms of responses to questionnaire items such as "knowledge of what is expected of me," "recognition in the past seven days," "my opinions count," and "opportunities (exist) to learn and grow (on the job)."

3. Baruch Lev, *Intangibles: Management, Measurement, and Reporting* (Washington, D.C.: Brookings Institution Press, 2001).

4. Interview with Fritz Henderson, then-CEO of GM, on CNN, July 10, 2009.

5. Charles S. Jacobs, *Management Rewired: Why Feedback Doesn't Work and Other Surprising Lessons from the Latest Brain Science* (New York: Penguin Portfolio, 2009), p. 36.

6. See James L. Heskett, Thomas O. Jones, Gary W. Loveman, W. Earl Sasser, Jr., and Leonard A. Schlesinger, "Putting the Service-Profit Chain to Work," *Harvard Business Review*, March–April 1994, pp. 164–174.

7. See, for example, Alex Edmans, "Does the Stock Market Fully Value Intangibles? Employee Satisfaction and Equity Prices," forthcoming in *Journal of Financial Economics*, available online March 30, 2011, and David H. Maister, *Practice What You Preach: What Managers Must Do to Create a High Achievement Culture* (New York: The Free Press, 2001).

8. John P. Kotter and James L. Heskett, *Corporate Culture and Performance* (Free Press, 1992).

9. Jeffrey Pfeffer, "Building Sustainable Organizations: The Human Factor," *Academy of Management Perspectives*, February 2010, pp. 34–45, at p. 35.

10. See James L. Heskett and W. Earl Sasser, Jr., *Southwest Airlines: In a Different World*, Case No. 910419 (Boston: Harvard Business School, 2010), p. 11.

11. Author's interview with Herb Kelleher, Dallas, TX, December 2008.

12. At Southwest, references to Employees and Customers are always capitalized.

13. This comment echoes the motto of Albert Heijn, the late former CEO of Dutch-based retailer Ahold, as reported by Phil Davison in Heijn's obituary, "Grocer who felt empathy for the shopper," *Financial Times*, January 22/January 23, 2011, p. 12: "You don't sell on behalf of your suppliers, you buy on behalf of your customers. I want my customers to feel fun, convenience and trust."

14. James L. Heskett, *Southwest Airlines 2002: Industry in Crisis*, Case No. 803133 (Boston: HBS Publishing, 2002).

15. This is a term regularly used by Herb Kelleher.

16. Sam Walton with John Huey, *Made in America* (New York: Doubleday, 1992), p. 21.

17. Lamar Muse, *Southwest Passage: The Inside Story of Southwest Airlines' Formative Years* (Austin, TX: Eakin Press, 2002), p. 100.

18. Personal correspondence from Herbert D. Kelleher, at the time Chairman of the Board, President, and Chief Executive Officer, Southwest Airlines Co., March 15, 1993. Used with permission.

Chapter 1

1. The Conference Board, "U.S. Job Satisfaction at Lowest Levels in Two Decades," January 5, 2010.

2. *Towers Perrin Global Workforce Study* (New York: Towers Perrin, 2005).

3. *Ibid.*, p. 30.

4. Peter M. Senge, *The Fifth Discipline: The Art and Practice of the Learning Organization*, Revised Edition (New York: Random House, 2006), p. xviii.

5. Larry E. Senn and Jim Hart, *Winning Teams, Winning Cultures* (Long Beach, CA: Leadership Press, 2006), p. 67.

6. Louis V. Gerstner, Jr., *Who Says Elephants Can't Dance?: Inside IBM's Historic Turnaround* (New York: HarperCollins, 2002), pp. 181–182.

7. The quote is from Marvin Bower, a longtime former managing director of McKinsey & Company, who put it this way in his book *The Will to Manage* (New York: McGraw-Hill, 1966), p. 22.

8. Larry E. Senn and John R. Childress, *The Secret of a Winning Culture: Building High-Performance Teams* (Long Beach, CA: Leadership Press, 1999), p. 17.

9. Terrence A. Deal and Allan A. Kennedy, *Corporate Cultures: The Rites and Rituals of Corporate Life* (Reading, MA: Addison-Wesley Publishing Company, 1982), p. 15.

10. Frances X. Frei, Robin J. Ely, and Laura Winig, "Zappos.com 2009: Clothing, Customer Service, and Company Culture," Case No. 9-610-015 (Boston: Harvard Business School Publishing, 2010), p. 4.

11. See, for example, Ruth Benedict, *Patterns of Culture* (Boston: Houghton Mifflin, 1934).

12. See Fritz J. Roethlisberger and William J. Dickson, *Management and the Worker: An Account of a Research Program Conducted by the Western Electric Company, Hawthorne Works, Chicago* (Cambridge: Harvard University Press, 1939), p. 88. The comment in parentheses is mine.

13. See Robert Kanigel, *The One Best Way: Frederick Winslow Taylor and the Enigma of Efficiency* (New York: Viking, 1997), p. 169. Ironically, Taylor (as opposed to his disciples) had a difficult time selling scientific management to practitioners. He actually made his fortune as a co-inventor of "high-speed steel," a hardened metal from which very efficient cutting tools could be fashioned.

14. George C. Homans, *The Human Group* (New York: Harcourt, Brace & World, Inc., 1950, quote at pp. 330–331.

15. Philip Selznick, *Leadership in Administration: A Sociological Interpretation* (Evanston, IL: Row, Peterson and Company, 1957), p. 17.

16. Terry E. Deal and Allan A. Kennedy, *Corporate Cultures* (Reading, MA: Addison-Wesley, 1982); Edgar H. Schein, *Organizational Culture and Leadership* (San Francisco: Jossey-Bass, 1985).

17. Joanne Martin, *Organizational Culture: Mapping the Terrain* (Thousand Oaks, CA: Sage Publications, 2002).

18. See, for example, William Ouchi, *Theory Z: How American Business Can Meet the Japanese Challenge* (Reading, MA: Addison-Wesley, 1981) and Richard T. Pascale and Anthony G. Athos, *The Art of Japanese Management* (New York: Simon & Schuster, 1981).

19. Caren Siehl and Joanne Martin, "Culture: A Key to Financial Performance?" in Benjamin Schneider, ed., *Organizational Climate and Culture* (San Francisco: Jossey-Bass, 1990) and John P. Kotter and James L. Heskett, *Corporate Culture and Performance* (New York: The Free Press, 1992).

20. Thomas J. Peters and Robert H. Waterman, Jr., *In Search of Excellence: Lessons from America's Best-Run Companies* (New York: Harper & Row, 1982).

21. Richard T. Pascale and Anthony G. Athos, *The Art of Japanese Management*, *op. cit.* Peters and Waterman noted that those originating the Seven S Framework had to adjust the names of the seven S's to fit the framework. As a result, shared values became equated with culture.

22. Peters and Waterman, *op. cit.*, p. 10.

23. James C. Collins and Jerry I. Porras, *Built to Last: Successful Habits of Visionary Companies* (New York: HarperBusiness, 1994).

24. See, for example, Louis V. Gerstner, Jr., *op. cit.*; Robert Slater, *Saving Big Blue* (New York: McGraw-Hill, 1999), pp. 97–107, and Jack Welch with John A. Byrne, *Jack: Straight from the Gut* (New York: Warner Business Books, 2001).

25. See, for example, John R. Emshwiller and Rebecca Smith, "Corporate Veil: Behind Enron's Fall, a Culture of Operating Outside Public's View. Hidden Deals with Officers and Minimal Disclosure Finally Cost It Its Trust," *Wall Street Journal*, December 5, 2001, p. 1, and Kay E. Zekany, Lucas W. Braun, and Zachary T. Warder, "Behind Closed Doors at Worldcom: 2001," *Issues in Accounting Education*, February 2004, pp. 161–117. The quote is from Zekany, Braun, and Warder regarding Worldcom, although much the same could be said for Enron.

26. See Hope Greenfield, "The Decline of the Best: An Insider's Lessons from Lehman Brothers," *Leader to Leader*, Winter 2010, Vol. 2009, Issue 55, p. 30, and Nicole Bullock, Francesco Guerrera, Patrick Jenkins, and Henry Sender, "Damning insight into corporate culture sheds light on fall of a Wall Street giant," *Financial Times*, March 13, 2010, p. 6.

27. Bruce Orwall, et. al., "Embattled CEO Expected to Step Down from U.K. Company," *Wall Street Journal*, July 26, 2010, p. A6.

28. Charles A. O'Reilly III and Jeffrey Pfeffer, *Hidden Value: How Great Companies Achieve Extraordinary Results with Ordinary People* (Boston: Harvard Business School Press, 2000).

29. George A. Ackerlof and Rachel E. Kranton, *Identity Economics: How Our Identities Shape Our Work, Wages, and Well-Being* (Princeton, NJ: Princeton University Press, 2010), at p. 15. See also Dan Ariely, *Predictably Irrational: The Hidden Forces That Shape Our Decisions* (New York: HarperCollins, 2010) for an overview of behavioral economics.

30. See, for example, Nirmalya Kumar with Pradipta K. Mohapatra and Suj Chandrasekhar, *India's Global Powerhouses: How They Are Taking on the World* (Boston: Harvard Business School Press, 2009) and Jeffrey K. Liker, *The Toyota Way: 14 Management Principles from the World's Greatest Manufacturer* (New York: McGraw-Hill, 2004).

31. Charles S. Jacobs, *Management Rewired: Why Feedback Doesn't Work and Other Surprising Lessons from the Latest Brain Science* (New York: Penguin Portfolio, 2009), p. 193.

32. Edgar H. Schein, *op. cit.*, p. 17.

33. Douglas McGregor, *The Human Side of Enterprise*, 25th Anniversary Printing (New York: McGraw-Hill Book Company, 1985), p. 7.

34. Charles A. O'Reilly III and Jeffrey Pfeffer, *op. cit.*, pp. 201–230.

35. T. J. Rodgers, William Taylor, and Rick Foreman, *No Excuses Management: Proven Systems for Starting Fast, Growing Quickly, and Surviving Hard Times* (New York: Currency Doubleday, 1992), p. 19.

36. O'Reilly and Pfeffer, *op. cit.*, p. 205.

37. See Douglas McGregor, *op. cit.*, pp. 33–57.

38. Robert Kinagle, *op. cit.*, pp. 496–497.

39. Personal correspondence to the author, received February 1993.

40. Mike Brewster and Frederick Dalzell, *Driving Change: The UPS Approach to Business* (New York: Hyperion, 2007), pp. 41–45.

41. For a description of Lincoln Electric's adaptation of Theory X concepts, see Frank Koller, *Spark: How Old-Fashioned Values Drive a Twenty-First-Century Corporation* (New York: Public Affairs, 2010). The quote is at p. 41.

42. Frank Koller, *Spark, ibid.*

43. Roethlisberger and Dickson, *op. cit.*, p. 552.

44. Abraham H. Maslow, *Motivation and Personality* (New York: Harper & Row, 1970).

45. For a highly readable exploration of these issues, see Daniel H. Pink, *Drive: The Surprising Truth About What Motivates Us* (New York: Penguin, 2009).

46. Warren Bennis in the Foreword to Douglas McGregor, *op. cit.*, p. iv.

47. Thomas J. Watson, Jr., *A Business and Its Beliefs: The Ideas That Helped Build IBM* (New York: McGraw-Hill, 1963), at p. 39.

48. Andrew Martin, "Give Him Liberty, But Not a Bailout," *The New York Times*, August 2, 2009, pp. BU1 and 6.

49. Jeffrey Pfeffer and Robert Sutton, "The Smart-Talk Trap," *Harvard Business Review*, May-June 1999, pp. 135–142, at p. 136.

50. "Cisco Systems' Mission and Values," a company document in use in 2001.

51. Edgar H. Schein, *op. cit.*, p. 187. The comments in parentheses are mine.

52. John Seabrook, "Rocking in Shangri-La," *The New Yorker*, October 10, 1994, pp. 64–78.

53. See Leonard A. Schlesinger and James Mellado, "Willow Creek Community Church," Case No. 9-691-102 (Boston: Harvard Business School Publishing, 1991).

54. This story has been told many times. See, for example, Richard S. Tedlow, *Giants of Enterprise: Seven Business Innovators and the Empires They Built* (New York: HarperBusiness, 2001), p. 358.

55. My paraphrase of John Rollwagen's comments in a videotaped interview, December 1980.

56. Bill George, *Authentic Leadership: Rediscovering the Secrets to Creating Lasting Value* (San Francisco: Jossey-Bass, 2003), pp. 72–73.

57. Pfeffer and Sutton, *op. cit.*, at p. 136.

58. Jack Welch with John A. Byrne, *Jack: Straight from the Gut* (New York: Warner Books, Inc., 2001), pp. 188–189.

59. I'm not the first one or the only one to reach this conclusion. See, for example, Larry Bossidy and Ram Charan, *Execution: The Discipline of Getting Things Done* (New York: Crown Business, 2002) on this topic.

60. See, for example, Leonard A. Schlesinger and Jeffrey Zornitsky, "Job Satisfaction, Service Capability, and Customer Satisfaction: An Examination of Linkages and Management Implications," *Human Resource Planning*, Volume 14, Number 2, pp. 141–149.

61. See Bruno S. Frey, *Not Just for the Money: An Economic Theory of Personal Motivation* (Brookfield, VT: Edward Elgar, 1997).

62. Corporate Leadership Council, *Driving Employee Performance and Retention Through Engagement: A Quantitative Analysis of the Effectiveness of Employee Engagement Strategies* (Corporate Executive Board, 2004), p. 17.

63. See Mark Huselid, "The Impact of Human Resource Management Practices on Turnover, Productivity, and Corporate Financial Performance," *Academy of Management Journal* 38 (1995).

64. See, for example, Rosabeth Moss Kanter, *The Change Masters: Innovations for Productivity in the American Corporation* (New York: Simon and Schuster, 1983) and Linda Grant, "Happy Workers' High Returns," *Fortune*, January 12, 1998, p. 8. For a study based on experiences among German firms, see Linda Bilmes, Konrad Wetzker, and Pascal Xhonneux, "Value in Human Resources," *Financial Times*, February 10, 1997, p. 10.

65. See, for example, Eric Van den Steen, "On the Origin of Shared Beliefs (and Corporate Culture), *Rand Journal of Economics*, Vol. 41, No. 4, Winter 2010, pp. 617–648.

66. Source: Study commissioned annually by the Great Place to Work Institute, web site: www.greatplacetowork.com/what_we_believe/graphs.php. For other comparisons of a similar nature, see Michael Burchell and Jennifer Robin, *The Great Workplace: How to Build It, How to Keep It, and Why It Matters* (San Francisco: Jossey-Bass, 2011), pp. 12–13.

67. The Conference Board, *op. cit.*

Chapter 2

1. Arkadi Kuhlmann and Bruce Philp, *The Orange Code: How ING Direct Succeeded by Being a Rebel with a Cause* (New York: John Wiley & Sons, Inc., 2009), p. 125.

2. Tony Hsieh, *Delivering Happiness: A Path to Profits, Passion, and Purpose* (New York: Business Plus, 2010), p. 152.

3. See James L. Heskett, *ING Direct*, Case No. 804-167 (Boston: Harvard Business School Publishing, April 2, 2004).

4. C. William Pollard, *The Soul of the Firm* (New York: HarperBusiness, 1996), at p. 45.

5. Nikos Mourkogiannis, *Purpose: The Starting Point of Great Companies* (New York: Palgrave Macmillan, 2006), especially p. 37.

6. See Bruce N. Pfau and Ira T. Kay, *The Human Capital Edge: 21 People Management Practices Your Company Must Implement (or Avoid) to Maximize Shareholder Value* (New York: McGraw-Hill, 2002), pp. 59–81.

7. Larry Bossidy and Ram Charan, *Execution: The Discipline of Getting Things Done* (New York: Crown Business, 2002), p. 109.

8. Gary Hamel, *The Future of Management* (Boston: Harvard Business School Press, 2007), pp. 83–117.

9. Marcus Buckingham and Curt Coffman, *First, Break All the Rules: What the World's Greatest Managers Do Differently* (New York: Simon & Schuster, 1999), pp. 15–16. The words in parentheses are mine.

10. The response to the first part of question 1 (the importance of strategy in the success "mix") was multiplied by the percentage response to question 2, the response to the second part of question 1 (the importance of execution) was multiplied by the percentage response to question 3, and the results were added.

11. Discussion on the blog "How Do You Weigh Strategy, Execution, and Culture in an Organization's Success?," James L. Heskett, "What Do You Think?" on the Harvard Business School *Working Knowledge* web site, June 2, 2010.

12. John Kay, *Obliquity: Why Our Goals Are Best Achieved Indirectly* (London: Profile, 2010).

13. Leonard L. Berry and Kent D. Seltman, *Management Lessons from Mayo Clinic: Inside One of the World's Most Admired Service Organizations* (New York: McGraw-Hill, 2008), p. 20.

14. *Ibid.*, p 254.

Chapter 3

1. Clarence Darrow, paraphrasing Charles Darwin during the Scopes trial in 1925. Scopes v. State, 154 Tenn. 105, 289 S.W. 363 (1927).

2. Charles I. Stubbard and Michael B. Knight, "The case of the disappearing firms: Empirical evidence and implications," *Journal of Organizational Behavior*, 27, pp. 79–100.

3. Based on an interview with James Kinnear, then CEO of Texaco, June 7, 1991.

4. James L. Heskett and Roger Hallowell, "Texaco, Inc.," Case No. 9-392-076 (Boston: Harvard Business School Publishing, 1994), pp. 2–3.

5. *Ibid.*, p. 7.

6. Based on an interview with Peter Coors, then president of Coors Brewing Company, January 10, 1991.

7. Much of the information in this section is based on work reported in John P. Kotter and James L. Heskett, *Corporate Culture and Performance* (New York: The Free Press, 1992).

8. *Ibid.*, p. 161.

9. Terry E. Deal and Allan A. Kennedy, *Corporate Cultures: The Rites and Rituals of Corporate Life* (Reading, MA: Addison-Wesley, 1982), p. 3.

10. Deal and Kennedy, *op. cit.*, pp. 107–127.

11. Dean Foust, "Where Headhunters Fear to Tread," *Businessweek*, September 14, 2009, pp. 42 and 44. Subsequent quotes are from the same article.

12. Boris Groysberg, *Chasing Stars: The Myth of Talent and the Portability of Performance* (Princeton, NJ: Princeton University Press, 2010), pp. 51–76. See also Boris Groysberg, Andrew N. McLean, and Nitin Nohria, "Are Leaders Portable?," *Harvard Business Review*, May 2006, pp. 92–100.

13. *Ibid.*, pp. 35–39.

14. Rob Goffee and Gareth Jones, "What Holds the Modern Company Together?" *Harvard Business Review*, November-December 1996, pp. 133–148.

15. See, for example, Boris Groysberg, Ashish Nanda, and Nitin Nohria, "The Risky Business of Hiring Stars," *Harvard Business Review*, May 2004, pp. 92–100, and Boris Groysberg, Lex Sant, and Robin Abrams, "How to Minimize the Risks of Hiring Outside Stars," *Wall Street Journal*, September 22, 2008.

16. Michael J. Mauboussin, *Think Twice: Harnessing the Power of Counterintuition* (Boston: Harvard Business Press, 2009), at p. 80.

17. Kotter and Heskett, *op. cit.*, pp. 89–93; Janice A. Klein, *Outsiders on the Inside: How Outsiders on the Inside Get Things Done in Organizations* (New York: John Wiley & Sons, Inc., 2004).

Chapter 4

1. James L. Heskett, "ServiceMaster Industries Inc.", Case No. 9-388-064 (Boston: HBS Publishing, 1987), p. 1, 4, 5.

2. The early development of IBM is described in Richard S. Tedlow, *Giants of Enterprise* (New York: HarperBusiness, 2001), pp. 187–245.

3. See Thomas J. Watson, Jr., *A Business and Its Beliefs: The Ideas That Helped Build IBM* (New York: McGraw-Hill, 1963), p. 39.

4. Bill George and Peter Sims, *True North: Discover Your Authentic Leadership* (New York: John Wiley & Sons, Inc., 2007), p. 189.

5. *Ibid.*, p. 5.

6. Jim Collins, *How the Mighty Fall and Why Some Companies Never Give In* (New York: HarperCollins, 2009), p. 148.

7. *Ibid.*, at p. 29.

8. James C. Collins and Jerry I. Porras, *Built to Last: Successful Habits of Visionary Companies* (New York: HarperBusiness, 1994).

9. Hiawatha Bray, "Apple sued over iPhone's antenna," *The Boston Globe*, July 2, 2010.

10. Richard S. Tedlow, *Denial: Why Business Leaders Fail to Look Facts in the Face—and What to Do About It* (New York: Portfolio, 2010), pp. 30–38.

11. *Ibid.*, pp. 78–95; See also Richard Tedlow, "Toyota Was in Denial. How About You?," *Bloomberg Businessweek*, April 19, 2010, p. 76.

12. Mike McNamee, "Credit Card Revolutionary," *Stanford Business*, May, 2001, p. 23.

13. Jim Collins, *How the Mighty Fall and Why Some Companies Never Give In* (New York: HarperCollins, 2009), p. 56.

14. *Ibid.*

15. Edgar H. Schein, *Organizational Culture and Leadership*, Third Edition (San Francisco: Jossey-Bass, 2004), p. 313.

16. Stanley M. Davis, *Managing Corporate Culture* (Cambridge, MA: Ballinger Publishing Company, 1984), p. 123.

17. See Ken Auletta, *Googled: The End of the World as We Know It* (New York: Penguin, 2009), pp. 322–336.

18. Matthew S. Olson and Derek Van Bever, *Stall Points: Most Companies Stop Growing—Yours Doesn't Have To* (New Haven: Yale University Press, 2008), pp. 33–42.

19. Illinois Tool Works, Inc. 2009 Annual Report.

20. Jim Collins, *op. cit.*, p. 76.

21. See, for example, conclusions based on an extensive field study by David H. Maister presented in his book *Practice What You Preach: What Managers Must Do to Create a High Achievement Culture* (New York: The Free Press, 2001), p. 79.

22. These relationships are documented in James L. Heskett, W. Earl Sasser, Jr., and Leonard A Schlesinger, *The Value Profit Chain: Treat Employees Like Customers and Customers Like Employees* (New York: The Free Press, 2003). Employee engagement typically is measured by an employee's willingness to recommend the organization to a good friend as a place to work. Ownership behaviors to look for include actual referrals provided to potential customers (or employees) as well as suggestions for new products or services or improved ways of doing business.

23. Quoted in Bill George and Peter Sims, *op. cit.*, p. 183.

24. Robert Slater, *Saving Big Blue* (New York: McGraw-Hill, 1999), p. 109.

25. Bill George, *Authentic Leadership: Rediscovering Secrets to Creating Lasting Value* (San Francisco: Jossey-Bass, 2003), p. 82. The comments in parentheses are mine.

26. *Ibid.*, pp. 97–107.

27. Louis V. Gerstner, Jr., *Who Says Elephants Can't Dance?: Inside IBM's Historic Turnaround* (New York: HarperCollins, 2002), pp. 181–182.

28. See Lisa Endlich, *Goldman Sachs: The Culture of Success* (New York: Simon & Schuster, 1999), pp. 89–90.

29. Rosabeth Moss Kanter, "IBM's Values and Corporate Citizenship," Case No. 9-308-106 (Boston: Harvard Business School Publishing, September 16, 2009), p. 1.

30. *Ibid.*, p. 2.

Chapter 5

1. James C. Collins and Jerry I. Porras, *Built to Last: Successful Habits of Visionary Companies* (New York: HarperBusiness, 1994), especially pp. 131–135.

2. *Ibid.*, pp. 131–132.

3. See James L. Heskett, W. Earl Sasser, Jr., and Joe Wheeler, *The Ownership Quotient: Putting the Service Profit Chain to Work for Unbeatable Competitive Advantage* (Boston: Harvard Business Press, 2008).

4. Corporate Leadership Council, "Business Case for Managing Employee Turnover," October, 2006, p. 3.

5. Corporate Leadership Council, *Driving Employee Performance and Retention Through Engagement: A Quantitative Analysis of the Effectiveness of Employee Engagement Strategies* (Corporate Executive Board, 2004), p. xiv. The same study estimates that in the same organization, highly engaged employees are half as likely to leave as the average employee (at p. 18).

6. Lisa Endlich, *Goldman Sachs: The Culture of Success*, Touchstone Edition (New York: Simon & Schuster, 2000), p. 210.

7. To calculate the productivity advantage for Southwest Airlines, it's necessary to estimate the airline's labor costs as a proportion of operating costs. I used an estimate of 25% of operating expense. According to Southwest's annual report, fuel costs as a percentage of operating expense ranged from 21.4% in 2005 to 35.1% in 2008 and represented either the highest or second-highest category of expense. If we assume that the other important category was labor, an assumption of 25% falls comfortably in the range between 21% and 35% of operating expense.

8. Quote verified by David Glass, April 10, 2002.

9. Corporate Leadership Council, *Driving Employee Performance and Retention Through Engagement: A Quantitative Analysis of the Effectiveness of Employee Engagement Strategies* (Corporate Executive Board, 2004), p. xiv. Note that this estimate is not exactly equivalent to the estimate of a 20% increase in productivity used here. But it is directionally correct and confirms and even understates field observations by the author.

10. Bo H. Eriksen, "How Employee Turnover Affects Productivity," working paper posted on January 16, 2010 on the Social Science Research Network web site.

11. Frederick F. Reichheld and W. Earl Sasser, Jr., "Zero Defections: Quality Comes to Services," *Harvard Business Review*, September-October 1990.

12. This is based on anecdotal evidence from my experience, although several studies have produced findings related to the assertion. They include Arif Hassan, "Human resource development and organizational values," *Journal of European Industrial Training*, Vol. 31, No. 6, 2007, pp. 435–448, and B. Lauterbach, J. Vu, and J. Weisberg, "Internal vs. external successions and their effect on firm performance," *Human Relations*, 52(12), 1999, pp. 1485–1504.

13. George A. Akerlof and Rachel E. Kranton, *Identity Economics: How Our Identities Shape Our Work, Wages, and Well-Being* (Princeton, NJ: Princeton University Press, 2010).

14. James L. Heskett, W. Earl Sasser, Jr., and Joe Wheeler, *The Ownership Quotient: Putting the Service Profit Chain to Work for Unbeatable Competitive Advantage* (Boston: Harvard Business School Press, 2008), p. 96.

15. *Ibid.*, p. 106, based on an interview conducted in November 2006.

16. Charles A. O'Reilly III and Jeffrey Pfeffer, *Hidden Value: How Great Companies Achieve Extraordinary Results with Ordinary People* (Boston: Harvard Business School Press, 2000), p. 118.

Chapter 6

1. James C. Collins and Jerry I. Porras, *Built to Last: Successful Habits of Visionary Companies* (New York: Harper Business, 1994), especially pp. 115–139.

2. *Ibid.*, p. 137.

3. USAA.com web site, January 20, 2011.

4. To illustrate the value of good service in seminars that I have conducted, I regularly ask USAA members in the audience to hold up their hands if they have ever received anything less than great service from the organization. Along with an absence of hands I get testimonials to the organization's service.

5. USAA.com web site, *Op. cit.*

6. nucorsteel.com web site, May 2010. Unless otherwise noted, the quotes in this section are drawn from the web site.

7. *Ibid.*

8. Nanette Brynes, "A Steely Resolve," *Businessweek*, April 6, 2009, p. 54.

9. Nanette Brynes, "The Art of Motivation," *Businessweek*, May 1, 2006, p. 57.

10. Jeffrey K. Liker, *The Toyota Way: 14 Management Principles from the World's Greatest Manufacturer* (New York: McGraw-Hill, 2004), xix.

11. Terrence E. Deal and Allan A. Kennedy, *Corporate Cultures: The Rites and Rituals of Corporate Life* (Reading, MA: Addison-Wesley Publishing Company, 1982), p. 3.

12. *Ibid.*, p. 7.

13. Peter M. Senge, *The Fifth Discipline: The Art and Practice of the Learning Organization*, Revised Edition (New York: Random House, 2006), p. 195.

14. For two examples, see Roger Connors and Tom Smith, *Change the Culture, Change the Game: The Breakthrough Strategy for Energizing Your Organization and Creating Accountability for Results* (London and New York: Portfolio/Penguin, 2011) and James L. Heskett, W. Earl Sasser, Jr., and Joe Wheeler, *The Ownership Quotient: Putting the Service Profit Chain to Work for Unbeatable Competitive Advantage* (Boston: Harvard Business School Press, 2008).

15. See Helen Rosethorn, *The Employer Brand: Keeping Faith with the Deal* (Gower: Farnham, UK, 2009).

16. For discussions of the effects of "workarounds" in health care organizations, see Anita L. Tucker and S. J. Spear, "Operational failures and interruptions in hospital nursing," *Health Services Research* 41(3): 643–662, and Anita L. Tucker and Amy C. Edmondson, "Why hospitals don't learn from failures: organizational and psychological dynamics that inhibit system change," *California Management Review* 45(2): pp. 1–18.

17. See Timothy Keiningham and Lerzan Aksoy, *Why Loyalty Matters* (Dallas: BenBella Books, Inc., 2009), p. 75.

18. For analyses of this phenomenon, see James L. Heskett, W. Earl Sasser, Jr., and Joe Wheeler, *The Ownership Quotient, op. cit.*

19. Bernardina Provera, Andrea Montefusco, and Anna Canato, "A 'No Blame' Approach to Organizational Learning," *British Journal of Management*, December 2010, 21(4): pp. 1057–1074.

20. Douglas McGregor, *The Human Side of Enterprise*, 25th Anniversary Printing (New York: McGraw-Hill Book Company, 1985), p. 241.

21. See Heskett, et. al., *op. cit.*, pp. 184–189.

22. See an interview of Richard Hackman with Diane Coutu, "Why Teams Don't Work," *Harvard Business Review*, May 2009, pp. 99–105, and Richard J. Hackman, *Leading Teams: Setting the Stage for Great Performances* (Boston: Harvard Business School Press, 2002).

23. Jeffrey K. Liker, *op. cit.*, p. 185.

24. Boris Gorysberg and Linda-Eling Lee, "Star Power: Colleague Quality and Turnover," *Industrial and Corporate Change*, 2010, 19(3): pp. 741–765.

25. See, for example, K. Y. Williams and C. A. O'Reilley, "Demography and diversity in organizations: A review of 40 years of research," *Research in Organization Behavior* (Greenwich, CT: JAI Press, 1998), pp. 77–140, and Jill E. Perry-Smith and Christina E. Shalley, "The Social Side of Creativity: A Static and Dynamic Social Network Perspective," *The Academy of Management Review*, January 2003, 28(1): pp. 89–106.

26. Bunter K. Stahl, Martha L. Maznevski, Andreas Voigt, and Karsten Jonsen, "Unraveling the Effects of Cultural Diversity in Teams: A Meta-Analysis of Research on Multicultural Work Groups," *Journal of International Business Studies*, 2010, 41(4): pp. 690–709.

27. Bo H. Eriksen, "Organizational Learning and Employee Turnover," working paper posted February 16, 2010 on the Social Science Research Network web site.

28. Adam Bryant, "It's the Culture That Drives the Numbers," *New York Times*, May 30, 2010, BU Y2.

29. See Anthony Rucci, Steven P. Kirn, and Richard T. Quinn, "The Employee-Customer-Profit Chain at Sears," *Harvard Business Review*, January–February, 1998, pp. 83–97.

Chapter 7

1. See, for example, Joanne Martin, *Organizational Culture: Mapping the Terrain* (Thousand Oaks, CA: Sage Publications, 2002).

2. In spite of this, two of the 11 hires in 2010 in Baltimore did result from employee referrals, even though that constituted a lower proportion than for either Minneapolis or Chicago.

Chapter 8

1. The source of this quote and much of the material in this chapter about 3M is *A Century of Innovation: The 3M Story* (St. Paul, MN: 3M Company, 2002). The italics in the quote are mine.

2. Gifford Pinchot III, *Intrepreneuring: Why You Don't Have to Leave the Corporation to Become an Entrepreneur* (New York: Harper & Row, 1985), pp. 138–139.

3. See *A Century of Innovation: The 3M Story* (St. Paul, MN: 3M Company, 2002), pp. 38–40. It is the source of the information appearing in this paragraph.

4. Susan Feyder, "3M sees slower growth next year," *Minneapolis Star-Tribune*, December 8, 2010, 1D.

5. Gal Tziperman Lotan, "Stanford team wins $200,000 in MIT Contest," *Boston Globe*, May 12, 2010, p. 87.

6. See James L. Heskett, W. Earl Sasser, Jr., and Joe Wheeler, *The Ownership Quotient: Putting the Service Profit Chain to Work for Unbeatable Competitive Advantage* (Boston: HBS Press, 2009).

7. See Clayton Christensen, *The Innovator's Dilemma: Meeting the Challenge of Disruptive Change* (Boston: HBS Press, 2000).

8. This reflects the concern of Youngme Moon, expressed in her book, *Different: Escaping the Competitive Herd* (New York: Crown Business, 2010).

9. Tim Brown with Barry Katz, *Change by Design: How Design Thinking Transforms Organizations and Inspires Innovation* (New York: HarperCollins, 2009), pp. 171–172.

10. See Gary Hamel with Bill Breen, *The Future of Management* (Boston: Harvard Business School Press, 2007), pp. 83–100, for a detailed profile of W. L. Gore.

11. Interview with John Martin, January 1992. Also see Leonard A. Schlesinger and Roger Hallowell, "Taco Bell Corp.," Case No. 9-692-058 (Boston: Harvard Business School Publishing Division, 1991).

12. Andrew Hargadon and Robert I. Sutton, "Building an Innovation Factory," *Harvard Business Review*, May–June 2000, pp. 157-166.

13. Gunter K. Stahl, Martha L. Maznevski, Andreas Voigt, and Karsten Jonsen, "Unraveling the Effects of Cultural Diversity in Teams: A Meta-Analysis of Research on Multicultural Work Groups," *Journal of International Business Studies*, 2010, 41(4): pp. 690–709.

14. For a detailed account of how Mayo Clinic has distinguished itself in both innovation and service, see Leonard L. Berry and Kent D. Seltman, *Management Lessons from Mayo Clinic* (New York: McGraw-Hill, 2008). The Clinic has subsequently created campuses in Scottsdale, Arizona, and Jacksonville, Florida.

15. Teresa M. Amabile, *Creativity in Context: Update to the Social Psychology of Creativity* (Boulder, Colorado: Westview Press, 1996), p. 15.

16. See, for example, Gifford Pinchot III, *op. cit.*

17. Michael Moritz, *Return to the Little Kingdom: Steve Jobs, the Creation of Apple, and How It Changed the World* (New York: The Overlook Press, 2009), p. 252.

18. *Ibid.*, p. 98.

19. Peter Burrows, "The Seed of Apple's Innovation," *Bloomberg Businessweek*, Online Edition, October 12, 2004.

20. "The World's 50 Most Innovative Companies," pp. 52–97, and "Innovation All-Stars," pp. 98–101, *Fast Company*, March 2010.

21. Susan Feyder, "3M sees slower sales growth next year," *Star Tribune* (Minneapolis–St. Paul), December 8, 2010, p. 1D.

22. Michael Moritz, *op. cit.*, p. 247.

23. Stefan Thomke and Barbara Feinberg, "Design Thinking and Innovation at Apple," Case No. 9-609-066 (Boston: Harvard Business School Publishing, 2009), at p. 2.

24. Michael Moritz, *op. cit.*, p. 339.

25. Scott Kirsner, "Why Apple is still generating buzz," *Boston Sunday Globe*, April 4, 2010, p. G1 and G3.

26. This story is told by Sculley in his interview with Leander Kahney, "Being Steve's Boss," *Bloomberg Businessweek*, October 25–31, 2010, p. 98.

27. *Ibid.*, p. 96 and 97.

28. See, for example, Randall Stross, "What Steve Jobs Learned in the Wilderness," *New York Times*, October 3, 2010, p. BU5.

29. Michael Moritz, *op. cit.*, p. 15.

Chapter 9

1. James L. Heskett, "Intuit: The TurboTax/MacInTax Crisis (A) through (D)," Cases No. 9-396-289, 9-396-296, 9-396-297, and 9-396-298, respectively (Boston: Harvard Business School Publishing, 1996).

2. *Ibid.*, Intuit (B), p. 3.

3. Bruce Orwall, et. al., "Embattled CEO Expected to Step Down from U.K. Company," *Wall Street Journal*, July 26, 2010, p. A6.

4. Two deaths have occurred during the airline's 40 years of operation. One person on the ground was killed when a Southwest plane skidded off the end of a runway. A passenger who was behaving suspiciously was inadvertently killed onboard a flight when other passengers tried to subdue him. The fact that this occurred before 9/11 may tell us something about the ownership tendencies of Southwest's passengers.

5. U.S. Department of Transportation, Bureau of Transportation Statistics Issue Brief 13, November 21, 2005.

6. Southwest Airlines company web site, Southwest.com.

7. Lisa Endlich, *Goldman Sachs: The Culture of Success*, Touchstone Edition (New York: Simon & Schuster, 2000), p. 15. The italics are mine.

8. *Ibid.*, p. 27.

9. Roben Farzad and Paula Dwyer, "Not Guilty. Not One Little Bit," *Bloomberg Businessweek*, April 12, 2010, pp. 31–38.

10. Peter S. Goodman, "In Case of Emergency: What Not to Do," *New York Times*, August 22, 2010, p. BU6.

11. United Nations Comtrade Data Base, January 20, 2010.

12. Carter Dougherty, "A Happy Family of 8,000, But for How Long?," *New York Times*, July 12, 2009, p. 1, 4 (SundayBusiness).

Chapter 10

1. Much of what follows regarding UPS is based on Mike Brewster and Frederick Dalzell, *Driving Change: The UPS Approach to Business* (New York: Hyperion, 2007), especially pp. 98–116. The quote is from p. 99.

2. *Ibid.*, p. 102.

3. See Geert Hofstede, *Culture's Consequences: International Differences in Work-Related Values*, Abridged Edition (Newbury Park, CA: Sage Publications, 1980), p. 12.

4. See David C. McClelland, *The Achieving Society* (Princeton, NJ: D. Van Nostrand Company, Inc., 1961).

5. See Peter F. Drucker, *The Practice of Management* (New York: Harper & Brothers, 1954).

6. Michael Hammer and James Champy, *Reengineering the Corporation: A Manifesto for Business Revolution* (New York: HarperCollins, 1993).

7. Abraham H. Maslow, *Motivation and Personality* (New York: Harper & Brothers, 1954).

8. Peter M. Senge, *The Fifth Discipline: The Art and Practice of the Learning Organization*, Revised Edition (New York: Random House, 2006).

9. Robert Simons, *Levers of Control: How Managers Use Innovative Control Systems to Drive Strategic Renewal* (Boston: Harvard Business School Press, 1994).

10. See, for example, Fons Trompenaars and Charles Hampden-Turner, *Riding the Waves of Culture: Understanding Cultural Diversity in Global Business* (New York: McGraw-Hill, 1998), pp. 13–14.

11. Jeffrey Liker, *The Toyota Way: 14 Management Principles from the World's Greatest Manufacturer* (New York: McGraw-Hill, 2004), pp. 257-258.

12. *Ibid.*

13. Richard D. Lewis, *When Cultures Collide: Leading Across Cultures* (Boston: Nicholas Brealcy International, 2006), pp. 32–34.

14. *Ibid.*, p. 41

15. *Ibid.*, p. 31.

16. This and material quoted in the following paragraphs are from the ISS corporate web site.

17. Interview with Lorenzo Zambrano, October 1997.

18. For more information about CEMEX's culture and how it is inculcated in newly acquired organizations, see Rosabeth Moss Kanter, Pamela Yatsko, and Ryan Raffaelli, "CEMEX (A): Building the Global Framework (1985-2004)," "CEMEX (B): Cementing Relationships (2004-2007)," and "CEMEX's Foundations for Sustainability," Cases 9-308-022, 9-308-023, and 9-308-024, respectively (Boston: Harvard Business School Publishing, 2007, 2009) and W. Earl Sasser, James L. Heskett, and Leonard A. Schlesinger, *Achieving Breakthrough Value. The Value Profit Chain: Sustaining the Gains*, CD 4 (Boston: Harvard Business School, 2002).

19. Rosabeth Moss Kanter, et. al., *op. cit.*, "CEMEX (A)," p. 12.

20. Rosabeth Moss Kanter, et. al., *op. cit.*, "CEMEX (B)," p. 5.

21. E-mail from former vice chairman Thomas Watson, January 13, 2011.

22. See, for example, Adrian Furnham and Stephen Bochner, *Culture Shock: Psychological Reactions to Unfamiliar Environments* (Methuen: London, 1986), xix.

23. Geert Hofstede and Gert Jan Hofstede, *Cultures and Organizations: Software of the Mind* (New York: McGraw-Hill, 2005), p. 286.

24. Jack Welch, *Jack: Straight from the Gut* (New York: Warner Books, Inc., 2001), p. 168.

25. Company web site, ben&jerrys.com. The italics are mine.

26. "Ben & Jerry's Ice Cream Chief Freese Leaving to Seek Other Opportunities," AP Newswire, February 10, 2010.

27. Richard D. Lewis, *op. cit.*, p. 134.

28. *Ibid.*, p. 102.

29. See, for example, *International Herald Tribune*, August 15, 1984.

30. Richard D. Lewis, *op. cit.*, p. 162.

31. *Ibid.*, pp. 172–173.

32. Lisa Endlich, *Goldman Sachs: The Culture of Success*, Touchstone Edition (New York: Simon & Schuster, 2000), p. 85.

33. James L. Heskett, "Girl Scouts of the U.S.A. (A)," Case No. 690-044 (Boston: Harvard Business School Publishing, 1989).

34. Richard D. Lewis, *op. cit.*, pp. 138–139.

35. Geert Hofstede, *op. cit.*, p. 273.

36. Geert Hofstede, *op. cit.*, pp. 262–263. The numbering of the items is mine.

Chapter 11

1. Nikos Mourkogiannis, *Purpose: The Starting Point of Great Companies* (New York: Palgrave Macmillan, 2006).

2. Adam Bryant, "Corner Office," *New York Times*, July 5, 2009, p. BU2.

3. The challenge is described in detail in Leonard A. Schlesinger and James Mellado, "Willow Creek Community Church (A)," Case No. 9-691-102 (Boston: HBS Publishing, 1991).

4. Willow Creek Association web site, January 20, 2011.

5. See Noel M. Tichy and Warren G. Bennis, *Judgment: How Winning Leaders Make Great Calls* (New York: Penguin Group, 2007), p. 68. This section is also based on personal conversations with Eleanor Josaitis.

6. Adam Bryant, *op. cit.*

7. J. Gregory Dees, Jed Emerson, and Peter Economy, *Enterprising Nonprofits: A Toolkit for Social Entrepreneurs* (New York: John Wiley & Sons, Inc., 2001), p. 11.

8. See Gary Loveman and Andrew Slavitt, "Habitat for Humanity International," Case No. 694038 (Boston: Harvard Business School Publishing, 1993).

9. See James L. Heskett, "Pioneer Human Services (A) and (B)," Cases No. MCG001 and MCG002, respectively (Pittsburgh: Manchester Craftsmen's Guild, 1999).

10. Heskett, *ibid.*, "Pioneer Human Services (B), p. 2.

11. *Ibid.*

12. *Ibid.*, p. 1.

13. pioneerhumanservices.org, January 21, 2011.

14. cityyear.org web site, January 20, 2011.

15. See James L. Heskett, Douglas Freeman, Roopchand Ramgolam, and Joshua Wallack, "Manchester Craftsmen's Guild and Bidwell Training Center: Governing Social Entrepreneurship," Case No. MCG005 (Pittsburgh: Manchester Craftsmen's Guild, 2000).

16. *Ibid.*, p. 10.

17. A large class-action lawsuit brought recently by employees against Walmart concerns alleged pay and promotion discrimination, not the issues cited here.

18. Richard S. Tedlow, *Giants of Enterprise: Seven Business Innovators and the Empires They Built* (New York: HarperBusiness, 2001), p. 348.

19. Chuck Bartels, "Wal-Mart offers staff online study, tuition discount," *Boston Globe*, June 4, 2010, p. B6.

Chapter 12

1. Source: International Telecommunication Union, *Key Global Telecom Indicators for World Telecommunications Service Sector*, 2010, ITU, www.int/ITV-D/ist/statistics/at_glance/KeyTelecom.html. It is interesting to note that Europe, for example, has 1.2 cell phone subscriptions per capita.

2. Harlan Cleveland, "Information as a Resource," *The Futurist*, December 1982, p. 37.

3. See James L. Heskett, *Managing in the Service Economy* (Boston: Harvard Business School Press, 1986), pp. 153–173 for an expansion of these ideas.

4. Interview with Ray Gottschalk, Senior Vice President and Managing Director, Alcone Marketing Group, June 17, 2010.

5. See Rob Goffee and Gareth Jones, "What Holds the Modern Company Together?," *Harvard Business Review*, November–December 1996, pp. 133–148.

6. Adam Bryant, "He's Not Bill Gates, or Fred Astaire," *New York Times*, February 14, 2010, p. B2.

7. Jena McGregor, "The Employee Is Always Right," *Businessweek*, November 19, 2007, p. 80.

8. Jena McGregor, "Zappos' Secret: It's an Open Book," *Businessweek*, March 23 and 30, 2009, p. 62.

9. See Nadira A. Hira, "You Raised Them, Now Manage Them," *Fortune*, May 28, 2007, p. 38.

10. Pew Research Center, "Millennials: Confident, Connected, Open to Change," February 2010.

11. Gary Hamel with Bill Breen, *The Future of Management* (Boston: Harvard Business School Press, 2007).

12. See Ken Auletta, *Googled: The End of the World as We Know It* (New York: The Penguin Press, 2009), p. 20.

13. *Ibid*, p. 288.

14. These quotes and the one in the next paragraph are from Hamel and Breen, *op. cit.*, pp. 108–117.

15. In 2009, Google ranked fourth behind SAS, Edward Jones, and Wegmans Food Markets. See Milton Moskowitz, Robert Levering, and Christopher Tkaczyk, "The List," *Fortune*, February 8, 2010, pp. 5–88.

16. Lindsey Gerdes, "Why New Grads Love Cisco," *Businessweek*, September 14, 2009, pp. 38–39.

17. Michael A. Costonis and Rob Salkowitz, "Traditional Jobs, Modern Mind-Sets," *New York Times*, June 13, 2010, p. BU9.

18. See the web site, wholefoods.com.

19. Michelle Conlon, "The Ideal Virtual Worker?," *Businessweek*, July 27, 2009, p. 65. (The words in parentheses are Conlon's.)

20. Thomas L. Friedman, *The World Is Flat: A Brief History of the Twenty-First Century* (New York: Farrar, Straus and Giroux, 2005).

Chapter 13

1. See John P. Kotter, *A Force for Change: How Leadership Differs from Management* (New York: The Free Press, 1990), p. 6.

2. Jim Collins, *Good to Great: Why Some Companies Make the Leap...and Others Don't* (New York: HarperBusiness, 2001), pp. 17–40.

3. A. G. Lafley, "What Only the CEO Can Do," *Harvard Business Review*, May 2009, p. 7.

4. In a recent interview, one of the first things mentioned by Ford's CEO, Allan Mullaly, as a way to monitor his company and its products was that he regularly drives his competitors' products. See Stacey Dale, "Ford on Path to Profit Growth," MarketWatch, wsj.com, February 8, 2011.

5. Curiously, when Henderson mentioned getting out of the office, he qualified the statement by saying "at least monthly." Some might consider that too infrequent for leading culture change. Source: gm.com/mission, July 16, 2009.

6. David Welch, "A Salvage Plan at GM," *Businessweek*, June 29, 2009, pp. 24–25.

7. Adam Bryant, "We're Family, So We Can Disagree: Xerox's New Chief Tries to Redefine Its Culture," *New York Times*, February 21, 2010, p. B9.

8. Richard Tedlow, "Toyota Was in Denial. How About You?," *Bloomberg Businessweek*, April 19, 2010, 76. See also Richard Tedlow, *Denial: Why Business Leaders Fail to Look Facts in the Face* (New York: Portfolio, 2010).

9. See Rob Goffee and Gareth Jones, "What Holds the Modern Company Together?," *Harvard Business Review*, November–December 1996, pp. 133–148.

10. See James L. Heskett, "GE: We Bring Good Things to Life," Case No. 899162 (Boston: Harvard Business School Publishing, 1999).

11. David Welch, "Ed Whitacre's Battle to Save GM from Itself," *Bloomberg Businessweek*, May 3–May 9, 2010, pp. 55.

12. See Michael Beer, *Organizational Change and Development: A Systems View* (Santa Monica, CA: Goodyear Publishing, 1980).

13. Two of the three examples in this section, Baptist Health Care and the New York Police Department, have appeared in a somewhat different form elsewhere. See James L. Heskett, W. Earl Sasser, Jr., and Joe Wheeler, *The Ownership Quotient* (Boston: Harvard Business Press, 2008).

14. Al Stubblefield, *The Baptist Health Care Journey to Excellence: Creating a Culture That WOWs!* (New York: John Wiley & Sons, Inc., 2005), p. 5.

15. This example is based on James L. Heskett, "NYPD New," Case No. 9-396-293 (Boston: HBS Publishing, 1997).

16. David Welch, *op. cit.*, p. 50.

17. David Welch, *op. cit.*, p. 51.

18. See Michael Beer, *High Commitment, High Performance: How to Build a Resilient Organization for Sustained Advantage* (San Francisco: Jossey-Bass, 2009), pp. 295–325.

19. Beer, *op. cit.*

20. John P. Kotter, "Leading Change: Why Transformation Efforts Fail," *Harvard Business Review*, March–April 1995, pp. 59–67. See also John P. Kotter, *Leading Change* (New York: The Free Press, 1996).

21. Al Stubblefield, *op. cit.*, p. 49.

22. Tom Krisher, "GM Chief Shakes Up Leaders," *Sarasota Herald Tribune*, March 3, 2010, p. 3D. The comments are attributed to Senior Associate Dean Jeffrey Sonnenfeld at the Yale School of Management.

23. David Welch, *op. cit.*, p. 54.

24. David Welch, "Akerson Grabs the Wheel," *Bloomberg Businessweek*, August 30–September 6, 2010, pp. 66–67.

25. The Compstat method is now being adapted to help identify medical "hot spots." These are locations that experience unusually high and costly, improper usage of hospital emergency rooms for routine treatment of chronically ill and, in some cases, indigent people. Such ER visits can be reduced through the development of patient wellness initiatives. See Atul Gawande, "The Hot Spotters," *The New Yorker*, January 24, 2011, 40–51.

26. See Steven D. Levitt and Stephen J. Dubner, *Freakonomics: A Rogue Economist Explores the Hidden Side of Everything* (New York: HarperCollins, 2005), pp. 127–130.

27. Arkadi Kuhlmann and Bruce Philp, *The Orange Code: How ING Direct Succeeded by Being a Rebel with a Cause* (Hoboken, NJ: John Wiley & Sons, Inc., 2009), p. 30.

28. A. G. Lafley, "What Only the CEO Can Do," *Harvard Business Review*, May 2009, pp. 61–62.

29. *Ibid.*, p. 62.

Chapter 14

1. Mayo Clinic proprietary market study, 2007, cited in Leonard L. Berry and Kent D. Seltman, p. 195.

2. See Jeffrey Pfeffer, "Building Sustainable Organizations: The Human Factor," *Academy of Management Perspectives*, February 2010, pp. 34–45.

3. Correspondence to the author from Herbert D. Kelleher, then Chairman of the Board, President, and Chief Executive Officer of Southwest Airlines Co., March 15, 1993.

Index